South American Eartheaters

South American Eartheaters

Thomas Weidner

English adaptation:
Mary Bailey

CICHLID PRESS

Photo cover: A fry-guarding female of *Geophagus altifrons* "Tapajós".
Endpaper: A group *G. altifrons* "Tocantins" and *Satanoperca leucosticta* in the aquarium.
Title page: A male *G. altifrons* "Tocantins".
Opposite page: *Retroculus lapidifer*. Photo: Frank Warzel.

All photographs by the author unless otherwise credited.

ISBN 0-9668255-1-9

Copyright © 2000 Cichlid Press
All rights reserved.
No part of this publication may be reproduced, stored in a retrieval system, or transmitted in any form or by any means — electronic (such as internet web sites), mechanical, photocopying, recording, or otherwise — without the prior permission of the author and publisher.

Cichlid Press
P.O. Box 13608
El Paso, TX 79913
www.cichlidpress.com

Contents

Forword and Acknowledgments 6
Introduction 7
Eartheaters in history 8
The natural habitat 20
The aquarium 30
Proper maintenance 43
Breeding behaviour 55
The genera 67
The species 71
Biotodoma Eigenmann & Kennedy, 1903 73
Geophagus Heckel, 1840 86
'*Geophagus*' *crassilabris* Complex 171
'*Geophagus*' *brasiliensis* Complex 191
Satanoperca Günther, 1862 206
Gymnogeophagus de Miranda-Ribeiro, 1918 248
Retroculus Eigenmann & Bray, 1894 281
Acarichthys Eigenmann, 1912 297
Guianacara Kullander & Nijssen, 1989 303
Glossary 326
References 328
Index 334

Foreword and Acknowledgments

The book you are reading is a monograph intended to provide an overview of the eartheaters of the South American continent. It covers the members of the genera *Geophagus*, *Satanoperca*, *Biotodoma*, and *Gymnogeophagus*, which are grouped together in the Tribe Geophaginii. Geophagine cichlids all possess a lobe-like appendage on the gill framework, a feature which is also found in the genera *Apistogramma*, *Apistogrammoides*, and *Mikrogeophagus*; these three genera are, however, classed as dwarf cichlids on account of their small size, and hence are not dealt with further here. On the other hand the acarichthyine cichlids (Tribe Acarichthyini), *Acarichthys* and *Guianacara*, are included, as for a long time they were regarded as eartheaters, even though they lack the gill appendage. In addition the genus *Retroculus* is considered, as it was for a long time included in the Tribe Geophaginii.

Unfortunately the large eartheaters of the South American continent have acquired a bad reputation among many aquarists, but this is totally unjustified, as they are without exception peaceful cichlids which can be kept without problem in a spacious community aquarium. Their behaviour, their presence, and their attractive coloration make them a worthwhile addition to almost any aquarium, and they do not deserve to be judged on the basis of the experiences of ignorant aquarists maintaining them incorrectly.

I would like to express my gratitude to Rainer and Angela Korpan, who introduced me to this fascinating hobby at the tender age of eight.

I would also like to thank the numerous photographers who have made a not inconsiderable contribution to the production of this book; and, of course, not forgetting the many hobbyists from whom I have received valuable tips on maintenance and breeding, and who have kindly provided me with eartheaters from their personal stocks.

In addition thanks are due to the companies Transfish, Planegg, Gerald Kellner, Mering, and Aquarium Glaser, Rodgau, who have given me every assistance in my search for eartheaters and have kindly supplied me with fishes.

I would particularly like to thank Frank Schäfer, a quite exceptional editor, who gave me every assistance in the correction of the text and the layout, and was an ever present help in bringing this book to fruition.

My sincerest thanks to my parents, Walter and Hildegard Weidner, who for more than 20 years have tolerated me and my watery hobby with the patience of saints. They have proved worthy "stand-ins", looking after my fishy friends during my absence, and been very understanding about the occasional "floods".

Last but not least, I would like to thank my partner, Petra Dotzer, as it was she

Introduction

The South American eartheaters are, by and large, easy to maintain provided the size of the aquarium is at least the minimum required by the species in question. They are amongst the most adaptable species of the South American continent. Adults are attractively coloured, long-lived, relatively easy to feed, and with luck can be induced to breed in almost any type of water. There is thus not the slightest reason for not trying them at least once — they are devoted parents with a fascinating behavioural repertoire that will never cease to amaze their owner. Do not make the mistake of judging them on the basis of their sometimes unfortunate common names or be put off buying them by the relative lack of colour in young specimens. The only reasons for not keeping eartheaters are insufficient tank size or aggressive tankmates, for although eartheaters sometimes attain a considerable size, they are unable to cope with bullying.

A further possible deterrent is the systematics of the group, which was very confused in the past, and remains confusing today, although the status of the different genera has been greatly clarified. However, travelling aquarists are forever bringing back new species which do not fit into the scheme devised for those already known. But what aquarist keeps only fishes whose taxonomy is crystal clear? In fact the only species that are kept are those whose appearance is attractive or which exhibit interesting brood-care behaviour. The South American eartheaters fit the bill on both counts!

Because eartheaters are relatively variable in their behaviour, the possibility exists that different individuals belonging to different aquarists, and kept under different conditions, will behave in different ways to those described here. But it is, when all is said and done, this variability that is the main attraction of our hobby. It may well be that you will make quite different observations of your own; if so, publicise them — every bit of information is important — and you will thus be making your own personal contribution to our knowledge of how to keep these fishes in captivity.

How to use this book

In the introductory section you will find general information on the history, systematics, geographical origin, and maintenance requirements of these cichlids. In the Species section the different taxa are described in detail. The references given at the end of the entry for each species are items that have appeared in the hobby literature and are concerned mainly with maintenance and breeding, although in the case of species little known in the hobby, original descriptions and general references are mentioned as well. A general bibliography is provided in the appendix, together with a glossary and, of course, an index.

Eartheaters in history

The first eartheater was scientifically described by Marcus Elieser Bloch more than 200 years ago, in 1791. At that time Bloch assigned these geophagine cichlids to the "catch-all" genus *Sparus*, naming them *Sparus surinamensis* after the region where they were collected. For almost half a century thereafter the species remained in that genus, until in 1840 the Austrian ichthyologist Jacob Heckel, in his work on "*Johann Natterers neue Flussfische Brasiliens nach den Beobachtungen und Mitteilungen des Entdeckers*" (Johann Natterer's new riverine fishes from Brazil, based on the observations and communications of the collector), assigned it to a new genus erected by him.

But in the meantime another eartheater, from the vicinity of Rio de Janeiro, had been described as *Chromis brasiliensis* by Quoy & Gaimard in 1824. The taxonomic status of this species remains unclear to the present day, as it does not conform with the normal eartheater habitus. The fishes sold under its current designation, *Geophagus brasiliensis*, actually include a number of different species, forming a species complex which will eventually probably be described as a separate genus.

Returning to 1840, Jacob Heckel laid the foundation, so to speak, of the classification of the geophagine cichlids, dealing with the eartheaters of central Brazil and grouping together all the species available to him at that time. In his work Heckel described seven species belonging to the *Geophagus* complex, and recognised the relationship that exists between the group of genera covered in this book on the basis of the structure of the epibranchials. In the following years considerable nomenclatural confusion reigned, and this persisted until the 1980s; even today

1. *Satanoperca acutipceps* from Rio Tauari — the four lateral spots are typical for *S. acuticeps*.
2. *Geophagus* cf. *altifrons* from Rio Aripuana.
3. *Satanoperca jurupari* (here a variant from Rio Capim) are ovophilous maternal mouthbrooders.

there is much debate, as new species are constantly being discovered and old ones rediscovered.

The seven species that Heckel assigned to the genus *Geophagus* were: *Geophagus altifrons, G. megasema, G. daemon. G. jurupari, G. acuticeps, G. pappaterra,* and *G. cupido*. Unfortunately Heckel was unaware of the close relationship between *Chromis brasiliensis* and the genus he had erected; and it would appear that he did not have access to Quoy & Gaimard's material, and hence followed Cuvier & Valenciennes (1831) in assigning the species to *Acara brasiliensis* without further investigation.

In 1848 Müller & Troschel described as *Acara heckelii* a species that is no longer included among the geophagines; this fish is today called *Acarichthys heckelii* (Müller & Troschel, 1848) and assigned to the acarichthyine cichlids. In the same year the same two authors described a further *Geophagus* species (*sensu* Heckel, 1840), namely *G. leucostictus*.

It was Castelnau who, in 1855, added further species to the catch-all genus *Chromys*. It comes as no surprise to find that this genus could not long be retained in its then form, as it contained a large number of very diverse cichlids which can easily be assigned to separate genera on the basis of visible external features alone. But at that time Castelnau assigned to that genus a number of eartheaters that in the years to come were reassigned to new genera. These were *Chromys lapidifera, C. proxima,* and a number of species now regarded as part of the *G. brasiliensis* complex: *C. obscura, C. unimaculata,* and *C. unipunctata*. Castelnau also assigned *C. ucayalensis* to *Chromys*, overlooking the fact that Heckel had already described this species as *Chaetobranchus flavescens* in 1840.

In 1862 the genus *Geophagus* Hekkel, 1840 was revised by Günther, who placed the species *Geophagus daemon, G. jurupari, G. acuticeps*, and *G. pappaterra* in his newly-erected genus *Satanoperca*. He was inclined to regard *Geophagus leucostictus* (Müller & Troschel, 1848) as a synonym of *Satanoperca jurupari*, and put a question mark next to the generic placement of this species. In the course of his revision he also described a new species, *Satanoperca macrolepis*, from Demerara, Guyana; nowadays this species is regarded as a synonym of *S. leucosticta*, but this synonymisation requires re-examination, as *Satanoperca* from Guyana appear to be more compressed than those from Surinam and French Guiana, moreover there are differences in the basic pattern and general coloration. In addition he regarded *Chromys proxima* as being closely related to *Satanoperca*, and this species was thus renamed *Satanoperca proxima*. Günther defined the genus *Satanoperca* as including all those species in which the base of the soft dorsal was unscaled. The species *Geophagus altifrons* Heckel, 1840 and *G. megasema* Heckel, 1840 were regarded by Günther as synonyms of *G. surinamensis* (Bloch, 1791), and distinct from *Satanoperca* on account of the scaled dorsal base — a distinction that remained unquestioned for a long time.

As part of his work Günther also erected the new genus *Mesops* for a newly-discovered species, *Mesops taeniatus* (now *Apistogramma taeniata* and the type species of the genus *Apistogramma*), and also assigned *Geophagus cupido* (Heckel, 1840) to the genus *Mesops*. He regarded many of the species identified by Castelnau, 1855, as *Chromys* as belonging to *Acara*, but at the same time he subdivided this genus into two groups, including *Acara brasiliensis* and its relatives in the group with five or fewer rows of scales on the cheek. Thus at that time we find *Acara brasiliensis, A. uniocellata*, and *A. obscura*. Meanwhile Castelnau's *Chromys unimaculata* was regarded as a synonym of *Acara brasiliensis*, and *Chromys unipunctata* (Castelnau, 1855) was assigned to the second group of *Acara* — those with more than five series of scales on the cheek. In describing *Acara gymnopoma* Günther produced, as was later discovered, another synonym of *Geophagus brasiliensis*.

In 1865 Kner realised that the cichlid described as *Chromis brasiliensis* by Quoy & Gaimard, 1824, and assigned to the genus *Acara* by Günther, 1862, was actually closely related to *Geophagus*, and included it in that genus as *Geophagus brasiliensis*.

Astonishingly at first cichlids were described only from the central Amazon region, even though the southern region was more easily accessible. Not until 1870 did Reinhold Hensel realise this fact, as a result describing six new southern species of *Geo-*

phagus: *G. pygmaeus*, *G. rhabdotus*, *G. scymnophilus*, *G. bucephalus*, *G. gymnogenys*, and *G. labiatus*. Today these southern eartheaters are better known under the scientific name *Gymnogeophagus*, and of the six species described by Hensel, only three are still valid, the other three having been synonymised with other species. But more of that later. In the same year Hensel also described *Acara minuta*, which was discovered in a pool at Porto Alegre, Rio Grande do Súl, Brazil, and which is now regarded as a further synonym of *Geophagus brasiliensis* (Quoy & Gaimard, 1824). Although his work covered both species, it was easy to overlook the fact that the two species were one and the same: the four specimens which he identified as *G. brasiliensis* (two of them likewise from Porto Alegre) were all more than 99 mm long, while the largest of the five specimens of *Acara minuta* was no more than 34 mm, not including the tail. If Hensel had followed Günther, 1862 in assigning all species without scales on the soft dorsal to the genus *Satanoperca*, then he would have placed *G. brasiliensis* in that genus as well. But he found that the transition between species with a scaled and scaleless dorsal was so gradual that no clear-cut distinction between the two genera was possible.

Likewise in 1870, in a report on two collections of fishes from the Marañon (= Amazon), Dr. Edward D. Cope noted that *Mesops taeniatus* (now *Apistogramma taeniata*) had been collected by John Hauxwell in the vicinity of Pebas, Ecuador, but published no further description of the specimens. In a later (1872) work Cope described *Geophagus amoenus* from the "River Ambyiacua" (= Rio Ampiyacú), Loreto Department, Peru). Today this name cannot be correlated with any species, as the type material has been lost and the species has not yet been rediscovered. Cope was well aware of the close relationship between his new species and *Mesops taeniatus*, but he did not accept Günther's division of *Geophagus* into *Mesops*, *Geophagus*, and *Satanoperca*, so he assigned it to *Geophagus*. In the same work he went on to describe a second *Geophagus*, *G. badiipinnis*, which is now regarded as a synonym of *Chaetobranchus flavescens* Heckel, 1840.

In 1875 the Austrian ichthyologist Franz Steindachner was of the opinion that some of the species described by Heckel (1840) represented no more than differences in sex and age. Moreover he concurred with Hensel — without, however, mentioning the latter's work — that the form of the scalation of the caudal base could not be used as a generic character. Being unaware of the earlier work of Cope (1872) and Hensel (1870), Steindachner returned to *Geophagus* the species described by Heckel (1840) and assigned to *Satanoperca* by Günther (1862) (*G. daemon*, *G. pappaterra*, *G. acuticeps*, and *G. jurupari*), but at the same time retained *Satanoperca* Günther, 1862 as a subgenus. In *Chromys proxima* Castelnau, 1855 (also assigned to

1. *Geophagus* sp. "Colombia" resembles *G. proximus* and *G.* sp. "Rio Negro I".
2. A male *Biotodoma cupido* "Santarém".
3. *Geophagus* sp. "Rio Areões" often exhibit two lateral spots.

Satanoperca by Günther, 1862) he saw no more than an old male of *Geophagus surinamensis*, and thus regarded the former as a synonym of the latter. *Geophagus cupido* Heckel, 1840 was now assigned to a subgenus *Mesops*, together with *G. (Mesops) taeniatus* and two new species, *G. (Mesops) thayeri* and *G. (Mesops) agassizii*; while *G. amoenus* Cope, 1872 was (probably correctly) synonymised with *G. (Mesops) taeniatus* Cope, 1870. Steindachner overlooked, however, the fact that his *Geophagus thayeri* had already been described by Müller & Troschel, 1848, under the name *Acara heckelii*.

In 1876 Steindachner described (in the "*Ichthyologischen Beitrage der Akademie Wien*") the first of the red-humped *Geophagus*, *G. crassilabris*, assigning the new species to he subgenus *Satanoperca*. The specimens were collected in a stream in the Isthmus of Panama.

In 1878, in an overview of the Peruvian fishes of the Amazon, collected by Professor Orton during an expedition from 1873 to 1877, Cope described *Acara subocularis*, now regarded as a synonym of *Acarichthys heckelii*.

In a work (1880) on the cichlids of the Cauca in Colombia, Steindachner identified as *G. brasiliensis* a cichlid which caused quite a stir in the 20th century and which we now know as *Geophagus steindachneri*, and which caused Eigenmann & Hildebrand a few headaches in 1909.

In 1891 Eigenmann & Eigenmann produced a list of the freshwater fishes of South America, again subdividing *Geophagus* into the subgenera *Mesops*, *Satanoperca*, and *Geophagus*. The species *G. thayeri*, *G. cupido*, *G. taeniatus* (syn. *amoenus*), *G. agassizii*, and *G. badiipinnis* were assigned to the subgenus *Mesops*. The subgenus *Satanoperca* contained *G. acuticeps*, *G. pappaterra*, *G. daemon*, *G. jurupari*, *G. crassilabris*, and the species originally described by Castelnau as *Chromys lapidifera* in 1855, now renamed *Geophagus (Satanoperca) lapidifer*; while to the subgenus *Geophagus* were assigned the six new species of *Geophagus* described by Hensel (1870) from southern Brazil, along with *G. brasiliensis* and *G. surinamensis*. In the same year Perugia described *Geophagus balzanii*, from the Rio Paraguay at Villa Maria, Mato Grosso, Brazil.

Three years later Eigenmann & Bray (1894) re-examined the American cichlids and published a revision, in whose introduction they stated that the genus *Geophagus*, along with a number of other genera, was in urgent need of revision, but that such a revision was beyond the scope of the current work because the authors quite simply did not have the necessary material available. These two authors did, nevertheless, describe a new genus, *Retroculus*, on the basis of a single specimen of the single species *Retroculus boulengeri*. It is strange that Eigenmann did not realise that three years previously he had examined the very same species as *Geophagus* (*Satanoperca*) *lapidifera*. The authors once again regarded *Mesops* as a subgenus of *Geophagus*, but with *G. cupido* as its type species. They further reiterated the view that *Satanoperca* and *Geophagus* could not be differentiated on the basis of dorsal fin scalation but without going into further detail. They further declared *G. acuticeps, G. jurupari, G. scymnophilus, G. surinamensis* to be valid species, while synonymising *Chromys* (or *Acara*) *unipunctata* Castelnau, 1855, *C. unimaculata* Castelnau,

1855, *Geophagus rhabdotus* Hensel, 1870, *G. bucephalus* Hensel, 1870, and *G. labiatus* Hensel, 1870 with *G. brasiliensis* (Quoy & Gaimard, 1824). It is, however, unclear what material they had available. In the same year Cope produced two more eventual synonyms in the form of *Geophagus brachyurus* (= *G. rhabdotus*) and *G. camurus* (= *G. gymnogenys*), from the Jacuhy River.

As the century approached its end, Boulenger (1895) described *Geophagus duodecimspinosus* from Paraguay; today this species is regarded as a synonym of *G. balzanii* Perugia, 1891.

As far as the geophagines are concerned, the beginning of the new century is associated with two notable men, the French ichthyologist Jacques Pellegrin, and the British naturalist Charles Tate Regan. Thus it was Pellegrin who, in 1902, in a work on the cichlids of French Guiana, described *Acara geayi*; and it was likewise Pellegrin who, in another work in the same year, once again drew attention to the fact that all these species, with the exception of *Acara geayi*, have a lobe-like appendage on the first epibranchial, and regarded them as all members of a single genus. Unfortunately he now used the name *Biotodoma*. Pellegrin regarded the position of the eyes as a primary generic character, but considered this less important than the low number of gill rakers or the position of the lateral line.

Curiously, in 1903 Pellegrin published the original description of *Geophagus camopiensis*, from the Camopi River, a tributary of the Oyapock River which forms the boundary between French Guiana and Brazil, as a *Geophagus* species. Likewise in 1903, Eigenmann and Clarence H. Kennedy described a new species of cichlid, collected by J. Daniel Anisits in Paraguay, as *Biotodoma trifasciata* (now *Apistogramma trifasciata*). These two authors suggested *Biotodoma* as a replacement name for *Mesops*, as Pellegrin had established that the name *Mesops* was preoccupied (used by Billberg in 1820 for another taxon) and thus no longer available for these cichlids. Interestingly Eigenmann & Kennedy assign a key role in their determination key to the epibranchial lobe on the gill arch, and describe these cichlids (the genus) as mouthbrooders, hence their choice of the name *Biotodoma*, "in allusion to their habit of carrying the young in the gills" (*biotos* (Greek) = living; *domos* (Greek) = home, house). In fact Cichocki (1977) established during research in the field that *Biotodoma cupido* is actually a substrate brooder.

In a series of publications between 1905 and 1906 Charles Tate Regan presented a revision of the South American cichlids, approaching the subject in closer detail than had Pellegrin. Regan did not agree with Pellegrin's opinion regarding *Mesops taeniatus*, and suggested the alternative generic name of *Heterogramma*, without designating a type species. Regan differentiated *Heterogramma* from *Geophagus* (!) *cupido* on the basis of the smaller number of dorsal spines (5-7 as opposed to 9-14) and in that the upper lateral line in *Heterogramma* lies appreciably closer to the dorsal (no more than a single row of scales distant) than in *Geophagus*.

In 1907 Eigenmann described an additional southern eartheater, *Geophagus australe*, from Buenos Aires (?), Argentina. And in 1909 Eigenmann & Hildebrand created a *nomen nudum* (= naked name), *Geophagus steindachneri*, as their article included neither a description nor a picture of this cichlid. A year later the same authors discovered that Franz Steindachner had incorrectly identified their new cichlid as a Colombian population of *Geophagus brasiliensis*. There was no question of synonymy: Steindachner had produced a scientific description and Eigenmann's identification and renaming (to *steindachneri*) constituted a proper description. Thus *Geophagus steindachneri* Eigenmann & Hildebrand, 1910 is a valid taxon in accordance with the International Code for Zoological Nomenclature. In 1922 Eigenmann & Hildebrand published a redescription of *G. steindachneri*.

In 1910 Eigenmann published a catalogue of the freshwater fishes of tropical South America in which he listed all the species known to date together with their synonyms. The work is worth mentioning not just on account of its completeness, but because it synonymises *Geophagus obscura* (Castelnau, 1855) with *G. brasiliensis* (Quoy & Gaimard, 1824).

In 1911 Haseman published a catalogue of cichlids collected during an expedition by the Carnegie Museum to South America, in which he described two new subspecies of *Geophagus brasiliensis*, *G. b. itapicuruensis* and *G. b. iporangensis*. In addition he did not recognise any subgenera within the genus *Geophagus*, and lists seven further species in the genus: *G. surinamensis*, *G. brachyurus*, *G. balzanii*, *G. cupido*, *G. gymnogenys*, *G. daemon*, and *G. jurupari*. He synonymises *G. acuticeps* with *G. daemon*, *G. pappaterra* with *G. jurupari*, and *G. brachyurus* and *G. camurus* with *G. gymnogenys*.

In 1912 two more red-humped eartheaters were scientifically described by Regan, under the names *Geophagus pellegrini* and *G. hondae* (*G. hondae* is now regarded as a junior synonym of *G. steindachneri* (Eigenmann & Hildebrand, 1910)). In the same year, in a description of the cichlids of British Guiana, Eigenmann erected the genus *Acarichthys*, with a single species, *Acarichthys heckelii* (Müller & Troschel, 1840). At the same time he stated that *Acara subocularis* (Cope, 1878), and *Geophagus thayeri* Steindachner, 1875, were synonyms of this species.

In 1913 Regan discovered that the name *Heterogramma* was preoccupied and published a description of the genus *Apistogramma*, to which he now transferred all the species previously included in *Heterogramma*. Thus the species formerly classified as *Geophagus* (*Mesops*) *taeniatus* (syn. *G.* (*M.*) *amoenus*), *G.* (*Mesops*) *agassizii*, and *G.* (*Biotodoma*) *trifasciatus* were now assigned to

Apistogramma, along with a number of other species not otherwise mentioned herein.

In the following years no significant work was performed on these cichlids on account of the First World War. Not until 1918 did A. de Miranda-Ribeiro describe a new genus, *Gymnogeophagus*, which he regarded as monotypic, with the type (and only) species *Gymnogeophagus cyanopterus*. Unfortunately he overlooked the fact that Perugia (1891) and Boulenger (1895) had both already described this species, as *Geophagus balzanii* and *G. duodecimspinosus*, respectively. For this reason *G. balzanii* is the type species of the genus *Gymnogeophagus*, and *G. cyanopterus* Miranda-Ribeiro, 1918 and *G. duodecimspinosus* Boulenger, 1895, are its junior synonyms.

In 1943 Brind described an aquarium population of *Geophagus steindachneri* as *G. magdalenae* — not surprisingly in the course of years of aquarium maintenance this population had undergone slight changes in its morphology, so that Brind thought he was describing a new species. *G. magdalenae* Brind, 1943 is now regarded as a synonym of *G. steindachneri* Eigenmann & Hildebrand, 1910.

In 1950 Fernandez-Yepez described *Geophagus mapiritensis* from the Rio Mapirito to the south of Maturín, Venezuela. There is no doubt that this species should now be assigned to the genus *Satanoperca*. But the rather complex question remains as to whether or not the taxon is valid. Gosse (1975) synonymised it with *Geophagus jurupari* Heckel, 1840 (he did not recognise the genus *Satano-*

perca as valid); Kullander (Internet: www. nrm. se) synonymises it with *Satanoperca leucosticta* (Müller & Troschel, 1848); while in an article by C. Schaefer (1992) there is a photo (by Uwe Werner) of a *Satanoperca* sp. (cf. *mapiritensis*). In my opinion *S. mapiritensis* should be regarded as a valid species until such time as a revision of the genus clarifies the matter, as on the basis of external characters it clearly differs from the two better known species.

In 1963 Gosse, in describing a further species of *Geophagus*, was of the same opinion as Regan and Pellegrin: he did not recognise the subgenus *Mesops*, nor at that time did he accept the name *Biotodoma* suggested by Eigenmann & Kennedy (1903). The new species was named after a Belgian naturalist, the Marquis de Wavrin.

It was likewise Gosse who, in 1971,

1. A male (upper fish) and a female *Geophagus* sp. "Tapajós - Orange Head".
2. A semi-adult male *Gymnogeophagus balzanii*.
3. An adult *Biotodoma wavrini*, imported from Venezuela.

revised the genus *Retroculus*, at the same time describing two new species: *Retroculus xinguensis* from the Rio Xingú, Brazil, and *R. septentrionalis* from the Rio Oyapock, French Guiana. He also determined that *Chromys lapidifera* Castelnau, 1855 was a senior synonym of *Retroculus boulengeri* Eigenmann & Bray, 1894, so according to the relevant rule of nomenclature the name *Retroculus lapidifer* (Castelnau, 1855) is valid.

In his 1976 revision of *Geophagus* Gosse split the genus up, resurrecting the genus *Biotodoma* Eigenmann & Kennedy, 1903, and at the same time removing two species — *Biotodoma cupido* (Heckel, 1840) and *B. wavrini* (Gosse, 1963) — from *Geophagus* Heckel, 1840. In this work he also described a new *Geophagus* species, *G. harreri*, from the Maroni system in the Guianas. Simultaneously he regarded *G. steindachneri* as a synonym of *G. hondae* and *G. mapiritensis* as a synonym of *G. jurupari*. He also evaluated specimens deposited in the Berlin Zoological Museum as the types of *Geophagus tuberosus* Müller & Troschel and of *G. olfersi* Müller & Troschel, species for which no descriptions exist, and identified them as *Geophagus brasiliensis*.

In the same work he revised the genus *Gymnogeophagus* Miranda-Ribeiro 1918, assigning to it not only the type species *Gymnogeophagus balzanii* (Perugia, 1891), but also *G. australis* (Eigenmann, 1907), *G. rhabdotus* (Hensel, 1870), *G. labiatus* (Hensel, 1870), and *G. gymnogenys* (Hensel, 1870), so that at present it includes a total of five valid species.

In 1986 Kullander reinstated the genus *Satanoperca* Günther 1862 in his book on the cichlids of the Peruvian Amazon, listing 12 characters by which the representatives of this genus can be differentiated from the genus *Geophagus*. He named *S. daemon* (Heckel, 1840), *S. acuticeps* (Heckel, 1840), *S. pappaterra* (Heckel, 1840), and *S. jurupari* (Heckel, 1840) as valid species, providing a redescription of the last-name species. In the same work he also resurrected *Geophagus proximus* (Castelnau, 1855), redescribing this species on the basis of material from Peru, the Trombetas drainage, the Tefé drainage, Lago Janauacá and Lago Amaña, demonstrating that this species has a very wide distribution.

In 1988 Reis and Malabarba performed a revision of the genus *Gymnogeophagus*, describing two new species, *G. lacustris* (from the coastal region of Brazil) and *G. meridionalis* (from the Rio Paraná and the Rio Uruguay system). In the same year Kullander and Ferreira described *Satanoperca lilith*, a new *Satanoperca* species from the Rio Negro drainage.

In 1989 Kullander and Nijssen published an extremely interesting work on the cichlids of Surinam, in which they redescribed *Geophagus surinamensis* (Bloch, 1791) and *G. harreri* Gosse, 1976, plus *Satanoperca leucosticta*, which was originally described as *Geophagus leucostictus* by Müller & Troschel (1848) and regarded as a synonym of *S. jurupari* by Günther (1862) — a synonymisation that had never been doubted in all the intervening years. But Kullander and Nijssen were able to detect a sufficient number of differences between this species and *S. jurupari* to regard them as separate species, and this was confirmed by ethological considerations: in the event *G. jurupari* (Heckel, 1840) is a maternal ovophilous mouthbrooder, while *S. leucosticta* (Müller & Troschel, 1848) is a biparental larvophilous mouthbrooder. In addition they described two new species: *Geophagus brokopondo* from the Afobaka region, and *G. brachybranchus* from the Nickerie drainage in western Surinam. In the same work they erected a new genus, *Guianacara*, with two subgenera, *Guianacara* and *Oelemaria*, and three new species: *Guianacara owroewefi* (type species of the subgenus *Guianacara*), *G. sphenozona*, and *G. oelemariensis* (type species of the subgenus *Oelemaria*). Also assigned to this genus was *Guianacara geayi* from French Guiana, originally described as *Acara geayi* by Pellegrin in 1902, and for a long time included in *Aequidens* before being recently (1980) transferred to the genus *Acarichthys* by Kullander. Today the genera *Guianacara* and *Acarichthys* together form the Tribe Acarichthyini, as they differ in several respects from the Tribe Geophagini.

In 1991 the number of described *Geophagus* was again increased by Kullander, who described a further species, *Geophagus argyrostictus* from the Rio Xingú. Just a year later two more species were described, this time from Venezuela, by Kullander, Royero & Taphorn: *Geophagus taeniopareius* and *G. grammepareius* — perhaps the two smallest eartheaters.

In 1992 Reis, Malabarba, & Pavanelli published the description of *Gymnogeophagus setequedas*, which was thought to have become extinct since the collection of the type material, but has since been relocated.

Finally, in 1998 Kullander erected a new subfamily, the Retroculinae, for the genus *Retroculus*. In his work on the phylogeny and classification of the South American cichlids he adduces valid reasons for transferring these cichlids to this new, extremely primitive, subfamily (see the section on the genus *Retroculus*, below). The cichlids of this subfamily are nevertheless included here, as for a long time they were assigned to the subfamily Geophaginae.

The natural habitat

Géry (1969) (drawing in Lowe-McConnell, 1975) was able to divide the South American continent into about eight different ichthyofaunal regions on the basis of natural barriers such as the Andes and the Guiana Shield. These natural barriers are of different ages and have thus had different effects on the overall evolutionary history of the fauna, including that of the eartheaters. Thus we find that some genera are found only in specific, limited, regions, while others have a very wide distribution.

The largest region is without doubt the **Amazon** drainage, which is also the largest interconnected river system on Earth, covering approximately 6.5 million square kilometres. The River Amazon, from which the region takes its name, discharges circa 175,000 cubic metres of water per second into the Atlantic over an area about 320 km wide. It originates as a tiny stream at an altitude of 5,000 metres, and is subsequently joined by other mighty rivers and smaller ones, plus innumerable streams and rivulets, over a length of 6500 km. From its source to Manaus it is known as the Rio Solimões, and by the time it reaches Manaus it is the largest river on earth; at its mouth it holds back the Atlantic for a distance of 200 km out to sea. Because in its lower course it has a drop of only 1 cm per kilometre it is possible to detect the effect of the rise and fall of the tides well upstream; every 12 hours the water level rises and falls by about 40 cm some 900 km inland at Santarém.

The average depth of the Amazon is 40-50 metres, and thus sea-going ships are able to travel along it for up to 3,700 km inland. The large southern tributaries such as the Rio Madeira, the Rio Tapajós, the Rio Tocantins, and the Rio Xingú have all formed lakes where they join the Amazon, as over the millennia their water has cut into the ground on finding itself held back by the rise in the level of the main river, which is itself "dammed" by the rising tide at its mouth. The Rio Madeira and the Rio Negro each empty practically as much water into the Amazon as the Congo empties into the Atlantic, and in terms of volume the Congo is the second largest river on Earth. The Amazon region is bounded by the Andes to the west, the Atlantic to the east, the Guiana Shield to the north, and the Brazilian Shield to the south.

The **Guianas** region, to the north of the Amazonian lowlands, is closely connected, in evolutionary terms, with the Amazon region. Its natural boundaries are the *tepuis* (table mountains) of Venezuela to the west, the Atlantic to the northeast and the Guiana Shield to the south. The Guiana Shield is a plateau that descends steeply to the north, to an inundation zone that extends to the Atlantic. Its rivers either empty directly into the Atlantic as in the case of the Essequibo and the Maroni or Corantijn, or, like the Rio Paru, are tributaries of the Amazon. The countries of this region (Surinam, Guyana, and Guiana) are, like the Amazon region, home to an almost unimaginable number of geophagine cichlids of the genera *Geophagus* and *Satanoperca*. Typical of the Guiana region is the genus *Guianacara*, whose name betrays its origins.

The **Orinoco** region encompasses practically all of Venezuela and a small part of Colombia, an area of 930,000 sq km in total. Originally the Amazon and Orinoco regions formed a single unit, before the Sierra Parima was uplifted in the southern part of the Orinoco region, forming a natural watershed. Astonishingly in its upper course the 1900 km long Orinoco feeds part of its water, via the Canal Casiquiare into the Rio Negro, and hence the Amazon. The Rio Orinoco is essentially a blackwater river, which becomes significantly more turbid in its lower course due to the sediment

1. The different ichthyofaunal regions of South America.
2. Eartheaters are rare near densely vegetated banks and under floating meadows. The upper Rio Guarico in Venezuela shortly before it flows into (the dammed) Lake Guarico.
3. A boat is the preferred means of transportation in Amazonia and in other parts of South America.

load derived from its floodplain. Its delta occupies an area of 13,000 sq. km. and is largely overgrown with mangroves, such that the transition zone contains chiefly fresh water. The region is bordered by the Andean *cordilleras* to the west, the Guiana Shield to the east, the already-mentioned Sierra Parima to the south, and the Atlantic to the north. The region harbours a considerable number of geophagine cichlids: *Geophagus* and *Satanoperca*, and, within the sphere of influence of the Guiana Shield, *Guianacara* as well.

A quite different group of eartheaters are found in the **Magdalena** region, named after the river of the same name. The northern cordilleras and their outliers form a natural river valley and the 1000 km long Rio Magdalena flows within this single valley to the Caribbean. The valley in some respects resembles the African rift valley, as it was formed by the sinking of part of the Earth's crust. Because it was formed only recently, geologically speaking, the waters of the Magdalena basin are relatively mineral-rich, and thus water hardness measures up to 10° dGH and the pH lies in the neutral zone. This region is "famous" for the red-humped eartheaters, above all *Geophagus steindachneri*, although both its close relatives are also found here even though *G. pellegrini* is found more in the trans-Andean region.

The **trans-Andean** region is separated from the Magdalena region by the Cordillera Occidentale, and forms a narrow coast strip along the edge of the Pacific. While its rivers are very cool and fast-flowing in their upper courses, as they near the Pacific they become calm, sediment-rich rivers flowing across the lowlands. By and large the water parameters correspond to those of the Magdalena region.

The Andean region and the Patagonian region have no relevance as regards eartheaters, or, indeed, to aquarists in general, as water temperatures are extremely cold, at least some of the time.

By contrast the **La Plata** Basin, whose main rivers are the Rio Paraná, the Rio Paraguay, and the Rio Uruguay, is an interesting region. It is the home of the *Gymnogeophagus* species, with *G. balzanii* the most northerly species, crossing the border into the Amazonian region. The La Plata drainage is the second largest river system in South America. To the west lie the Andes, and to the north the Mato Grosso, forming natural boundaries on these two sides. The region is famous worldwide for the Pantanal National Park: a region of swamps which is home to numerous reptiles and aquatic birds. This paradise is, however, threatened by a hydroelectric project and intensive agricultural use.

The Rio Paraná and the Rio Uruguay enter the Atlantic at Buenos Aires, and thus, just as at similar latitudes in the northern hemisphere, the southern part of the region is subject to seasonal variations in temperature, with seasons comparable to those of southern Europe, a fact that should be borne in mind when keeping the southern species of *Gymnogeophagus* in the aquarium. These species require a sort of "winter break" at lower temperatures in order to regain their vigour, and if deprived of this winter rest they will become susceptible to disease and their life expectancy will be significantly reduced.

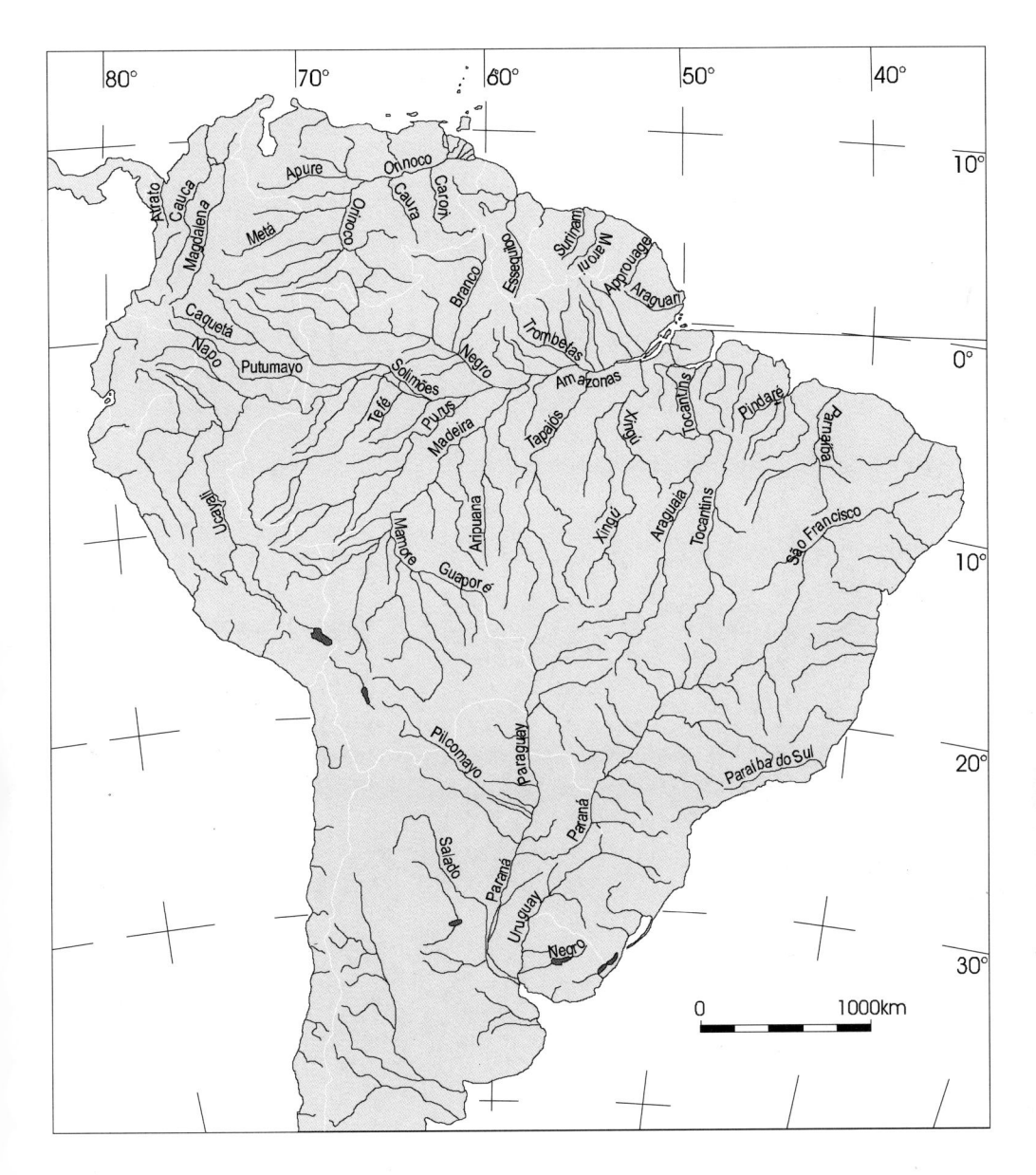

The final region is **eastern Brazil**, which is characterised by the fact that the majority of its rivers empty into neither the La Plata nor the Amazon system, but directly into the Atlantic. This region is divided into a northern and a southern part. With regard to keeping the cichlids (or other fishes) from the southern part (Rio Grande do Sol province), the same applies as for the southern part of the La Plata system. The northern part of eastern Brazil is characterised by a specific type of vegetation and its many endemic cichlids. The land often dries up completely to form desert areas. In the larger rivers, however, i.e. those which flow all year round, it is possible to find eartheaters and other cichlids. Thus members of the *Geophagus brasiliensis* complex are found throughout eastern Brazil, from the Rio Itapicurú to the Rio de Ribeiro de Iguapi. The longest river in the region is the Rio São Francisco, at 3200 km.

Types of Water

Despite the vastness of the region, in all parts the flowing waters fall into three principal categories, which may influence the maintenance requirements of the fishes that live in them. It was Harald Sioli who, in 1950 and subsequently, demonstrated that the nature and composition of the water in a river are dependent on geology, climate, lithology, and topology. The colour of

1. The Igarapé Ambroso near Alenquer — mainly juvenile eartheaters are found in such shady habitats.
2. Satellite photo of the confluence of the Rio Negro with the Rio Solimões near Manaus. Photo: NASA.
3. Following the Amazon river from Manaus going towards Santarém one needs to fly about 20 minutes before the blackwater of the Rio Negro completely mixes with that of the Rio Solimões (whitewater).
4. The mixing zone of a clearwater and a whitewater river. Both Rio Guariquito (clearwater) and Rio Guarico (whitewater) flow very gently; the effect is that their mixing area resembles a "hazy day" underwater.

a river and its transparency are, so to speak, a function of, and dependent on, the landscape across which it flows and the type(s) of sediment washed into it from the surrounding land. It should also be noted that the diverse smaller tributaries of a large river can significantly affect its appearance. For example, the Rio Tapajós is essentially a clearwater river, but because gold prospectors have tipped and washed vast quantities of sediment and mercury into the Rio Jamanxim, which empties into the Tapajós, that formerly clearwater river is increasingly becoming a whitewater stream. Another example is the lower course of the Rio Negro, downstream of its confluence with the Rio Branco. Because of its low nutrient levels the upper course of the Rio Negro is very unproductive at a primary level, and thus harbours few fishes; by contrast the Rio Branco is a whitewater river with a high sediment burden and is thus very rich in nutrients — and the result is a larger variety of species.

Whitewaters are characterised by an enormously high fish density, but are the least transparent (10-50 cm visibility). For the most part the classic whitewater rivers rise in the Andes. Because the rocks in question are relatively young the rivers can acquire a heavy load of sediment. An additional factor is the fact that the steep eastern slopes of the Andes have one of the highest levels of rainfall on earth. Obviously the heavy precipitation erodes the soil and washes it into the rivers, which then carry it away downstream. As a result the Amazon, a classic example of a whitewater river, carries an estimated thousand million tonnes of sediment down to the Atlantic every year. Another result of this sediment burden is that the course of the Amazon is constantly altered over the centuries as the inorganic sediment is deposited along the way and then eroded again.

The pH of this type of river is relatively high, at 6.2-7.2. Many eartheaters live in whitewaters, but it is neither necessary nor desirable to try and create a whitewater habitat in the domestic aquarium. From an optical viewpoint a clearwater aquarium is preferable, and numerous eartheaters are found in this type of water as well.

Clearwaters contain mostly dissolved inorganic substances and visibility ranges from one to four metres, while at the same time the water is a yellow to olive-green colour. Depending on the source of the water the pH may range from 4.5 to 7.8; thus the clearwater rivers of the Amazonian lowlands, which originate in tertiary rocks, have a pH of only 4.5, while the waters flowing from the highlands of central Brazil and the Guiana Shield have a pH of between 5.5 and 6.6. In addition the waters flowing across the calcium-rich limestone and gypsum deposits to the north and south of the lower Amazon may have an average pH of 7.8.

The fish population density varies tremendously depending on the pH. Because it is almost impossible for submerse vegetation to thrive at low pH values, then fishes can survive only if they occupy specialised feeding niches, as do, for example, the eartheaters. High pH values may also lead to lower fish densities.

Clearwater rivers are typically found where the soil is loamy and contains iron, and the surrounding vegetation forms the lofty Amazonian forest. Typical examples are the Rio Xingú, the Rio Tocantins, and formerly the Rio Tapajós, as well as the right-bank tributaries of the upper Rio Madeira, which all originate in the Brazilian Shield and originate in carboniferous rocks. These rivers also contain numerous areas of rapids, which complete the picture of a clearwater river.

A few eartheaters are regarded as **blackwater** species, for example *Satanoperca daemon*, in which egg development is possible only at a pH of less than 5.0. This species is thus more or less restricted to blackwaters, which typically have a pH of 3.7-4.9 and are olive to (black) coffee-brown in colour, with good transparency (visibility, generally speaking, one to three metres). The pH is lowered by the presence of organic substances in the form of humic acids, such that blackwater rivers also exhibit a certain paucity of fishes. Primary production takes place only on a limited basis on account of the lack of nutrients, for which reason such rivers are often referred to as hunger rivers. The organic content of the blackwater rivers derives from the stunted woodland known as *caatinga* and *campina*, which is the predominant vegetation on the tropical podsols. Other typical features of these rivers are paucity of calcium and magnesium salts in the underlying rock strata, as well as a coarse-grained sandy substrate. These regions are also noted for their high humidity and precipitation. The picture is completed by vegetation with a low nutrient requirement. Typical blackwaters include the Rio Negro, the Rio Arapiuns, and the Rio Tefé, in which various eartheaters are to be found.

Because the South American eartheaters are largely adaptable species, no particular type of water can be identified as their primary habitat. In addition, the large rivers which are their preferred habitat in general contain a mixture of water types. Nevertheless there are a few basic elements that always form part of the eartheater biotope. As can be deduced from their common name, the substrate will be sandy, or at least soft, so that it can be sifted for edible organic material. It is irrelevant whether it is swampy, muddy, or sandy. There will also be rocks and/or roots to provide shelter from predators. Because during the rainy season many of the rivers of South America flood the surrounding area far beyond their banks, then all of a sudden vast amounts of roots on a muddy substrate are available as shelter, while during the dry season there is nothing but a sandy bottom with no cover.

Eartheaters are found mainly in the larger rivers and, during the rainy season, in the inundation zone. The smaller streams and rivulets, by contrast, are the habitat of their smaller relatives, the dwarf cichlids of the genus *Apistogramma*, etc. Taking the fish habitats listed by Fink & Fink (1979), the following biotopes can be termed preferred eartheater habitats: open water in rivers and lakes, side channels and backwaters, and the bank zones of these bodies of water; including grassy banks with water meadows, wooded banks, mud banks, and above all sandbanks. These cichlids are also found in grassy or wooded wetlands, as well as in fast-flowing large rivers with a solid substrate of sand and rocks, as can often be found in the so-called *cachoeiras* (rapids).

From these brief remarks we can conclude that the larger geophagine cichlids must possess a degree of tolerance as regards environmental conditions, as although each of the various species occupies only one of these biotopes as its primary habitat, eartheaters are often encountered in areas where they are not expected.

However, there are also variations within a species, dependent on the

age of the fish concerned. Some species visit specific areas to spawn if a specific factor is necessary to ensure reproductive success. This may be an element of water chemistry, for example a lower pH, that favours egg development; or an area that offers plenty of shelter from predators. It is very easy to observe how particularly large numbers of juveniles are to be found in areas with numerous dense thickets of plants, tangles of roots, or even piles of leaf litter. Of course this applies equally to a large number of aquarium fishes as well as to earth-eaters. Later on, as the fishes grow older, they can no longer find shelter from large underwater predators in such areas, and so they move to the bank zones where the water is only a few centimetres deep and thus offers adequate protection from large predators. By contrast adult individuals prefer deeper water, as their size means they no longer figure on everybody's menus, and with increasing age they are better able to defend themselves. Besides which adults are more vulnerable to predatory birds in the bank zone.

Of course these data do not apply to each and every species, as geographical barriers and specialised biotopes may require the fishes to "remain faithful" to their ancestral habitat and habits.

1. *Satanoperca daemon* are very sensitive to the quality of the aquarium water.
2. Some eartheaters, such as e.g. *Retroculus*, prefer fast flowing waters. The photo shows the rapids (*cahoeira*) above São Luis do Tapajós.
3. Sunset over the Amazon River near Alenquer.

The Aquarium

Although the eartheater group includes relatively small species of about 10-12 cm, the aquarium should have a capacity of not less than 200 litres. If species such as *Retroculus* spp., *Geophagus altifrons*, or *Satanoperca daemon* are to be kept, then the bottom area should be at least 150 x 50 cm. There are, of course, no upper limits to tank size. If one is intending to keep eartheaters and install a new aquarium in the home, then it should be borne in mind that the natural habitat of these fishes is the sandy zone, and thus the bottom area of the aquarium is of particular importance, and a large bottom area is advantageous. A deep aquarium can also be beneficial, in that it is easier to arrange, using skilful decoration, to provide an effective simulation of a natural biotope and thus be visually more attractive.

In addition a large bottom area generally permits observation of more natural behaviour (including territorial behaviour) than is possible in a small aquarium. In this respect the depth of the aquarium plays a subordinate role, and is important really only for aesthetic reasons — for example, an adult *Geophagus altifrons*, with a body depth of 10-15 cm, does not look particularly good in a 40 cm deep aquarium, especially when the substrate and the hood reduce the actual depth of water to 30 cm.

The aquaria generally available in the trade today are assembled using silicone sealant, and there is sometimes a choice as regards the mode of construction and the colour of the sealant. The method of construction is by and large not relevant; a longer guarantee period may be involved — but only at a higher price, and cheaper tanks normally last for just as long. Black silicon has the advantage that algae cannot discolour the joins.

The aquarium should be sited in as dark a spot as possible, as direct sunlight will encourage algal growth. In addition it should be borne in mind that the aquarium should be situated in a relatively quiet place, and not, for example, behind a door that is constantly being opened. A location subject to such disturbance will often cause stress in the aquarium occupants, sooner or later leading to ill-health. When installing a large aquarium the load-bearing capacity of the floor and base should be taken into consideration, as a 500 litre aquarium generally weighs some 600 kg when filled.

Equipment

Once the aquarium size has been decided, then the necessary equipment must be considered. The other way round is less sensible, as the equipment required is a function of aquarium size. The most important elements of the equipment are the heating and filtration, and the aquarist should not skimp on cost or space (for the filter) as regards these items.

Where the maintenance of eartheaters is concerned the lighting is of lesser importance. Large geophagine cichlids require only muted lighting in the aquarium, although in the wild they sometimes encounter brighter illumination from the sun. But if you try to simulate this in the aquarium then you will soon discover that the fishes react by being timid or even frightened. There are two ways of avoiding this: firstly, the aquarium can be decorated with plants that form extensive growth at the surface, for example *Cryptocoryne usteriana* and various *Vallisneria* varieties, in order to create shade. Or the problem can be approached from an electrical viewpoint, i.e. by simply providing very little lighting, e.g. a single 36 watt tube for a 600 litre aquarium. That is, of course, rather dim, and may take some getting used to in a well-lit living-room. The spectrum of the lighting is less important, and can be to suit the aquarist's personal aesthetic requirements.

Rather more attention should be paid to the heating, which maintains the aquarium at the appropriate temperature that constitutes one of the basic life requirements of our cichlids. But remember that the different genera often have different temperature requirements. For example, *Gymnogeophagus* require a maximum temperature of 18° C during their quiescent winter period, but this can be raised to 25° C during the breeding season. By contrast eartheaters from the Amazonian lowlands can tolerate 34° C for several weeks and may actually require such high temperatures to induce courtship. The two groups should thus not be kept together.

But what type of heating is advisable for the eartheater aquarium? Heating cables buried in the substrate have the advantage of ensuring even heat distribution throughout the aquarium, and are generally safe from the attentions of "normal" fishes. But bear in mind that you are going to be keeping fishes that are quite likely to clear away the sand in part of the aquarium, exposing the cable to possible damage (e.g. chewing by the eartheaters while feeding) and ultimately short-circuiting of the heater.

The safest form of heating for the eartheater aquarium is undoubtedly the internal combined heater-thermostat. Modern models have an extra safety mechanism to switch them off when not immersed. Older models, not thus equipped, can overheat and burn out, fracturing the glass tube and leading to a short circuit, if you forget to disconnect them from the mains during water changes. If you are the owner of such a model, then please invest in a new one with an "out-of-water cut-out", for your own safety.

The wattage of the heating will depend on the ambient room temperature and the water temperature required. For example, if a 500 litre aquarium is to be heated to 30° C, in a room at 18° C, then in general 300

31

watts of heating will be required, while if the temperature difference is only 7° C then 200 watts will suffice. If the aquarium is properly tended, and daily checks made, then you will be bound to notice if the tank is too cool, and increase the wattage of the heating. Your dealer will undoubtedly be able to help you tailor your heating to your specific requirements.

The filtration is undoubtedly the part of the equipment deserving of the greatest attention. Eartheaters are fishes which in nature feed almost continuously during the daylight hours and this point should not be underestimated in the aquarium. In a fully-matured and properly-maintained aquarium these cichlids will find plenty of nourishment in the substrate, as well as taking the food offered, and will continue to forage in the substrate until there is truly nothing edible to be found there. Do not

1. The eartheaters' habitat consists of an open sand bottom and therefore the aquarium should be decorated sparingly. A few plants, bogwood, and rocks should be placed in the tank to give the fishes some sort of shelter. *Corydoras* or other South American cichlids are appropriate companions.
2. Eartheaters produce a lot of waste which has to be removed efficiently. Large filters are not a luxury; the photo shows a custom-made three-compartment trickle filter.
3. The eartheater communities should consist of compatible species. *Retroculus lapidifer* and *Geophagus argyrostictus* both are found in fast flowing water, grow to a similar maximum size, and require the same type of food.

underestimate the resulting quantities of wastes. The filter must therefore be of adequate size, and, to provide suitable biological filtration, have an appropriate turnover rate. Basically, the aquarium volume should be turned over by the filter at least once per hour. But bear in mind that the nominal turnover rate may be affected by the choice of filter media. The siting of the filter relative to the aquarium must also be taken into consideration. For example, if an open filter is positioned beneath the aquarium, then the pump will need to be very powerful in order to pump water back into the aquarium. In addition the period the filter has been in use should not be ignored, as clogged filter media can significantly diminish the turnover of a filter. For these reasons you should choose a filter rated for a turnover of 2-3 times the aquarium volume per hour.

Essentially, a power filter is the best choice. Internal filters have the advantage that, being sited in the aquarium, they do not require hoses (which may accidentally become detached and lead to flooding). The disadvantage of internal filters is their small capacity. By contrast, external filters generally offer a greater volume and the option of using a variety of media. In practice a combination of the two systems may be the optimal solution. Whatever type of filter you in fact choose, the return should always be sited at or above the water's surface to optimise oxygen uptake.

In addition there are air-driven filtration systems whose installation in large aquaria generally requires a degree of practical skill, as they need to be cut to fit the aquarium in question. Moreover air-driven systems are normally fitted internally, and because they take up a lot of space and are not particularly pleasing visually, they are more suitable for breeding aquaria or fish-rooms.

Finally, there is the possibility of using a trickle filter, but the cost of buying such a filter may outstrip your budget. But with a little practical skill, and a reasonable understanding of water pressure in tubes and containers, it is possible to build your own. But we will not go into that in greater detail here.

In conclusion, it should be mentioned that very long aquaria (more than 2.5 metres) require two filters, one at either end, as a single filter is unlikely to provide optimal filtration in an aquarium of such length. Whether two externals, two internals, or one of each, are used, is a matter of personal choice.

Filtration equipment also includes diaphragm air-pumps, which have, however, tended to be forgotten recently because of the fashion for well-planted aquaria. But, because eartheaters require plenty of swimming space and open sand, dense planting is not appropriate to their aquarium, hence additional aeration by means of an air-pump is a viable option. This type of artificial aeration can give you peace of mind: if, for whatever reason, the pump or the filter malfunctions, then there will still be adequate oxygenation of the aquarium. If you don't like the sight of the bubbles, then you have the option of positioning a flat stone, e.g. a slate, in front of the diffuser in order to reduce the disturbing visual impact.

Decor

The decor of a biotope aquarium for eartheaters should be carefully thought out, as skilfully designed "interior architecture" will provide the fishes with a greater sense of security, and they will reward you with increased vitality and brighter coloration. If you first learn about the natural lifestyle of the cichlids then the task will be that much easier. Although these are fishes of open sandy areas, in captivity they like to have cover to at least one side in the aquarium. For this reason the tank should by preference have a background — avoid using the aquarium as a room-divider! Because wallpaper is a less than fitting adjunct to the aquatic scene, the backdrop should form an integral part of the aquarium decor. There are a number of possibilities. Firstly, you can stick a pictorial background (underwater scene) to the outside of the rear glass — such backgrounds can be obtained at any aquarium store. However, it is difficult to find a background to match the internal decor; moreover one can quickly become bored with such backgrounds and they then become more irritating than biotope-correct in their effect. It is better to have a neutral background, e.g. dark-coloured cardboard. The actual colour — black, blue, brown, green, etc. — is again a matter of personal taste. Another option is, of course to paint the outer side of the rear glass with waterproof paint, but this has the disadvantage that it is then very difficult to change the background. A further possibility is to make a "showcase", about 10 cm thick to provide perspective, and set with bits of rock, bark, and cork, and position this behind the aquarium. The disadvantage of this is the wasted space behind the tank — an additional 10 cm of aquarium width would be better. Probably the best solution is to use a compressed cork internal background attached to the bottom and end glasses to keep it in place. Don't forget that cork — especially such a large piece of cork — is incredibly buoyant, and use large heavy stones in front of it, to hold it in place. This background can then be decorated with plants such as *Anubias*, and will in addition prevent the reflections which often spoil the effect of an aquarium. Cork sheet can be obtained via the aquarium trade, and buying this type will ensure that the cork does not contain adhesives that might contaminate the aquarium water. A few years ago preformed backgrounds made of polyurethane foam were introduced into the hobby, which were fitted inside the aquarium and were astonishingly realistic. These had a number of disadvantages, however — high price, loss of swimming space, and sometimes less cover for the fishes. You can, of course, apply polyurethane foam to the rear glass yourself, but the background cannot then be varied at a later date.

The choice of substrate also requires some consideration, as this will be an important feature of the cichlids' habitat in the aquarium. Grain size should under no circumstances exceed 2 mm, and the finer the better. One can even use a grain size of well below 0.5 mm in an eartheater aquarium, as even with a layer 5 cm thick there is no possibility of the substrate "going bad" because the fishes will constantly turn it over in their search for food. The grain size needs to be that small because the fishes are in the habit of passing it out through their gills. If the sand taken into the mouth is ejected via the mouth opening, then this indicates that the sand is too coarse. It is, of course, permissible to have a small amount of coarser gravel as a bottom layer, in order to make the substrate less uniform, but the bulk should always be fine sand. This brings additional benefits: if the eartheaters can expel sand via their gills, then this could free their gills of large parasites. One may also surmise that they swallow a certain amount of sand, which may not only serve to aid digestion but also have a cleansing effect on the flora of the digestive system. It should perhaps be noted here that there is no cause for concern that the fishes will disrupt the decor or even the substrate with their activities. They do, as their common name of eartheater implies, "process" the substrate, but they usually do this so evenly that the surface of the sand normally remains level. A few species, for example *Geophagus taeniopareius*, may sometimes construct pits during the breeding season, but this does not last for long.

As regards additional decoration, almost any material available from the trade or in nature can be used. But do bear in mind that the aquarium is not meant to be a display cabinet for decorative materials. It is best to stick to a mixture of rocks and wood, but not just any old rocks and wood. Wood which is to be used in the aquarium should have been weathered for sufficient time, such that it will no longer release any toxic substances into the water. Bogwood is ideal, as its long immersion in peaty soil means that it will release only tannins into the water, giving the water a brownish coloration. These tannins will not negatively affect the health of fishes from tannin-rich waters, which includes many (but not all) geophagines. On the contrary, it has even been suggested that tannins stimulate the immune system and may even trigger breeding. In addition they may help lower the pH to the level required (for acid-water species) and have a buffering effect. It is also possible, of course, to use local roots or wood, but great care is required, as such wood may contain unsuitable substances. The presence of toxins is sometimes indicated by sudden darkening in coloration and nervous behaviour.

Rocks should, essentially, contain no calcium carbonate or other minerals that might lead to an undesirable increase in water hardness. It is best to stick to one type of rock, as a variety will make the aquarium look "fussy" and create an unnatural effect — only rarely is a mixture of rocks found in the same place in nature. Smooth stones are vastly preferable to rough ones, as fishes can injure themselves on sharp edges and substrate-spawning species require a smooth spawning substrate. A few stones should be positioned on the open sand, as such places are often preferred as spawning sites. But avoid siting heavy rocks directly on the bottom glass, as this could lead to breakage.

Plants may, of course, be considered as additional decor. There is no reason not to include plants when keeping eartheaters, as they are generally not hostile towards vegetation. But fine-leaved plants should nevertheless be avoided, as they soon become coated in mulm from the sifting. The best plants are those with broad leaves, but given the rather muted lighting preferred by geophagine cichlids, it is best to select plants that are happy with little light, for example *Anubias*, various Cryptocorynes, *Hygrophila, Vallisneria, Microsorium pteropus* (Java fern), and some *Echinodorus*. The plants should either be well-rooted before the fishes are introduced, or else their roots should be protected by large stones, as eartheaters are prone to uprooting poorly-rooted plants — the result is either an aquarium full of floating plants or lots of work repeatedly replanting them. Then again,

1. Eartheaters are not solitary fishes and should be kept in small groups of at least 4 individuals.
2. Regarding their temperament and feeding habits *Biotodoma cupido* and *Satanoperca acuticeps* resemble each other and they can therefore be kept in the same aquarium.

true floating plants such as *Riccia* or *Salvinia* can be used to improve our eartheater aquarium still further, as they provide additional shade, which suits the cichlids down to the ground.

Water Parameters

While it is very easy to cater for the requirements of our fishes as regards the aquarium equipment and decor, providing the correct water parameters can be quite a different matter. In some regions mains water, straight from the tap, is very close to the legal limits defining drinking water, and some of the parameters used to decide whether or not water is potable can often be determined only by specially equipped laboratories, which makes things even more difficult.

The values cited in books are normally just for the parameters that can easily be measured by aquarists, e.g. hardness, pH, conductivity, and aspects of water quality such as ammonia, nitrite, and nitrate levels. As regards hardness, pH, and conductivity, mains water rarely exceeds, respectively, 30° dGH, pH 8.0, and 1000 µS/cm. These can be regarded as upper limits of tolerance for eartheaters, although lower values are beneficial — especially for breeding — and sometimes absolutely essential for good health.

The values for nitrogen cycle by-products, e.g. ammonia, nitrite, Nitrate, are even more important. There should never be measurable levels of ammonia and nitrite, as these are highly toxic for fish. Nitrate, one of the end-products of the breakdown of wastes during the nitrogen cycle, may be present in mains water up to a maximum legal limit (50 mg/l in some countries); and in some areas the water comes from the tap with a nitrate content very close to that legal limit. And that is where our problems really begin. The oxidation of the metabolic wastes of our fishes raises the nitrate content of the water, and the level can quickly rise to in excess of 100 mg/l. Elevated nitrate values may in turn be detrimental to the health of the fishes. Optimally maintained aquaria should never have a nitrate level higher than 50 mg/l.

While these parameters can be measured at home, this is not possible for a number of other adverse chemicals, for example organic compounds which are permitted in only minute traces in mains water as they can be harmful to living organisms even at very low concentrations. These compounds include pesticides, herbicides, and fungicides used in agriculture to protect crops and livestock. These may get into our water supplies and we have little idea what effect they may have. And they can be measured only at great expense in specially equipped laboratories — assuming there is any method for detecting them at all.

In the face of this appalling scenario there are nevertheless ways of providing water ideally suited to the aquarium. First, however, you must ask yourself whether you want to breed the fishes or just keep them. Though you should bear in mind that we are talking about life forms designed to live under specific optimal conditions and that we have a duty to simulate those conditions in the aquarium. Even if we do not wish to breed them, our fishes will reward our efforts with better colours and livelier behaviour, which alone will make it all worth while.

The first method of preparing unsuitable water is via a reverse osmosis (RO) unit. During the reverse osmosis process the water is forced through a semipermeable membrane through which dissolved trace elements and mineral salts cannot pass. The resulting water can be up to 95% pure. The advantages of RO are that it is easily performed, and that all dissolved substances are removed, including organics. The disadvantage is that there is a high wastage element, with, depending on the type and configuration of the unit, 4-10 litres of mains water required to produce 1 litre of processed water. While this may be acceptable for a single aquarium, the economic and environmental aspects must be taken into consideration where a whole fishhouse is concerned. In such cases an industrial unit may seem preferable as this will provide a better product-to-waste ratio. But when you see the price of such units you may rapidly change your mind.

Another method is deionisation, which removes ions (charged particles) (i.e. inorganic compounds) but not organic substances. A further minus is the complexity of the process, as the resins used in a deioniser need to be regenerated using soda lye (caustic soda solution) and hydrochloric acid, both dangerous chemicals requiring careful handling. The main advantage is the favourable ratio between usable water and waste — about 20:1. The minerals that cause hardness, phosphate, sulphates, and ionised nitrogen compounds are removed, but organic compounds are not, so additional filtration through activated carbon is advisable, as this may remove most of the organics.

Neither of these two processes produces water immediately suitable for aquarium use, as it will be "dead" water with no buffering capacity. Although this may seem illogical, the water must be partially hardened, for example by the admixture of some tap water, as otherwise the pH will be unstable and may drop to a level lethal to the fishes. As a general rule of thumb, 5-20% (the exact percentage to be established by experiment) tap water should be added to produce a hardness reading of about 3° dGH.

It should also be noted that RO or deionised water should not be used for water changes without prior aeration. This is mainly meant to drive out the carbon dioxide and to replace it with oxygen which the fishes require for respiration. This can be rectified using an air-pump and diffuser, which, of course, requires temporary storage of the water in a suitable container.

If lowering of the pH is required, then this can be achieved by using peat as a filter medium; this has the additional advantage of adding humins to the water, which is generally beneficial for geophagine cichlids.

I strongly advise against the use of acids to lower the pH, as it is difficult for the non-expert to regulate the dosage and effect properly, and this may lead to an adverse change in the redox potential to the possible detriment of the fishes. Moreover sudden changes in pH can also be harmful to living organisms.

The aquarium trade offers a wide variety of methods for maintaining the nitrate content of the aquarium water as low as possible. I personally use a denitrification filter or denitrifying resins in the normal filtration system. Discuss the various possibilities with your dealer, as the method chosen needs to be suited to the aquarium in question.

The following are the (easily measurable) water parameters for an eartheater aquarium: general hardness 3-10° dGH; carbonate hardness 3-10° dKH; pH 6.0-7.0; conductivity up to 300 µS/cm; ammonia and nitrite nil; nitrate 50 mg/l max.; phosphate and sulphate minimal. These parameters will suit the bulk of species, but some may have different requirements, as indicated in the specific text in the chapters dealing with the various species groups.

Maintenance

Once the aquarium has been set up, and the fishes and plants intro-

1. Aquaria with *Biotodoma* spp. or small *Geophagus* species (here: *Geophagus* sp. "Areões") can have a denser growth of water plants as long as the swimming space does not become too limited.
2. Although, in the natural habitat, *Retroculus* are found on bare bottoms they seem to be more at ease in richly decorated aquaria.

duced, there are, of course, some maintenance tasks required.

1. Daily checks that all the electrical equipment is functioning properly. I.e. measure the temperature with a thermometer and make a visual check that the filter is running properly.

2. Depending on the fish population, internal filters need to be cleaned at least once every three weeks, as such filters will be acting mainly as mechanical filters with little biological function. Long-term biological filters with an appropriate volume must be only partially cleaned in order to retain their effectiveness, as complete cleaning would result in the loss of the entire bacterial population responsible for the biological breakdown of wastes. In the worst case scenario the filtration would have to be matured again from scratch, i.e. new colonies of the beneficial bacteria established, and this could lead to problems in the aquarium (e.g. high ammonia and nitrite) in the interim. If activated carbon is used then this should be replaced every 6 weeks as it will be unable to adsorb any further pollutants. It cannot be simply washed and re-used.

3. Dead leaves should be removed to avoid unnecessary pollution of the water and work for the filter.

4. Adult fishes should be fed a varied diet two to three times per day, and given as much as they will eat in 3 minutes. Two days a week can be

"fast days", to encourage vitality. Juveniles should be fed several times a day without fast days. Newly-hatched fry, once free-swimming (yolk sac used up), should have food constantly available. Any uneaten food should be siphoned off every evening.

5. Every week 25% of the water should be changed for fresh. If this is not possible then a third should be changed every 14 days at the most. If the tap water is unsuitable for use without prior treatment, then a supply of treated water should be kept at the ready so that water changes can be performed quickly and easily when required.

6. Trace elements should be added regularly, as tap water commonly lacks, or contains too small a concentration of, all the trace elements fishes require.

7. If — and this is unlikely in an eartheater aquarium with a fine sand substrate — any mulm accumulates in corners, then this should be siphoned off during each water change.

8. The fishes should be checked every day for any signs of disease. The sooner disease is spotted, the more likely that treatment will be successful.

9. If the plants are regarded as being of intrinsic value, then the lighting (tubes and/or lamps) should be replaced every six months.

10. For aesthetic reasons the front glass should be kept clear of algae.

Proper maintenance

In this chapter several elements that apply to all species are explained. Specific characteristics and maintenance requirements are covered in the review of the individual species.

Selection and Purchase

Before you can become a successful keeper of geophagine cichlids, you must, of course, obtain your fishes, and that is where the problems generally begin. Hardly any normal retail outlet stock fishes of this group, and hence it is usually necessary to travel long distances in order to obtain your eartheaters.

If you are lucky enough to have a good dealer locally then you may be able to get the odd species or two. But the few shops that do stock them often do so under incorrect names, so that sometimes when you get them home you are disappointed to discover they are not the desired species. So when buying from a dealer, it is a good idea to check that the name is currently valid, and whether the locality where they were caught is known. There is nothing basically wrong with buying a fish without knowing how large it will grow, but because the available space in the aquarium may be limited, it can be helpful to know whether you are buying *Geophagus taeniopareius*, which grows to a maximum of 15 cm, or *Geophagus altifrons*, which can attain more than 30 cm. In fact these two species are easily differentiated even as juveniles, but the beginner with *Geophagus* may initially require a little help, and correct labelling on the dealer's tank not only inspires confidence in the shop but also avoids unwelcome surprises later.

Locality details can also be helpful in identifying a fish when it cannot be assigned to a particular species on other grounds, or when it is imported for the first time. Moreover they can be useful when it comes to obtaining additional specimens to increase the size of the group, and prevent any confusion subsequently when it comes to selling or giving away the young. Assuming the species is a distinct species, then the strain can be kept pure and hybridisation avoided.

Don't forget that many aquarists breed eartheaters, so it may be worth attending a meeting at your local aquarists' club, where you may make valuable contacts and obtain useful addresses. You may thus be able to obtain fishes from a professional or amateur breeder, and this has the additional advantage that you will usually be able to see the adults, which makes it easier to decide if the species is suitable for your own aquarium at home. You can buy juveniles of just a few centimetres without having to worry about what they will grow into. And in addition you will be able to obtain invaluable information on their behaviour, preferred diet, and the basics of their maintenance. The breeder will often have concrete data on the source locality — he may even have caught the fishes himself; you may be able to obtain unusual species apparently not normally stocked by the trade, perhaps because they do not exhibit their full splendour in the trader's tank and are thus incorrectly regarded as not worth stocking.

If you cannot locate an amateur breeder, then it is worth asking your dealer if he knows one, as he may be able to obtain fishes specially for you from such a source. Additional useful contacts can sometimes be made via aquarium magazines, trading lists, and fish clubs that specialise in geophagines or cichlids in general.

Once you have decided on a species, then you should examine the fishes closely before purchasing. Whitish patches or white spots, dark coloration, and/or threadlike faeces are all sure signs of disease. In addition the fishes should be lively and not exhibiting frayed finnage or other injuries. It is also worth asking the seller to offer the fishes a little food so that you can see if they are all feeding. Another way of checking the health of a particular specimen is to look at the ventral profile, which should be slightly convex. Never in any way concave, as this may denote intestinal parasites, although a slight concavity may merely indicate that the fish has been underfed for a long time. In such cases it is worth looking at the size of the eyes in relation to other body proportions: if a thin

1. Such leaf-layers are often home to juvenile eartheaters who use them as shelter.
2. The Caño San Diego in the *llanós* of Venezuela is a classic blackwater biotope. However, eartheaters could not be found.

specimen has relatively large eyes and a concave ventral profile, then the beginner should leave it where it is. It is often the case that these cichlids are very poorly fed as juveniles. Given a balanced and nutritious diet (with repeated small portions throughout the day), using high quality food, then there should be no long-term effects on the health of the adult fish or its ability to produce healthy offspring; but the beginner is often not capable of dealing with the problem and may rapidly find the fish nothing but a source of trouble.

Tankmates

A few points must be considered if eartheaters are to be housed with other fishes, although basically they can be kept with all other types of fishes. It is just a case of identifying and avoiding potential problems right from the start:

1. All the fishes should have "normal" maintenance requirements; problem species or those with specialised needs, of whatever type, require a species aquarium.

2. Fishes with different habitat preferences or requirements, e.g. Rift Valley cichlids, are not suitable tankmates.

3. Tankmates should be of a certain minimum size, as if they are too small they may be accidentally eaten by the generally rather large cichlids.

4. Aggressive species such as many Central American cichlids are

unsuitable companions, as geophagine cichlids are not designed for continuous warfare.

5. Large piscivores such as certain catfishes and predatory characins (e.g. piranhas) are unsuitable tankmates for obvious reasons!

6. Feeding the various species should not be a lottery: all the occupants of the aquarium should require the same or a very similar diet such that they all receive adequate nourishment.

7. Slow-moving or shy fishes, for example various labyrinth fishes of the genera *Ctenopoma* and *Betta*, are unlikely to obtain enough food and may starve.

8. On the other hand, when keeping *Biotodoma* or *Satanoperca* it is best to avoid greedy or rapid-feeding tankmates, as members of these two cichlid genera are very slow feeders and may likewise go hungry.

9. Naturally fin-nippers (such as some barbs) should be avoided, as they may harass the cichlids.

Ideal complementary fishes for eartheaters include mailed catfishes and loricariids, and these will also help keep the aquarium clean, though it should not be forgotten that these catfishes will require additional food, they are not just waste disposal units! Just like other fishes they require a varied and nutritious diet.

Almost any American or African characin is suitable (provided fin-nippers are avoided), as long as their temperature and water requirements match those of the eartheaters. Provided there is no objection to mixing fishes from different biotopes, then barbs (no fin-nippers!) and some of the rainbowfishes of the Australian continent are suitable tankmates for eartheaters. But the easiest of all is to house them with other South American cichlids. Provided the tank is large enough to satisfy the territorial requirements of all concerned, then other peaceful South American cichlids of reasonably similar size are good tankmates. Large thugs (e.g. *Cichla*, '*Cichlasoma*' *festae*) should, however, be avoided, as should dwarf species which would be stressed by the presence of appreciably larger fishes.

Feeding

Goulding, Carvalho, and Ferreira (1988) carried out stomach contents research on fishes of the Rio Negro between 1979 and 1987, and the specimens they examined included 911 eartheaters (*Geophagus*, *Satanoperca*, and *Biotodoma*). The authors investigated a variety of habitats, such that specialised trophic behaviours, restricted to specific habitats, were also included. They tabulated their results separately for a number of different food types (e.g. detritus, fish), including only those species where at least 25% (volume) of stomach contents comprised the material in question, to exclude those taxa for whom the material was an insignificant dietary item. The stomach contents of eartheaters were found to be chiefly detritus (including contained micro-flora and -fauna) and aquatic invertebrates (insect larvae, crustaceans, etc.). Only in exceptional cases did they find terrestrial invertebrates, plant material, and once, in a single region, fish, in the stomach of an eartheater. Because such a large number of specimens were examined the data can be regarded as valid.

So what does this signify as far as aquarium maintenance is concerned?

As their common name denotes, these cichlids are fishes which forage for edible organic material in the upper layers of the substrate (sand or mud). This zone contains huge numbers of microscopic plant and animal organisms, and is the niche exploited by our eartheaters. And because both plant and animal food is ingested, this dual requirement must be provided for in the aquarium. I.e. a good quality dried food containing both animal and vegetable elements is a good start, although this alone is not an adequate diet. Various frozen foods, such as *Artemia*, glassworms, mosquito larvae, *Mysis*, krill, and *Daphnia* will help provide the variety required to maintain good health. However, be careful of bloodworm and *Tubifex*, as these filter-feeders commonly originate from extremely polluted waters and may contain pollutants. There is no reason not to feed such foods occasionally, but they are unsuitable as a staple diet. The best foods are small pond foods, which can be offered fresh as well as frozen. And although it seems incredible that 20 cm cichlids would enjoy newly-hatched *Artemia*, this is indeed the case with eartheaters, and always worth a try.

If you wish to give your fishes a special treat then you can offer them a home-made vegetable mixture of salad greens, fruit, vegetables, with about 20% fish fillet as an attractant. The ingredients should be processed in a blender and then bound together using gelatine or agar-agar. Vitamins, red paprika, and high protein baby food may be added. If you like you can also add Spirulina powder. The end-product should be deep-frozen.

Of course finding foods that the fishes will eat is to some extent a matter of experiment, and you must not expect them to leap upon the vegetable mix immediately, as they are bound to be suspicious of it, as with all strange foods.

Unsuitable foods include freeze-dried foods, as these float for a very long time on the surface and these fishes prefer to take their food from the bottom. I must also advise against the use of beef heart and meat from warm-blooded creatures in general. There may be breeders who swear by it, but in my view it is quite obvious that fishes eat only aquatic organisms, which does not include cows! In general we should not feed fishes on types of food that they would not find in their natural habitat. The fact that the fish eats a food does not mean it enjoys eating it or that it is good for its health. Humans will eat insects rather than starve, but these and similar such gourmet items are not to the general taste.

Eartheaters should be fed as varied a diet as possible in order eventually to bring them into spawning condition. This is best achieved by feeding them as many different foods as possible and in alternation, on a little and often basis. This also applies under normal conditions, as in the natural habitat each food organism must be hunted down or picked up individually. It should also be mentioned here that sandsifters such as geophagines have an almost limitless food supply available, even though large morsels are rarely to be found. In addition in the wild these cichlids find an inexhaustible supply of micro-organisms and other small life forms in the upper layer of the substrate, and these too are required to satisfy the appetites of these rather large cichlids.

A few genera such as *Satanoperca* and *Biotodoma* are unable to take in their daily food requirement at one sitting, at least if there are other fishes in the aquarium. They are slow eaters which require patient feeding, i.e. two to four meals per day using small portions of a variety of foods, and offering as much as may be eaten in five minutes. One or two fast days per week will make them more

1. *Satanoperca* sp. "Jarú".
2. *Retroculus* species possess very large ventral and pectoral fins which should be considered as adaptations to their environment. Aided by these powerful fins they are able to move swiftly in the fast flowing water of rapids and they are propped up on their ventrals when resting on the bottom.

active, as in nature the food supply is relatively meagre and unlike the "land of milk and honey" of the aquarium, where nutritious food falls, manna-like, from above. Fast days will also help bring them into spawning condition, as in the wild the spawning cycle is related to the food supply, plus obese individuals may become sterile and inactive.

Moreover juveniles grow appreciably better if they are fed small portions several times per day. But in their case fast days are inappropriate, as the breeding season usually coincides with a glut of food. Free-swimming fry which are already feeding should be kept practically "up to their necks" in food. In this regard, bear in mind that the area of movement of the fry will still be very restricted at this stage, i.e. the food must be brought to the fry rather than vice versa. Moreover, because of their small digestive volume they will rapidly become hungry again. If they are not fed enough during their first days then this may affect them throughout their lifetimes. Of course, frequent feeding of high-protein food may have a detrimental effect on water quality, which must be rectified, if necessary, with daily water changes.

Sexing and Breeding

Naturally this section deals only with general aspects, and more detailed information will be found in the chapter on the various species.

In general it is true to say that males grow larger than females and have longer or more pointed fins. Moreover male eartheaters look generally more bulky and thickset. Adult females appear more rounded and in practice have less vivid coloration. But, of course, these distinctions are of use only if you have several individuals and both sexes for comparison.

A few species, however, exhibit marked sexual dimorphism and dichromatism, for example the "red-hump" eartheaters and the *Gymnogeophagus* of southern tropical South America. In these species the males are more colourful and may also exhibit a nuchal hump, which may vary in its degree of development depending on sexual and social status.

Males and females can also be differentiated by behaviour. When sexually ripe individuals of the same sex meet, they start to mouth-wrestle after a short period of lateral threat. There may also be snapping at the flanks and fins until the weaker individual eventually flees. If, however, individuals of opposite sex meet then the lateral threat phase predominates. There may also be mouth-fighting and flank/fin biting, but the subordinate individual (usually the female) never flees very far away and after a short time the entire ritual is repeated. Pair formation is now in full swing and nothing stands in the way of a possible spawning. If the fishes have been optimally fed and are not dominated by another species, then breeding is possible, even in the community aquarium.

Unfortunately there can be no general rule of thumb as regards water parameters as some species can be induced to breed in relatively hard water, while others have very specific requirements as regards water quality. In general, however, biological purity is the most important factor, plus the temperature should be above 25° C except for *Gymnogeophagus*. It should be self-evident that ammonia and nitrite levels should be zero. The nitrate level should not exceed 50 mg/l in the long term and oxygen content should be adequate. These are the most important parameters.

Difficulties may arise if a species aquarium is provided, as the fishes may become too timid, rendering the addition of one or more companion fishes necessary. Such fishes will on the one hand encourage the breeding species better to defend its brood, and on the other prevent the parents from falling out and eating the eggs or fry.

A number of authors have suggested that artificial rearing may lead to deterioration of brood-care instinct in subsequent generations with loss of the natural behaviour. I have never myself observed this, although I have reared rare species artificially and then bred further generations naturally. It should, however, be mentioned that if artificial breeding is repeated for generation upon generation, this may indeed affect natural behaviour. Far more important, however, is the fact that artificial rearing means natural behaviour cannot be observed and recorded, with the loss of much valuable information which could perhaps have been used in species differentiation.

Diseases

Basically, an eartheater can suffer any of the normal fish diseases, hence it is essential to observe new purchases closely and if possible, quarantine them for three to four weeks. Quarantine, of course, has the advantage of avoiding infection of established stock and making it easier to perform any treatment required.

Whether a fish is ill can best be seen from its feeding behaviour. If a fish feeds only hesitantly then it is either stressed or sick. But if a fish will not feed then do not rush to treat it: wait for a few hours and then try feeding it again. If it is still not interested then treatment can be considered.

In order to make an accurate diagnosis the hobby literature can be consulted, or professional advice (vet, fish health expert) sought as regards diagnosis and treatment. Often the diagnosis will be fish tuberculosis, but this utterance must be treated with great circumspection, as the infection rate in tropical ornamental fish is about 95%. This is in itself tragic, but the advice that accompanies the diagnosis, is devastating: the entire population of the affected aquarium should be destroyed. But that is out-and-out nonsense, as a well-maintained, correctly fed, and unstressed fish will never succumb to fish TB and die. In general the real problem is with secondary infections arising from poor husbandry. So although the tuberculosis pathogen may be present in histological sections from dead fishes, the pathogens responsible for the secondary infection will already have left the host and can thus no longer be detected. This is why sick, but still living, fishes should be killed and investigated immediately in order to obtain a definitive diagnosis rather than relying on post-mortem investigation of specimens that died of the disease.

So, if fish TB is diagnosed as the cause of death, bide your time, ensure living conditions are optimal, and do not add any new fishes to the affected aquarium. If you have more than one aquarium and want to be quite sure, then make sure that nothing from the infected aquarium has any contact with any healthy tank. This includes nets and similar items that are often shared between tanks, and your hands, which should be well washed with soap after contact with infected water.

The following covers just a few treatments for common diseases in eartheaters, as the subject is too wide to discuss in detail here (please consult the bibliography for further reading).

Ichthyophthirius — whitespot disease: a commonly encountered disease caused largely by stress due to, among others, too cold water. A typical transportation disease. The infection rate in wild fishes is virtually 100%.

Symptoms: clamped fins; shimmying; scratching on decor and

1. and 2. *Satanoperca daemon* are very sensitive to bad water parameters and need a balanced diet. Is one of their requirements not met then they usually suffer from stress, usually visibly expressed in the skin lesions which are very hard to cure and only when all requirements are fulfilled.

equipment; slightly prominent, tiny, round whitish spots on the body and above all the fins.

Treatment: Proprietary medication, dosage as stated in the instructions. In mature (biologically active) aquaria daily re-dosing at half rate may be necessary with some medications, especially when active carbon filters are used. The fishes should be free of pathogens after seven days at most.

Diseases of the digestive tract: widespread in wild-caught specimens. Caused by nematode worms or endoparasitic flagellates.

Symptoms: white threadlike faeces; loss of appetite; emaciation; shimmying; dark coloration and skulking behaviour.

Treatment: Ideally alternating prophylactic treatment every three months with an anthelminthic such as Piperazin (to counter the worms) and metronidazole (for the flagellates). Both drugs are available from the veterinarian, who will advise as to dosage. Treatment is best administered via food, hence the need for prophylactic treatment as a fish that has stopped eating is generally past saving.

Warning: Never use both drugs simultaneously, but allow about 14 days between the individual treatments.

Hexamitiasis — hole-in-head-disease: infestation of the digestive tract with the flagellate Hexamita.

Symptoms: emaciation, dark coloration, whitish threadlike faeces. Infection (possibly secondary) of the sensory pores on the head (and sometimes the lateral line) resulting in holes filled with whitish pus.

Treatment: Only prescription drugs work, and it is not difficult or dangerous but you need to contact a veterinarian. Sometimes metronidazole (prescribed by vet) may work but common aquarium drugs, such as Hexa-Ex, are not effective at all. The best cure is to make certain that the affected fish is relieved from all stress and maintained under proper conditions. Other cichlids placed in the same tank with the sick fish may become affected as well.

Treatment is extremely protracted and requires a degree of patience (Weidner, 1994; 1997). First of all optimal maintenance conditions must be provided. In this instance this means soft water (< 8° dGH) which should also have an acid pH (between 6.0 and 6.8). Add a good trace element preparation to the water. Eliminate any possible causes of stress. Feed with mosquito larvae treated with a suitable antibiotic, such as Phenoxyethanol, or with Metronidazole in order to ward off secondary infections. Next feed with a high quality food which has been soaked in a liquid vitamin supplement, plus the vegetable mix mentioned earlier in this chapter, as well as frozen and dried foods that have previously been fortified with a vitamin supplement.

Once the causes have been eliminated then the healing process can be assisted. The fish should be caught with as little stress as possible and laid on a damp cloth. Next the affected areas should be dried with kitchen towel or "Q-tips" (cotton buds) and a healing ointment such as gentian violet or mercurochrome applied, avoiding the eyes and gills. Allow this to take effect for a short period and then return the fish to the aquarium. It goes without saying that you need to work quickly, but without rushing. You have at least three minutes before the fish must be returned to the aquarium. The ointment will wash off in the aquarium but will not affect water quality. Under some circumstances the treated fish may shed its body mucus after treatment, and this is the result of the netting and contact with the damp cloth, and has no effect on the health of the fish. After a few days the edges of the lesions should be visibly darker, and within a few weeks no trace will remain. Large "holes" may need further application(s) of ointment.

Neither the author nor the publisher can accept any responsibility for the effects of any treatment. It is advisable to consult an expert and/or the appropriate literature.

Breeding behaviour

General Observations

Any attempt to compare the behavioural characteristics of fish groups will rapidly lead to the realisation that there are limits to what is possible. This may sometimes be because the equipment required is too expensive, but more often it is a problem that repeatedly besets ichthyology — restricted habitat and consequent unnatural behaviour. No-one can hope to come even close to simulating the native waters. In addition fishes are capable of adapting to new situations, so findings should be treated, and generalisations made, with considerable circumspection. One small example is provided by the wild fish which at the first sign of disturbance in its native waters flees into open water or hides in the dark shelter of the branches of a rotting tree. If such a fish is captured and brought home for the aquarium, then a change in its behaviour will very soon be discernible. Provided it is properly maintained, the fish will, for example, rapidly learn when to expect food to arrive. And then all danger will be forgotten as the fish waits in the spot where the food is normally introduced. From this we can see that zoological ethology is directly linked to ecology and physiology. Behaviour in the aquarium can at best be regarded as an approximation to that in the wild. Ultimately abiotic (non-living) environmental factors (e.g. topography of the habitat, water parameters, seasonal rhythms) and biotic (living) ones (e.g. mate, food supply, predators, parasites, and plants) may have a considerable effect on the manner in which the organism reacts to its environment as a whole.

Just like humans and other life forms, fishes react to diverse stimuli sensed by a variety of receptors (such as eyes, acoustico-lateralis system, taste-buds). When a fish perceives a stimulus then its response (e.g. whether to attack, flee, or feed) will be decided by inherited and learned behavioural elements. Because every juvenile fish within a species inherits the same behavioural elements from its parents, but subsequently "learns" different things, then deviant behavioural patterns are often encountered.

Thus during researches (into breeding) in the restricted environment of the aquarium differing observations are commonly made as regards behaviour such as courtship, spawning, and brood care. These facets of behaviour are, of course, genetically fixed, but nevertheless different aquarists frequently make contradictory observations. For example, *Crenicichla* are generally regarded as relatively aggressive. Males can be very rough towards females. Ripe females display a red belly to males, and the redder the belly, the less aggressive the reaction of the male. In addition the male's readiness to spawn is increased by the sight of the female's belly so that the urge to breed is increased on the one hand, and the urge to fight is reduced on the other. Because these are largely monogamous cichlids there will thereafter be only minor problems with their main-

1. A brooding pair of *Biotodoma cupido* "Santarem". Photo: Peter Lucas.
2. '*Geophagus*' sp. of the '*Geophagus*' *brasiliensis* complex of unknown origin. A guarding male with his offspring.

tenance. So if the aquarist has the good fortune to own a compatible pair, then he will regard *Crenicichla* as only moderately aggressive.

Cichlids certainly possess a broad spectrum of behaviour as regards courtship and battle. Because here too individual facets of behaviour may have a considerable effect, it is wise to refrain from making broad generalisations. Exceptions may arise to every rule. Thus an otherwise harmless cichlid can terrorise an entire aquarium, as, quite simply, no adequately-matched opponent is present. In the case of sexually ripe individuals in particular there is always a likelihood of surprises or of situations arising that can change at a moment's notice. Again, an example: a pair of eartheaters wish to breed and are defending a territory. If there is another pair of equal strength present in the same aquarium, then the two pairs will divide the aquarium equally between them, but if the pairs are not equally matched then the territory of the stronger pair will be larger. But once the pair has spawned and is leading young, then it may be that the territory will become smaller again, as it is now only the area immediately around the shoal of fry that is regarded as territory, as to defend a greater expanse would require too much effort. There are many additional variations on this theme, as other tankmates (and their strength) and the topography of the aquarium may play a significant role.

Despite what has been said by way of introduction, it is generally possible to categorise the behaviour of species or species groups, always bearing in mind the exceptions to the rules. A number of points that can be regarded as "normal" are discussed below. Only a small number of deviations are likely to be seen as regards courtship and the various brood-care mechanisms, as these are innate behaviours, while a wide spectrum of variation can be seen in both interspecific and other elements of intraspecific behaviours, as these are often learned. For precisely this reason it is important to study fishes during brood care, as this may reveal the degree of relationship of species to one another.

Interspecific Aspects

Although some species, e.g. *Geophagus altifrons*, can attain a large size. They take virtually no notice of significantly smaller, healthy, fishes. Thus eartheaters are commonly found with small characins in the natural habitat. Of course it may happen that careless individuals may fall victim to eartheaters, but such cases are generally "accidents". Larger fishes are generally avoided. These statements apply equally in the aquarium. The type of "assertiveness" that we see in the heroine cichlids is unthinkable. It is true that they are generally capable of commanding due respect during the breeding season, but well-built aggressive species will usually win the day even with brood-caring eartheaters, hunting down up and eating the fry. The eartheater mouth is, moreover, not designed for fighting, and lacks the so-called canines with which some species can inflict actual wounds on an "enemy". It can thus be seen that geophagine cichlids are fundamentally absolutely neutral towards other species.

Intraspecific Aspects

All geophagine cichlids are relatively sociable creatures, which form small groups even in adulthood. This fact can very easily be seen in the aquarium, as individuals kept singly become very apathetic and listless. If, however, a small group of up to 10 individuals is maintained, they become remarkably more lively and active. This could, of course, be regarded as being due to an increase in competition, but field observations indicate that eartheaters do generally move around in groups in the wild as well. The individuals within such a group do maintain a certain distance from one another, but a relationship between these conspecifics is clearly discernible. Breeding pairs seek out a territory some way away in order to maintain a distance from conspecifics and also predators. Solitary individuals are rarely seen, and are usually old or sick and unable to keep up with the group. The basic rule is, "Where there is one, there will be more than one!" If a healthy individual gets separated from its group, then it will immediately seek out another to which to attach itself, and it is most unlikely to meet with an aggressive reaction from the "new" group.

As in all cichlids, natural intraspecific aggression is present, but is limited to conspecifics or species of similar appearance/coloration and then only if these are sexually mature adults during the breeding season, or if the "personal distance" of 20-30 cm is compromised. Quarrels of this sort invariably have a harmless outcome, however, as they are usually just a matter of mutual threat — lateral display, spreading of the opercula, and beating of the tail. Only occasionally do they go as far as mouth-fighting, and then the weaker individual rapidly yields, before any harm is done. Mouth-fighting in eartheaters is in some ways reminiscent of the well-known arm-wrestling, only in this case the lips are pressed against those of the opponent (or more rarely the opponents lip is grasped with the teeth), and mutual pushing ensues. The stronger fish pushes the weaker backwards, and the battle appears to be decided when an imaginary line is crossed. The weaker fish then yields.

Courtship

Courtship, i.e. the phase during which the opposite sexes meet and mutually prepare for spawning, follows by and large the same pattern in all geophagine cichlids. Geophagine cichlids are monogamous cichlids whose pairing may continue beyond the actual spawning and brood care, although the continued relationship is not as marked as in some other cichlids. If one individual is removed from the aquarium then the remaining partner will immediately look for a new mate. It may also happen that a single male will spawn with a variety of females.

When these cichlids encounter a potential mate, then both fishes initially greet each other with mouths stretched wide open and remain facing each other for a while, before proceeding to mutual circling. Next comes lateral display, with the two fishes side by side and head to tail, with fins spread wide. During this lateral threat the mouth is always kept wide open. Next violent beats of the tail are used to fan water over each other while they circle each other several times as is seen in some East African cichlids. There may also be gentle flank-nipping at this stage. This behaviour may be triggered by one of the pair — usually the female — swimming away. In this event the male follows and the ritual is repeated at another spot only a few centimetres away. If one of the partners has already selected a definite spawning site then the other will be enticed to that site by this "leading" behaviour.

In a number of species, or where the partners are evenly matched, mouth-fighting may take place. This is always the case where the fanning of water has produced no decision. If mouth-fighting proves unavoidable, then some species seize each other's lips with their teeth and test their strength that way, while others simply press their lips together and "shove" each other across the aquarium in order to demonstrate their "qualifications" as a mate. Ultimately each partner needs to be absolutely sure that the other is capable of defending the spawn, and later the brood, in order guarantee the perpetuation of the species.

The female next cleans a stone, or some other suitable substrate, on which her eggs will be laid. While she is doing this the male constantly circles her, and during this phase endeavours to impress her by being particularly aggressive towards fish of other species, attacking them and putting them to flight from the immediate vicinity. After each attack he immediately swims back to his "intended" and resumes circling her. After a little while the female interrupts her cleaning and the two partners display over again. Just before spawning the male too begins to take part in the cleaning.

A number of species do not require a solid spawning substrate as they instead spawn on the sand. In such cases the courtship battles are virtually identical, but thereafter it is usual for one of the partners to create a small pit in which the eggs are ultimately laid. Many species also dig one or more pits, at this stage or later, in which to place the larvae after hatching.

The duration of courtship depends, in essence, on the subsequent course of the reproductive behaviour, i.e. how closely the pair need to be bonded in order to breed successfully. A degree of synchronisation between the partners is essential where success depends on the participation of both. This requires a long period of "getting acquainted" — up to 14 days before spawning finally takes place — whereas in species where only one partner is involved in brood care then courtship and spawning may take place in the course of a single "working day". For this reason open-brooders possess the greatest behavioural repertoire during courtship. In open-brooding species the parents must be optimally attuned to one another, as only then will they be able to cooperate to rear the brood successfully. The corresponding synchronisation of their "gestures" — tail-beating, frontal and lateral display, head-jerking, flank-nudging — can almost be described as a dialogue between the pair. Ultimately the partners must be able to recognise one other via these gestures, for example when one of them returns to the eggs/brood after an absence. In such instances the partners often greet one another with head-jerking or brief lateral display, although there may be huge differences from pair to pair.

Brood-care mechanisms

Before looking at brood-care mechanisms it is important to be aware of a number of facts about the eggs of cichlids, to know about the different modes of spawning. Firstly, there is a distinction between the eggs of open-, cave-, and mouth-brooding species, with concealed spawners included among the open-brooding cichlids as only a very few species lay their eggs in unprotected sites. If "enemy fishes" are present then preferred sites are usually narrow crevices or places concealed from view, as these are easier to defend. There is no difference in egg structure between open and concealed spawners, although they differ from the other types (which in turn differ from each other).

The eggs of mouth-brooding species are generally roundish, large, very rich in yolk, and only slightly adhesive (but see ovophilous and larvophilous mouthbrooders, below). In addition the zona radiata (eggshell) is significantly thinner (3-5 µm) than that in substrate-spawning fishes (5-15 µm), as they are exposed to fewer mechanical demands in the mouth. In substrate-spawning cichlids the zona radiata externa (outer eggshell) is always adhesive to some extent. At present it is thought, on the basis

1. The eggs of *Geophagus* cf. *brachybranchus* (a larvophilous mouthbrooder) shortly before hatching. The dark pigments can be recognised, which are the signal for the parents to assist the larvae in freeing themselves from the egg shell.
2. Both parents actively assist the larvae by "chewing" the eggs. The larvae are then taken up in the parents' mouth.
3. While one parent forages and digs new pits, the other (in this case the male) broods the larvae.

of histochemical evidence, that acid and neutral mucopolysaccharides are responsible for the adhesiveness (Riehl, 1991). The eggs of substrate-spawning eggs have been differentiated into two groups, l-type and p-type eggs, by Wickler (1956). L-type eggs are produced almost exclusively by open-brooding cichlids and are generally oval in shape. They adhere directly to the substrate by the long side (l-side) of the zona radiata externa and do not have adhesive threads ("stalks").

By contrast p-type eggs have a polar ("p", i.e. at one end) attachment in the form of an adhesive thread. It is this "stalk", and not the egg itself, that adheres to the substrate. In contrast to l-type eggs they cannot easily be attached to horizontal substrates but are usually deposited on vertical or overhanging surfaces. Thus p-type eggs are produced mainly by cave-brooders. *Biotodoma cupido* is an exception, as its p-type eggs are laid on a horizontal surface but are lighter than water and thus float up, with the stalks acting as anchors to prevent the eggs from drifting away. P-type eggs have a number of advantages over l-type:

1. More eggs can be laid on the same surface, as the area required for the stalks to adhere is smaller.
2. The oxygen supply (from parental fanning with the pectoral fins or from natural water currents) is significantly increased. Fungussing is almost impossible.
3. Because the micropyle (the point on the egg where the sperm can penetrate) is at the opposite end a higher fertilisation rate results.

Among the geophagine cichlids we find practically every type of brood safeguard to prevent premature picking up of the larvae. It is important to realise that initially the eggshell serves not only to protect the embryo from mechanical damage, but also to prevent the glutinous liquid yolk from running away. A certain period of time is required before the yolk has developed an enveloping layer, which again protects the yolk mass from mechanical influences. The time required for this skin, known as the periblast, to form is between 24 and 36 hours, depending on temperature. This is the earliest point at which the larvae can leave their shells, and is also linked to pigment formation, so that the parents can tell that it is now possible to free the larvae from their shells.

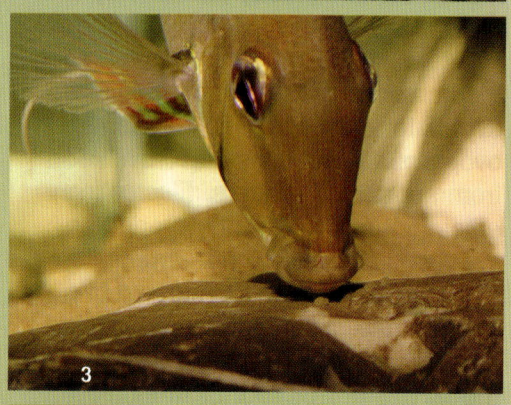

Basically the larvae must initiate hatching themselves, the parents can do no more than assist once the process has started. The hatch-ready embryos are able to produce an enzyme that soften the shell. Researches to date indicate that the same enzyme is involved in all fishes, and that it is a protease. This protease requires zinc in order to be effective and the optimum pH, for the species investigated, is in the slightly alkaline zone. Hatching is essentially a two-stage process: firstly the zona radiata is dissolved chemically from within, and secondly the larvae mechanically breaks through the gelatinous envelope surrounding the zona radiata, which is very thin and thus easily ruptured.

Because the gills are not yet formed at this stage, wriggling movements are used to obtain oxygen, which is absorbed via the skin. These movements also stimulate the parents to collect the larvae into the protection of their mouths. For these reasons even the most highly-evolved larvophilous mouthbrooder, *Gymnogeophagus balzanii*, can never pick up eggs, as on the one hand the well-developed attachment coat of the eggshell would be an impediment to ovophilous mouthbrooding, while on the other hand the necessary stimuli to collect up the brood are absent. The evolution of mouthbrooding in these fishes is complete.

Other younger (from the viewpoint of evolutionary biology) species are still at the stage where they can bring forward the time when they pick up the larvae. A number of species can be seen to repeatedly move the fry around and keep them in the mouth for a while before spitting them back into a pit. These species can be regarded as "young" larvophilous mouthbrooders in the broadest sense, which still have the major part of their development in front of them.

Ovophilous mouthbrooders behave in an essentially similar manner, only in this case the egg takes centre stage. As already mentioned at the beginning of this section, the embryos of ovophilous mouthbrooders possess attachment organs which would make mouthbrooding difficult.

1. *Geophagus proximus* is an ovophilous biparental mouthbrooder. In the foreground the female with the genital papila clearly visible.
2. A female laying eggs. In the background the male is waiting to take up the eggs.
3. The freshly laid eggs are immediately taken up in the mouth.
4. Both parents *G. proximus* brooding.
5. A spawning pair of *Geophagus altifrons* "Tocantins". In the foreground the male is fertilizing the eggs which were just laid. After fertilisation the eggs are picked up first by the female. With this pair the male only sporadically picked up eggs or larvae, usually after 5 or 6 days.
6. *G. altifrons* from the Rio Tapajós turned out to be a biparental, ovophilous mouthbrooder.

Because the yolk sac is sometimes extremely large, there is a longer period before the larva hatches in which the periblast forms and the attachment organ can regress. However, because the eggs of phylogenetically "young" ovophilous mouthbrooders still possess a sticky coat it is not possible to pick up the eggs during spawning. Some species pick the eggs up only after a certain period of time has elapsed, others lay an entire clutch and pick the eggs up only in conclusion to spawning. The most highly-evolved ovophilous mouthbrooders pick up their eggs in batches during spawning.

As far as the aquarist is concerned, the easiest way to differentiate the two types of mouthbrooding is to examine the spawning substrate in closer detail immediately after egg/larva collection. If there are empty eggshells — a whitish gelatinous mass — on the spawning substrate, then the species is a larvophilous mouthbrooder. But if the substrate looks freshly-cleaned then the species is ovophilous.

While in East African cichlids mouthbrooding is by the female in the majority of cases, this is not the case with the South American eartheaters. It is true that the female always plays an important part in the mouthbrooding, but in such cases the male role is not limited simply to territorial defence. Males are commonly seen to participate in the mouthbrooding, particularly in the case of larvophilous species. In these cichlids the male can time and again be seen to be carrying the bulk of the brood in his mouth towards the end of the brood care period. But even in the highly specialised ovophilous mouthbrooders both sexes often share the brooding.

This method has two significant advantages: first of all, the larvae in time become too large for all to find room in a single mouth, and secondly, neither of the pair is excessively weakened by the long brooding period. The latter is very easily demonstrated by the fact that the brood is always swopped between partners at feeding time, so that both parents can feed. Now and then it is possible to observe how both parents spit their larvae into small pits for temporary protection, so both can feed at the same time.

The genera

The genera dealt with in this book all have quite obvious external characteristics that permit their species to be assigned to the appropriate genus. But there are also morphological and anatomical differences which can be used to differentiate the genera. From a scientific viewpoint these morphological and anatomical characters are indispensable in diagnosing a species, while the external characteristics are far more important as far as aquarists are concerned.

The subfamily Geophaginae comprises those South American cichlids in which specialised morphological and anatomical development of the gill rakers and pharyngeal bones enable the fishes to sift particles of food from inorganic material such as sand. Additional skeletal characters permit the fishes to be assigned to a particular genus within the subfamily.

Thus the cichlids of the tribe Geophagini have a so-called epibranchial lobe, a "flat anteroventral expansion of the first epibranchial, lined by a wide band of connective tissue" (Kullander, 1986). This lobe is present in the genera *Geophagus, Satanoperca, Biotodoma,* and *Gymnogeophagus*, as well as in the dwarf cichlid genera *Apistogramma, Apistogrammoides, Mikrogeophagus,* and *Taeniacara*. The last 4 genera are generally regarded as dwarf cichlids and will not be discussed further here.

The rheophilic cichlids of the genus *Retroculus* (subfamily Retroculinae (Kullander, 1998)) are, however, mentioned here, as they were formerly regarded as part of the tribe Geophagini.

The genus *Geophagus* Heckel, 1840, *sensu stricto*

Type species: *Geophagus altifrons* Heckel, 1840.

Relatively deep-bodied cichlids with a flat ventral profile. There is a lateral spot, of variable size, in the middle of the flank; this is small or absent in *G. altifrons* but can attain enormous proportions in *G. megasema* and *G. proximus*. The lips are fleshy and the mouth slightly subterminal. In some species there is a pattern of bars on the flanks. The dorsal is more or less scaled. The ventrals may be greatly elongated in some species. *Geophagus* have scaled dorsal and anal fins and more than two rows of teeth in each jaw.

The *'Geophagus' crassilabrus* complex

Males of the "red-hump eartheaters" from northwestern South America and Panama exhibit a striking, normally reddish, nuchal hump, which can attain enormous size depending on the status of the individual within a group.

The red-hump eartheaters can be differentiated morphologically from *Geophagus sensu stricto* on the basis that the distal part of the first epibranchial is not ossified. The caudal is not particularly thickly scaled. The pectorals are rounded and shorter than the head.

The *'Geophagus' brasiliensis* complex

The "pearly eartheaters" (*'G'. brasiliensis* and its immediate relatives) from southeastern Brazil are extremely robust in their structure. In adults the body is very deep; the dorsal fin is narrow; the posterior edge of the caudal is straight. In contrast to all other members of the Geophagini, these species are more similar in cross-section to the cichlasomine cichlids. The species look — and are — very robust. Adult specimens may develop a nuchal hump. The pectorals are spotted and at least as long as the head.

The genus *Satanoperca* Günther, 1862

Type species *Satanoperca daemon* (Heckel, 1840).

An alizarinrot/alcianblau staining according to Dingerkus and Uhler (in Plösch, 1991) show (red-coloured) bones through cleared tissue.
1. *Satanoperca* sp. "Tocantins".
2. *Gymnogeophagus balzanii*. The cleared tissue of the nuchal hump is very distinct (there is no bone to support the structure). *Gymnogeophagus* also lacks real supraneurals (arrow; compare with *Satanoperca*).

the subsequent processing/reproduction may distort the natural colours. In addition some species of *Geophagus* include a number of different populations: these should be regarded simply as populations and referred to by their geographical origin, not regarded as new species. There are enough already!

If you make, or have already made, further observations, then please record them. Every contribution is important at this moment in time. There may come a time when it is necessary for us to breed these fishes in our aquaria because there are no longer any left in the wild!

1. *Geophagus* sp. "Araguaia - Orange Head" is a monogamous, larvophilous mouthbrooder.
2. Brooding pair *Biotodoma cupido* "Santarém". While the female mainly cares for the spawn, the territory is defended by the male (above the female). Photo: Peter Lucas.

The species

This section catalogues all the species I know of to date, including those that are not yet scientifically described. But I cannot guarantee that the list is complete. The information that follows is based on personal knowledge and experience together with data collected from other aquarists, plus valuable information extracted from the literature. Although the information thus assembled has been used to present a picture of each species, these should not be regarded as definitive, but rather as representing a range of possibilities and perspectives. In the final analysis, the conditions under which these cichlids are kept and bred may be decisive, affecting almost all of the resulting data. A few examples may serve to demonstrate this:

The sizes given: high nitrate values resulting from neglected water changes can often result in stunting. Other aquarists, with optimal tap water, a tendency towards overenthusiastic feeding, but at the same time frequent water changes, are capable of producing fishes that bear no resemblance to their wild ancestors. Hence the sizes given are normal values such as are seen in nature.

The behaviour described: Nature has equipped cichlids with aggressive tendencies, and these can lead to different observations under different conditions. It may thus happen that some individuals turn into real bullies if they have no equally-matched opponent in their aquarium. On the other hand, in other company individuals of the same species may prove so timid that they rarely come out for food and thus waste away. The way in which the aquarium is setup (i.e. arranged internally) may have quite different effects on behaviour: for example, excessively bright lighting or a lack of hiding places (caves and overhangs) can create nervous fishes.

The preferred natural habitat: the best time to make observations is, of course, the dry season. But conditions are sometimes quite different during the rain season: torrents turn into broad lake-like areas, sandy zones disappear so deep beneath the water that hardly any light reaches the bottom. The eartheaters now shun these sandy regions, as during the rainy season they do not provide the shelter offered by shallow water during the dry period. Instead they move to the inundation zone — a complete change of biotope, for suddenly we find our eartheaters over a densely vegetated substrate.

Typical appearance: the text that follows describes the eartheater species on the basis of coloration. The details provided are for normal coloration and are only for guidance. To cite just one problem: diet can have a significant effect on coloration, with carotene-rich foods resulting in a reddish base colour and heavy feeding on green foods making the fishes increasingly greenish. Coloration is of only limited use in differentiating species, and for this reason one should be wary of regarding slight deviations in colour pattern as denoting new species. Care is required above all when it comes to colour photos: the type of film used and

The caudal is heavily scaled almost to its posterior edge. The lateral line extends onto the caudal fin. The pectorals are somewhat rounded and visibly shorter than the head.

Finally two additional genera should be mentioned, although these currently form the tribe Acarichthyini. The acarichthyine cichlids exhibit many similarities to the geophagines, and because they were formerly assigned to that tribe, they too are included here.

The genus *Guianacara* Kullander and Nijssen, 1989

Type species *Guianacara owroewefi* Kullander & Nijssen, 1989.

Guianacara (the so-called "saddleback cichlids") is a relatively recently described genus which was subdivided into two subgenera, *Guianacara* and *Oelemaria*, by the authors in the original description. The two subgenera can be differentiated by the form of the "saddle" and the dorsal fin. The subgenus *Guianacara*, on the one hand, has a true "saddle" spot extending downwards from base of the dorsal (often reduced to a small dorsal spot in older specimens), while *Oelemaria* has a more central lateral spot. Likewise in the subgenus *Guianacara* the anterior dorsal spines have prolonged membranes, while this is not the case in *Oelemaria*.

In both subgenera the anterior dorsal spines may be dark, depending on mood. In all species the body is oval in cross-section, relatively deep, and only moderately elongate. The dorsal is low and the posterior edge of the caudal is straight. The lips are relatively fleshy, the mouth terminal, low on the head, and relatively small.

The genus *Acarichthys* Eigenmann, 1912

Type species *Acarichthys heckelii* (Müller & Troschel, 1849).

Many of the characters of *Acarichthys heckelii*, the single known species, correspond to those of the geophagine cichlids, e.g. some aspects of the coloration, the small scales, and the body shape.

A. heckelii exhibits an almost circular black spot on the central flank, which never extends upwards to the dorsal fin. The upper head profile rises relatively steeply. The first soft dorsal rays in adult specimens possess threadlike extensions, and the first soft anal rays may likewise be prolonged.

The members of this genus are elongate cichlids which are only moderately deep-bodied. All species have an ocellus on the upper part of the caudal peduncle.

Satanoperca have unscaled dorsal and anal fins, while the caudal is fully scaled. They have one or two rows of teeth in each jaw.

The genus *Biotodoma* Eigenmann & Kennedy, 1903

Type species *Biotodoma cupido* (Heckel, 1840).

Biotodoma are moderately deep-bodied with an oval body shape. The coloration is likewise typical of the genus: a black stripe running through the eye from the nape to the corner of the preoperculum. There is a round ocellus on the upper flank, close to the soft dorsal. The mouth is terminal and relatively small. A number of fine lines may be visible on the flanks.

The two described species of *Biotodoma* have the epibranchial lobe less well developed than in *Geophagus* and *Satanoperca*.

The genus *Gymnogeophagus* Miranda-Ribeiro, 1918

Type species *Gymnogeophagus balzanii* (Perugia, 1891).

At up to 25 cm TL the type species is the largest member of this genus of relatively small species. *Gymnogeophagus* are moderately compressed laterally. The upper head profile rises gently to very steeply. The dorsal fin is only moderately high. The head is unscaled (*gymnos* (Greek) = naked). All the cichlids of this genus originate from southern Brazil south to Argentina and require a "winter rest" (from breeding). A lateral spot is present in all species.

Gymnogeophagus species can be differentiated from all other geophagine cichlids by the absence of a supraneural (a small bone at the front of the dorsal fin).

The mouth is terminal and the head of older specimens by-and-large rectangular. There are numerous small conical teeth in both jaws, with the outer teeth larger than the inner. The teeth are recurved distally and not noticeably arranged in rows.

The genus *Retroculus* Eigenmann & Bray, 1894

Type species *Retroculus lapidifer* (Castelnau, 1855)

The genus comprises three species, all from areas of rapids in Brazil. These very large cichlids are noted for a deep anterior body. The eyes are positioned high on the head. The swimbladder is reduced, which means that these fishes are rather ungainly when they swim in open water. The mouth is underslung and the lips fleshy. The premaxillary is longer than the lower jaw. There is no lateral spot, but instead, depending on mood, there may be a number of stripes or a marbled pattern of dark bands on the flanks. There is a round ocellus on the soft dorsal. In general these fishes rest on their powerful elongated pelvic fins.

Biotodoma Eigenmann & Kennedy, 1903

Derivation of scientific name: *biotos* (Gr.) = life; *domos* (Gr. = house). The author was of the opinion that these fishes were mouthbrooders.

Distribution: The genus is widespread in Amazonia, the Orinoco region, and the adjoining Guianas.

Characters of the genus: *Biotodoma* are moderately deep-bodied with an oval, laterally compressed body. There is a round black ocellus, surrounded by a number of whitish zones, on the posterior part of the body. The two described species, *B. cupido* and *B. wavrini*, together with an undescribed form from Guyana, can easily be differentiated from one another by the position of this lateral spot. Geographical varieties of *B. cupido* are known (see also Remarks, below). The body base colour is best described as grey-blue to light beige. A number of fine lines are often visible on the flanks. A black band runs through the eye, from the nape to the lower edge of the operculum. There

73

are always numerous iridescent bluish lines and spots beneath the eye. The lips are not fleshy. The mouth is terminal and very small, and thus rather atypical of eartheaters. Likewise the feeding method does not correspond to that of eartheaters.

Ecology: The members of the genus are found above all in the bank zones, over sandy and/or muddy substrates. Areas with wood and/or layers of leaf litter are preferred habitats. Stony bottoms and fast-flowing waters are avoided. The water is generally moderately acid and extremely soft. Members of this genus prefer clear- or whitewaters. Only *B. wavrini* has been shown to occur in blackwater. Field observations by Cichocki (1976) have shown that a *Biotodoma* species from the Essequibo system spawns during low water conditions and that these fishes, and their spawn, can survive periods of low oxygen content. This may be a method of protecting the spawn from enemies, as likely predators generally avoid areas with a depleted oxygen content.

Ethology: There is still some confusion regarding the spawning behaviour of *Biotodoma* species. Thus older literature indicates that there may be cave-brooders as well as open-brooders. *Biotodoma* species are substrate-spawners whose eggs have a special attachment apparatus (Wickler, 1956). Depending on species, the eggs are designated p-type or I-type. *Biotodoma* species form a parental family: both adults generally share the brood care, with the female playing the main role in care of the spawn while the male guards the territory. If one partner is lost then the other is able to take over its role. These are very peaceful fishes which are little inclined to aggression outside the breeding season, although during brood care they can become very aggressive and are quite capable of driving away predators larger than themselves.

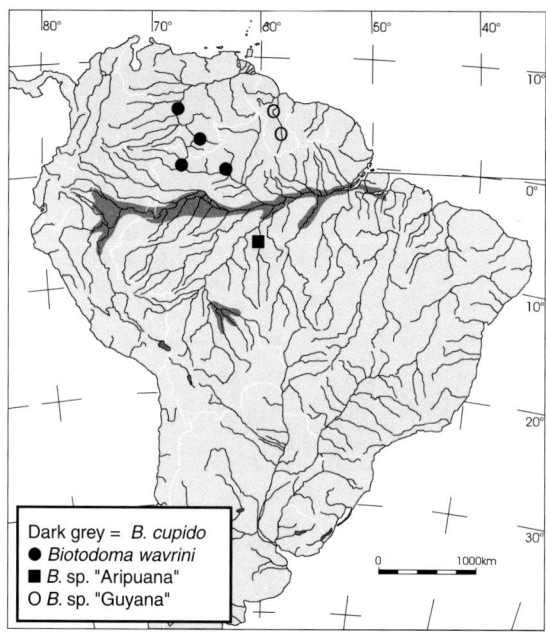

Remarks: The fishes from Peru (according to Kullander, 1986, the typical form of *B. cupido*), Brazil (Tapajós, Guaporé, Negro, Tefé, and Tocantins drainages), and Guyana, which have hitherto all been sold as/labelled *B. cupido*, probably include at least two species. It may be that ethological work by aquarists can contribute to the clarification of the status of the various species within the genus, which

Dark grey = *B. cupido*
● *Biotodoma wavrini*
■ *B.* sp. "Aripuana"
○ *B.* sp. "Guyana"

has been brought into question by observations made on the various populations. A broad window of opportunity for aquarists to make a contribution to science.

Biotodoma cupido Heckel, 1840

Original description: Ann. Wiener Mus. 2(1): 399-401.

Derivation of scientific name: cupido, from Cupid, the Roman god of love and son of Venus. Perhaps referring to the beauty of the fishes — the author does not provide any explanation.

Distribution: In Peru B. cupido is found in, among others: Rio Javari (or Yavari) (Hongslo, 1971); Rio Ucayali and Rio Ampiyacu (Kullander et al., 1981); Rio Napo and Rio Mazan (Kullander et al., 1984); Rio Nanay (Kullander et al., 1983; Hein 1998; Staeck & Linke, 1985); Rio Tahuayo (Kullander et al., 1986); Rio Samiria (Kullander et al., 1986). Localities in Brazil include: Rio Tefé (Stawikowski, 1993); Rio Curuá (Stawikowski et al., 1996); and Rio Tapajós (Kilian & Seidel, 1991; Knowles, 1964; Marlier, 1963; Stawikowski et al., 1992, 1996; Warzel et al., 1992; pers. obs., 1996). In addition, Loubens found B. cupido in Bolivia in 1984, in the Rio Guaporé at the mouth of the Rio Machupo. There are unconfirmed reports of the species in the Rio Tocantins and Rio Araguaia in Brazil, but it has not been established whether these were indeed B. cupido.

Habitat: The habitat of B. cupido is characterised as extensive sandy or muddy bays with no current to mention. The species seems to prefer shallow sandy regions with low predation pressure. Only sporadically encountered among piles of wood and leaf litter, or over stony substrates, but the virtual impossibility of study during the rainy season may have produced a distorted picture.

Size: Males are fully grown at about 14 cm, while females remain about 2 cm shorter.

Characters of the species: In B. cupido the lateral spot lies above the upper lateral line, only a short distance from the dorsal, and is bordered anteriorly and posteriorly by a number of whitish areas. A number of narrow vertical bars are visible on the flanks. The body base colour is light brownish with a silvery sheen. Depending on locality, older specimens may, however, exhibit very beautiful markings on the body, iridescing in all the colours of the rainbow. Peruvian specimens have a distinctly yellow zone behind the operculum, while fishes imported from the Santarém region have bright yellow-orange flanks and a bluish green sheen all over the body.

Sexual dimorphism: Only adults exhibit clear differences: males have iridescent bluish horizontal lines beneath the eye, while in females these lines are broken up into dots. Unfortunately only dominant females exhibit these typical markings, while younger or subordinate females have just one faint interrupted line. Males grow somewhat larger and are more slender than females. It is virtually impossible to sex half-grown specimens.

Maintenance: *B. cupido* is a rather unaggressive fish which appreciates peace and quiet in the aquarium. Rapid swimmers, greedy feeders, and aggressive species are not ideal tankmates, although it should be noted that during the breeding season significantly larger fishes will be driven away. Spawning is unlikely if *B. cupido* is dominated by other species. The diet should be tailored to the requirements of these cichlids, i.e. particle size should not be too large. Diffuse lighting will greatly enhance the coloration of the fishes and their well-being. Although in the wild there is often little or no cover in the way of roots and other wood, the aquarium should be amply provided with this type of hiding place, which *B. cupido* greatly appreciates as shelter. The filtration should not be too powerful, as strong currents are not enjoyed. These fishes are relatively sensitive to pollution, but will tolerate a nitrate level of up to 50 mg/l. Water enriched with humic acid will simulate the conditions in nature. Given an aquarium capacity of at least 200 litres, and provided the pH is maintained below 7.0 and the hardness at less that 10° dGH, then much long-term enjoyment can be expected from these truly gorgeous cichlids.

Breeding behaviour: Because of the broad distribution highly variable observations have been made on the breeding behaviour of B. cupido, and it is almost certain that not all of these actually refer to that species but are instead the result of confusion with different Biotodoma from Guyana. While Kuhlman (1984) reports that the species bred by him (possibly from Guyana) spawned in a pit in the sand and the eggs adhered to the sand along their long side, Arendt (1995) describes a substrate-spawner in the strict sense, and how the species maintained by him (from Santarém) produced eggs with a "polar" attachment, which adhered firmly to the substrate by means of little bundles of threads, such that they waved in a vertical position in the current when fanned. The accompanying description of courtship and brood-care behaviour indicates B. cupido from Santarém. Pair formation begins with lateral threat and frequent mouth-fighting. Eventually a mutual search for a spawning site takes place, with the female making the actual decision. The female then thoroughly cleans the chosen substrate (a flat stone), while the male is already defending the

1. In the female the bluish lines below the eye are split up in spots. This is a distinct sexual character of Biotodoma cupido "Santarém".
2. The igarapé Acara opposite of Santarém, where B. cupido "Santarém" was collected.
3. A male B. cupido "Santarém". Photo: Peter Lucas.
4. This B. cupido (?) probably comes from the Araguaia.
5. Because this B. cupido was imported from Peru, one can assume that this population is very close to the holotype.
6. This individual from Peru exhibits only thin blue lines below the eye.
7. Juvenile B. cupido "Peru", about 5 cm long.

territory. After a few "dummy runs", which can take place over a number of hours or even days, the female begins to lay her eggs. The eggs, once laid, are periodically fertilised by the male when not involved in territorial defence. Simultaneous egg deposition and fertilisation is very rare. The spawn ultimately occupies an area 5-6 cm in diameter and consists of about 200 close-packed eggs. All of the eggs are attached at one end by a tiny "stalk" and move to and fro, as Arendt described, in the current like a grassy meadow in the wind. This means that the individual eggs must have either neutral or positive buoyancy, as with negative buoyancy they would sink to the substrate and the stalks would be superfluous. The female generally hovers several centimetres away and fans fresh water over the eggs with her pectoral fins. If she is obliged to chase away an invading predator, then the male immediately takes over the care of the spawn and begins to fan. Only when a suitable opportunity arises is he relieved by the female. Both male and female are capable of defending the spawn and territory alone for a long period. Both parents swim to and fro over the eggs and gently mouth them to remove any adhering particles. After about 2 days at 28° C the larvae either penetrate the egg-cases independently or are freed from them by the parents. The parents next move the larvae, which are incapable of swimming at this stage, around a number of pre-dug pits. As previously, it is mainly the female who hovers over the pit, again fanning with her pectorals. After a further 8 days the fry are free-swimming and can now be fed with newly-hatched *Artemia*. The fry of *B. cupido* grow relatively slowly and do not reach the 3 cm mark for about 2 months. At least 18 months are required to attain sexual maturity.

Further reading: Arendt (1995: 85-88); Koslowski (1984: 17); Kuhlmann (1984: 14-17); Kullander (1986: 147-154); Stawikowski (1995a: 82-85).

Biotodoma wavrini (Gosse, 1963)

Original description: Bull. Inst. R. Se. Nat. Belg., 39 (35): 1-7

Derivation of scientific name: In honour of the Belgian explorer, the Marquis de Wavrin.

Distribution: This species is found mainly in the Orinoco region (including the borders with Amazonia), in particular in the Rio Inírida (Stalsberg, 1991; Hongslo, 1977): Caqo Alisal (Hongslo, 1985); the Rio Negro drainage in Venezuela (Hongslo, 1981); the Rio Negro drainage in Brazil (Römer *et al.*, 1991; Staeck, 1981) at the confluence with the Rio Urubaxi and the Rio Ererê (Goulding, 1987); Rio Preta de Eva (Marlier, 1964, in Gosse, 1975).

Habitat: Slow-flowing waters with a decidedly low pH, as with *B. cupido*. Usually with wood and leaf litter, and a sandy or muddy substrate. This species apparently prefers blackwaters.

Size: Up to a maximum of 12 cm, hence not quite as large as *B. cupido*.

Characters of the species: More elongate body and rather more pointed snout than in *B. cupido*. The lateral spot lies below the upper lateral line, i.e. between the two lateral lines. In addition the lateral spot is framed by two comma-like light areas. The body base colour is silvery green and there are no other markings on the body. There is a band on the nape, starting between the dorsal insertion and the eye, which then runs diagonally through the eye and thereafter vertically downwards, ending at the leading edge of the operculum. In adult specimens the soft parts of the unpaired fins have a reddish tinge, while the spinous portions are slightly iridescent bluish. There is an iridescent bluish area behind the eye, broken up into spots.

Sexual dimorphism: Very difficult to determine. Males are somewhat larger and have more elongate spines in the dorsal, caudal, and ventrals. In this species too the males have fine blue lines below the eye, while in females the lines are broken into spots. In adult males a very narrow, iridescent blueish stripe maybe visible along the base of the anal. This stripe can be very striking in the half-dark at "lights on".

Maintenance: The specimens imported to date have not proved very hardy in the aquarium and have always eventually disappeared from the trade and from the hobby. Because usually only very small individuals are available in the trade, they need to be grown on in a species tank (at least 200 litres capacity) with small characins. The characins will serve to make the cichlids feel less timid and masters of the aquarium, so that they receive sufficient food. This species is moderately aggressive intraspecifically. Confrontations may occur, but these usually pass with no harm done. Adult specimens, by contrast, command general respect and can keep even larger fishes at a distance during the spawning preparations.

The best diet is small frozen foods such as lobster eggs, *Cyclops*, *Artemia*, and *Daphnia*, plus glassworms and mosquito larvae, with several feeds per day. Once the fishes are settled they will also take good quality dried food without further ado. A maintenance temperature of 26° C is a fair approximation to natural conditions. If the fishes are unwell then it is advisable to raise the temperature to 30° C. The pH should not fall below 5 or rise above 7, and the hardness should not be appreciably greater than 5° dGH. This species reacts quickly and badly to pollution with nitrogenous compounds, and even the nitrate level should never be above 30 mg/l in the long term. Bright light is to be avoided under all circumstances. Ample hiding-places and cover must be provided in the form of plants and bogwood.

Breeding behaviour: To date no definite data are available on the spawning behaviour of *B. wavrini*. It can be assumed, however, that the species requires a very low pH to bring it into spawning condition, as this most closely resembles conditions in nature.

I have, nevertheless, been able to observe a pair during courtship and establishing a territory. While pair formation was rather unexciting, the fishes became extremely aggressive thereafter. They occupied a 50 x 50 cm territory and guarded this with extreme vehemence against all tankmates. The female in particular seemed to have even greater ambitions: she would allow only one male in her immediate vicinity and encouraged him to defend the territory by repeated lateral ramming. After such assaults the male himself invariably likewise became very aggressive and chased the other fishes into their own corners. Interestingly, throughout the entire courtship phase the female's favourite spot was right in the rising bubbles from the diffuser, and it was this area that she defended most fiercely. Unfortunately I was unable to establish whether she preferred this spot because it would provide any subsequent eggs with adequate oxygen, as they never actually spawned.

Further reading: Gosse (1975: 71-76); Staeck (1992: 72-78); Stawikowski (1995a: 82-85).

Biotodoma sp. "Aripuana"

Distribution: Klingner and Seidel caught this species in 1997 (pers. comm.) where the Rio Aripuana enters the lake at its mouth, about an hour's journey by boat upstream of

Novo Aripuana. In this area the river is split into multiple channels by numerous small islands, and fast-flowing reaches alternate repeatedly with slow-flowing areas.

Habitat: Like all other known *Biotodoma* species, *B.* sp. "Aripuana" prefers areas of calm water. Klingner (pers. comm) was able to observe this *Biotodoma* over sand, mud, and leaf litter in slow-flowing reaches of the Rio Aripuana. Wood was also repeatedly seen underwater between the islets.

The water of the Rio Aripuana is clear, although small tributaries carry whitewater and muddy the main river in places. In the shallow areas

1. An adult *Biotodoma wavrini*, imported from Venezuela. Such large individuals of *B. wavrini* are found only sporadically in the trade because they are very sensitive to transport. The main attractions of this eartheater are the metallic sheen on its body and its delicate anatomy.
2. *Biotodoma wavrini* from an unknown locality. Photo: Ad Konings.
3. Subdued lighting enhances the beauty of *Biotodoma* sp."Aripuana".

preferred by *Biotodoma* the water was very warm (30° C).

Size: Males attain up to 12 cm, while females remain somewhat smaller.

Characters of the species: This species cannot be differentiated from *B. cupido* by either body shape or markings. Just like the latter species, *B.* sp. "Aripuana" has a clearly visible suborbital stripe, bluish lines beneath the eye, and very fine vertical lines on the flanks. The operculum itself and the region behind are yellow-orange, while the rest of the body is metallic greenish.

The lateral spot is sited above the upper lateral line, but unlike that of *B. cupido* it has an elongate shape, lies directly below the line of the back, and is bounded above by a white line and below by two white areas.

Sexual dimorphism: Judging from the few specimens that have been imported, males of *B.* sp. "Aripuana" have a more distinct and longer lateral spot, while that of females in general appears smaller. It has not yet been possible to ascertain whether in this *Biotodoma* the bluish suborbital lines are interrupted in females.

Maintenance: This species does not differ from other *Biotodoma* species as regards maintenance. If the aquarium is set up in accordance with Klingner and Seidel's observations of the natural habitat, then there is no barrier to successful maintenance as long as a varied and balanced diet is provided.

Breeding behaviour: The brood care of this species has not yet been observed.

Remarks: The possibility cannot be excluded that this fish is a form of *B. cupido*, but on the basis of the typical form of the lateral spot, which differs from that of *B. cupido*, it can be assumed that this is a new, undescribed, species.

Biotodoma sp. "Guyana"

Distribution: The Essequibo system in Venezuela (Cichocki, 1972).

Habitat: Our knowledge of the habitat of *B.* sp. "Guyana" rests on observations by Cichocki, who in 1972 studied this species in a small tributary of the Rio Essequibo. The study site was a small stream opposite Bartica, whose shoreline was occupied by red mangroves (*Rhizophora mangle*). The habitat was strongly affected by the tides, but nevertheless contained totally fresh water. The bottom was covered with detritus and consisted largely of grey muddy sediment. There was no underwater vegetation. Because the stream was subject to the influence of the tides, Cichocki measured the fluctuating relative levels of oxygen and carbon dioxide during the various phases. He thus established that at the time of low water the oxygen content dropped to less than 4 mg/l, while the CO_2 content rose simultaneously to almost 7 mg/l. During this phase Cichocki was able to make the following observations: 1. At extreme low water (only a few centimetres deep) both parents transported their already-hatched brood into deeper water, and subsequently back again. 2. When the oxygen content reached its lowest level the female assumed nocturnal coloration and "slept" in the immediate vicinity of the nest, while the male likewise "made himself comfortable" a short distance away. This behaviour represents an exceptional adaptation to the habitat, as the raised carbon dioxide level has a limiting effect on the activity of the organism and renders the area "taboo" for active brood-predators. Under such circumstances the parents do not need to tend the brood even during the day; they can switch to "stand-by mode" while remaining in the immediate vicinity of the brood.

Size: Males grow to about 14 cm, while females are full-grown at 12 cm.

Characters of the species: In *B.* sp. "Guyana" the lateral spot lies on the upper lateral line and is usually enclosed by four white spots. Body shape and markings are by and large similar to those of *B. cupido*, although *B.* sp. "Guyana" appears rather more elongate. The dorsal spines have threadlike extensions.

Sexual dimorphism: Similar to that of the two described species.

Maintenance: It is not necessary to imitate the influence of the tides in the aquarium, regardless of the observations in the wild. It is far more important to consider the benefits of good water quality, providing a pH of 6.5-7.0 and a hardness of less than 10° dGH. This species too requires muted lighting and plenty of cover in the form of bogwood and rocks. Feeding and tankmates as for *B. cupido*. Finally, it should be noted that in contrast to the two other members of the genus, this species actually prefers a stronger current.

Breeding behaviour: According to Cichocki *B.* sp. "Guyana" is a substrate brooder, which spawns directly on sand, depositing its eggs, which are attached on their long side, in long irregular rows. The female's role is exclusively brood care, while the male defends the territory at a considerable distance away. If any invader approaches the nest despite the male's efforts, then the female attacks the potential brood-predator with rapid and aggressive ramming and is very successful in driving such enemies away. Cichocki was unable to see any fanning behaviour by the female during the two days between spawning and the larvae hatching. Perhaps the influence of the tides provided sufficient oxygenation. The fry became free-swimming four days after hatching and were then escorted by both parents. In the event of any danger, both parents spread their pelvic fins and jerked them to and fro. The fry then hugged the bottom and oriented themselves

1. In *Biotodoma* sp. "Aripuana" the extremely elongated lateral spot is located near the base of the dorsal fin.
2. A typical blackwater biotope in Venezuela.
3. The white, elongate rays in the caudal fin are a very attractive character of *Biotodoma* sp. "Guyana".
4. A wild-caught male *Biotodoma* sp. "Guyana".

with their heads towards the lateral spots of the parents, from which we may deduce that the spot has a specific signalling function.

These observations on brood-care behaviour correspond closely to those made by Kuhlmann (1984) in the aquarium, which suggests that Kuhlmann in fact kept and bred this species from Guyana, and not *B. cupido* as surmised by him.

However, Grad (1987) reported that his *Biotodoma* species from Guyana was a cave-brooder. The female remained in the breeding cave (an upturned flowerpot) for the whole of the first 5 days, while the male defended the territory very aggressively. After 5

84

days Grad was able to see larvae on the floor of the cave. Unfortunately he does not report whether the eggs were deposited on the wall or the ceiling of the cave, or even perhaps in a pit dug in the floor. After a total of 11 days the brood became free-swimming and were escorted by both parents.

Further reading: Cichocki (1976); Grad (1987: 176-177); Koslowski (1984: 17); Kuhlmann (1984: 14-17).

85

Geophagus Heckel, 1840

Note: The red-hump eartheaters (*'Geophagus' crassilabris* and its immediate relatives) and the pearl eartheaters (the *'Geophagus' brasiliensis* complex) are dealt with separately, as a forthcoming revision of these cichlids will remove them from *Geophagus sensu stricto*.

Derivation of scientific name: *geos* (Gr.) = earth; *phagein* (Gr.) = eat; thus eartheater, with reference to their behaviour, taking food from the substrate.

Distribution: The members of the genus *Geophagus* occupy a large part of Amazonia, the Guianas, and the Orinoco region, where they are found in a large variety of waters.

Ecology: *Geophagus* are an extremely adaptable group. Their specific habitat is a sandy or muddy substrate, but it is irrelevant whether the water is still or fast-flowing. Naturally some species have a preferred habitat, but there are always a number of atypical (habitat-wise) specimens living in the peripheral zones. Thus areas with a rocky substrate are sometimes colonised, likewise places with large piles of dead wood. Rapids, and almost dry residual pools during the dry season, are also *Geophagus* habitats, and they are found in white-, black- and clearwaters. Juveniles are often encountered in the shallow shore zones or among leaf litter, where they find shelter from predators. Adult specimens prefer deeper water by and large.

Likewise temperatures between 22 and 35° C are tolerated (only for a short while at the extremes), with the optimum in the 25-30° C range. Only one type of habitat is largely avoided — *igarapés*, small forest streams which can be rather cool owing to the constant shade of the forest giants.

Characters of the genus: *Geophagus* can very easily be distinguished from other geophagine cichlids by the steep upper head profile and the relatively deep body. The body is only moderately compressed laterally. The eye is sited rather high on the head. The terminal mouth opening, which is very small in relation to the size of the body, runs horizontally. The dorsal and anal fins are always scaled, while the anterior half of the cheek is scaleless. There is always a lateral spot on the centre of the flank, its size variable according to species. By contrast there is no spot on the caudal peduncle. The flanks also exhibit a more or less distinct vertical barring, which in some species is found only immediately below the dorsal base, while in others it extends right down the flanks. This pattern is more distinct in juveniles, but fades in adults and becomes mood-related. As regards base colour, there are no hard and fast rules for the *Geophagus* genus as a whole, and hence coloration is dealt with as a specific character for each species.

Ethology: Outside the breeding season all species move around the bottom in loose association, constantly searching for food. Field observations tend to confirm this, as single specimens are rarely seen. It may often appear that only single specimens are present, but although the distance between individuals may be considerable, there are always conspecifics nearby. Only one species appears to be an exception: *G. harreri*, which apparently associates with bands of *Guianacara*, where it is "camouflaged" by its similar basic pattern and presumably benefits in some as way as yet not understood.

Geophagus are cichlids with two contrasting aspects: although during the breeding phase they can put to flight significantly larger and more aggressive species, the rest of the time they wouldn't hurt the proverbial fly and are generally peace-loving. Although lateral threat is the order of the day, in contrast to other cichlid species this seems to be just for show. During the spawning phase, the smallest *Geophagus*, *G. taeniopareius*, can dominate a 150 cm aquarium without harming tankmates. All members of the genus defend their territories simply by threat or short charges; they never cause injury to other fishes.

Within the genus we find every possible type of reproductive strategy up to and including cave-brooding, as well as a number of hybrid forms; details of these will be found in the sections for each individual species.

Remarks: *Geophagus*, more *Geophagus*, and no end in sight — both importers and travelling aquarists are forever bringing in new local variants. In general these populations are given the name of the locality where they were caught and traded/passed on with details of that locality. This practice is absolutely necessary, as so far it is impossible to say which populations belong to an already-described species and which are sufficiently distinct to be regarded as new, as yet undescribed, species. Every major river system in Brazil, whether it be the Rio Madeira, the Tefé, the Xingú, Tocantins, Araguaia, Trombetas, Tapajós, Pará, or whatever, is home to sibling species, each perhaps part of a species complex. To date it remains unclear whether these are one or a number of very closely-related species. This phenomenon is particularly striking in the species identified as *Geophagus altifrons* and *G. surinamensis sensu stricto*. Practically every river system contains not just individuals with a small or no lateral spot, relatively long snout, and speckled tail (*G. altifrons*), but also specimens which appear very thickset and have a large lateral spot and speckled tail. Other populations have an elongate body shape and a streaked pattern on the caudal. Every sort of intermediate variation is possible, such that the number of populations to be investigated is becoming virtually innumerable. Aquarists are left with no choice but to bide their time, wherever possible identifying their *Geophagus* by locality or special characteristics when passing them on to others.

However, ethological distinctions can be a great help in differentiating the species, and to this end it is absolutely necessary to observe the fishes during brood care. It may well be that the more thickset specimens with a large lateral spot have different breeding behaviour to *G. altifrons*, an ovophilous mouthbrooder, demonstrating that they are different species. As long ago as the 1970s it was noted on a number of occasions that some species were larvophilous or delayed ovophilous mouthbrooders. It was assumed from this that these fishes were all from the Guianas, Colombia, or Venezuela, but it cannot be ruled out that they included specimens from Brazil which today are identified as *G. surinamensis*, *G. brachybranchus*, or *G. brokopondo* on the basis of external characters but may turn out to be new species. That apart, the rapids of each river are home to sibling species which can be assigned to *G. argyrostictus*, *G. taeniopareius*, or *G. grammepareius*, in the broad sense or sometimes belong to a species complex of narrow-barred, thickset, earth-eaters (*Geophagus* sp. "Tapajós Orange-Head". To what extent all these forms can be assigned to particular species remains unclear so far.

From the above it can be assumed that in the years to come the number of described *Geophagus* species (currently 11) will be significantly increased, as already a number of species are known that are quite clearly distinct from those thus far scientifically described.

1. A male *Geophagus altifrons* from the Rio Tocantins.
2. When *G. altifrons* guard larvae or fry, or when they are in an aggressive mood, the dark vertical bars on the flanks become more prominent.
3. An adult male *G. altifrons* "Tapajós". The elongated fin filaments are not necessarily a sexual character because they can be found in males as well as in females.

Geophagus altifrons
Heckel, 1840

Original description: Ann. Wiener Mus. 2 (1): 385-387.

Derivation of scientific name: *altus* (Lat.) = high; *frons* (Lat.) = forehead. The specific name refers to the high forehead (i.e. steeply-rising upper head profile) of these fishes.

Distribution: Widely distributed along the Amazon system, including the northern and southern affluents. The type locality is the confluence of the Rio Negro with the Amazon. Other recorded localities include the Rio Trombetas (Kilian & Seidel, 1991); Rio Tapajós (Andersen, 1994; Stawikoswki, 1992, 1996; Warzel, 1995; pers. obs., 1996); Rio Tocantins (Werner, 1989); Rio Araguaia (Werner, 1989); Rio Uatuma (Kullander, 1987); Rio Guamá (Stawikoswki, 1988); Rio Capim (A. Werner, pers. comm); and Rio Xingú (Stawikowski, 1988). All of these river systems contain other, as yet undescribed, *Geophagus* species, which are sympatric and sometimes syntopic with *G. altifrons*. It would be a serious error to regard all *Geophagus* from the region as being *G. altifrons*. Far better to classify all *Geophagus* from the Amazon region on the basis of locality and markings.

- Geophagus altifrons
- G. sp. "Altamira"
- G. sp. "Rio Areões"

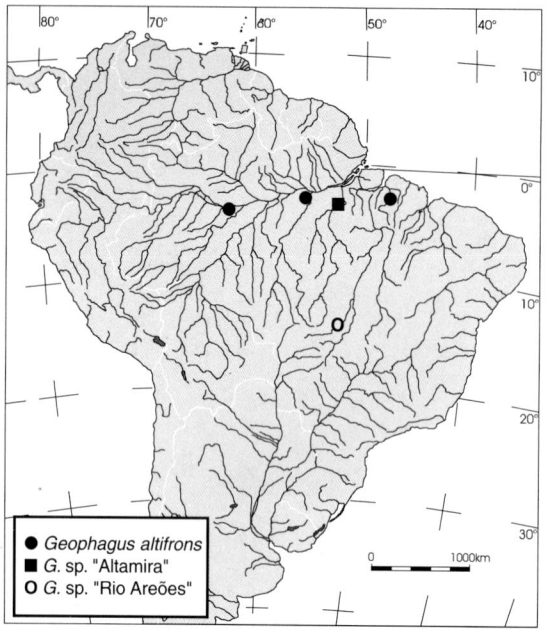

Habitat: Because of the huge distribution area general remarks on the habitat are possible only with reservations. The species can be found not only in areas with a sandy substrate but also in zones with coarse gravel and rocks. Juveniles appear to inhabit shore regions in the main, probably as a defence against possible predators. Tangles of wood and zones with vegetation are not part of the normal environment, but may be resorted to for shelter. The species is found only occasionally in blackwaters, instead inhabiting chiefly clearwaters with a high oxygen content; it may, however, also be found in whitewaters, but not in high population densities.

Size: One of the largest members of the genus. Individuals from some populations can attain a good 30 cm, and the norm is well in excess of 20 cm.

Characters of the species: According to current wisdom G. altifrons can easily be distinguished from other species by the absence of a lateral spot. A lateral spot is, however, to be seen in a number of specimens, but encompassing only a small number of scales. Juveniles always exhibit a lateral spot, but from 5 cm upwards this becomes gradually smaller until it completely disappears or only a hint remains. In addition a dark zone, from the operculum to the midpoint of the body and at approximately mid-height, can be seen in individual that are unwell or in aggressive mood. The caudal and dorsal fins are speckled with tiny spots and exhibit no streaking. Because there are so many different populations a description of coloration is impracticable, and the reader is referred to the photos.

Sexual dimorphism: Extremely difficult to establish, and a matter of guesswork outside of the breeding season. Females remain somewhat smaller and their fins are not so prolonged as those of males. During the breeding season females become rather corpulent with an almost angular ventral profile. After heavy feeding the blunt genital papilla of the female may appear even when spawning is not imminent.

Maintenance: Because of their considerable size these cichlids may attain, they should be kept only in aquaria at least 150 cm long. A substrate of fine sand should be provided, which the fishes can sift at will, as well as a few large flat stones laid on the sand, plus a few pieces of bogwood to serve as cover. A few isolated plants, such as *Cryptocoryne usteriana* or *Anubia barteri barteri* can also be included, and will be left alone by the fishes. *Echinodorus* (swordplants) are less suitable, as *G. altifrons* will tug at them and rapidly render them untidy and unattractive. From this it can be assumed that *G. altifrons* is not entirely disinterested in green food, and hence vegetable food should be offered as well as plenty of "carnivore" food in the form of a variety of frozen foods (mosquito larvae, crustaceans, plus raw fish and mussel meat). Scalded lettuce or squashed peas are suitable. Because these fishes fall greedily upon all food offered, powerful filtration is required in order to cope with the abundant metabolic wastes they produce. In general *G. altifrons* is "happier" with a slight current than in still water. Water chemistry plays a subordinate role, as in contrast to some other members of the genus, these fishes are not particularly fussy (sensitive) as regards pH and hardness.

Breeding behaviour: If the individual flat stones are positioned near the front when setting up, then there will be a better chance of being able to observe spawning at close range, as such stones are preferred spawning substrates. If necessary, however, they will also spawn on sand, but this is only very rarely the case. Spawning is preceded by a period of intense courtship, in which the pair position themselves side to side and head to tail with their fins spread to bursting, and beat the latter violently. Frontal threat sometimes takes place as well, and in this case the gillcovers are also often spread wide. Mouth-wrestling is very rare. Once courtship is finished the female thoroughly cleans the spawning substrate; the male engages in this activity only sporadically, his main task being defence of the territory. During this phase and the actual spawning the fishes may be extremely aggressive. The cleaning of the spawning substrate may take hours or even days.

G. altifrons is an advanced ovophilous mouthbrooder, in which the female lays 2-8 eggs at a time in a straight line; the eggs are next fertilised by the male and then immediately taken into the protective mouth of the mother. It may also happen that the female picks up the eggs before they have been fertilised, in the event that the male is busy with territorial defence. In such instances the male nevertheless emits sperm over the chosen substrate, and the female then picks it up retroactively. Egg deposition and fertilisation by the male always take place in straight passes, with no circling movements

G. altifrons "Tocantins"

G. altifrons "Manaus"

G. altifrons "Xingú"

G. altifrons "Trombetas"

such as are seen in the cichlids of the African Rift Valley.

A maximum of up to 350 eggs are laid, but a brood of 100 is to be regarded as a "good size". The actual spawning takes place very peacefully and harmoniously. The female broods the eggs and fry for only about 10 days (depending on temperature), until they are free-swimming. After 10 days at 28° C the yolk sac is already very small and the larvae are capable of taking freshly-hatched *Artemia*. In very densely populated aquaria, however, the female may keep the fry in her mouth for a very long time, and after 14 days at 28° C the fry are already so emaciated and weakened that no small effort is required to rear them successfully.

From time to time it may be found that females, despite being sexually mature, eat their first brood. But experienced females likewise sometimes eat their brood if they feel stressed for some reason or other. When the fry are finally released they are already 3-4 mm long. The female continues to take the fry back into the shelter of her mouth for a long time, until their increasing size means there is no longer room for them. Parental leading of the fry has not been seen. Instead the fry seem to orient more on one another and to lead their mother! Only when danger threatens does the female swim to the fry and open her mouth, and then the stragglers too swim to mother to be taken in by her. If a few get left outside, they swim to and fro close to their mother's head and keep contacting her until, stimulated by this contact, she opens her mouth again for a while, until the last youngster has taken refuge inside. Hitherto all indications have been that this is an ovophilous maternal mouthbrooder.

The post-spawning brood care appears, however, to vary with the individual or to be affected by outside influences, as while I was unable to observe any pair bond during my first spawning of *G. altifrons* "Rio Tocantins" and the female alone was responsible for brood care, there were variations later on. Thus, when the aquarium population density was higher, the same male guarded a territory in which the female remained, and I even saw the male take over the larvae on the fifth day, although from the eighth day on the female alone brooded and the male played no further part. Males of *G. altifrons* "Maraba" defend a small territory, and in it the female, right from the start. The most pronounced territorial behaviour is seen in males of *G. altifrons* "Tapajós", which defend the brooding female and a territory very aggressively. While the female remains constantly in the shelter of a root or other cover, the male tirelessly patrols around her refuge, attacking any potential predator.

In this case too I observed that on the occasion of the first brood the male was seen to be brooding on the sixth day. I should add, however, that the first spawning took place at a total length of 15 cm and the brood comprised more than 250 fry,

G. altifrons "Tapajós"

G. cf. *altifrons* "Aripuana I"

G. cf. *altifrons* "Tocantins"

G. altifrons "Marabá"

93

requiring both parents to participate in the rearing of so many. When the larvae were taken away from the female, leaving the male still brooding a few, then after a few hours the male handed the remaining fry over to the female and from then on she alone brooded, while the male reverted to guarding her and the territory. Once the fry were released, then if the female moved too far from the shoal while chasing away some predator, then the male would remain near the brood and, if danger threatened, take them into his mouth. On average the female retained the fry in her mouth for longer than the male. If the brood was lost, then after as little as three weeks the pair were ready to spawn again. If the fry were reared successfully, then further spawning was delayed for about two months.

Darda (pers. comm.) reported his male *G. altifrons* "Manaus" as extremely aggressive towards the female. Although the pair spawned together, the male was so violent in his behaviour towards the female that she generally dared venture out only at feeding time. Until the seventh day Darda could detect only the female brooding. But when the fry left their mother's mouth, he repeatedly saw the male picking up stragglers and brooding them. Occasionally the male even went so far as to steal a few fry, after persuading the female to release them by gentle flank-nudging or snapping at her mouth.

Remarks: *G. altifrons* is the type species of the genus *Geophagus*.

Further reading: Stawikowski (1989a: 476-480); Weidner (1994a: 39-42).

Geophagus sp. "Altamira"

Distribution: Stawikowski *et al.* caught this species in the vicinity of Altamira on the Rio Xingú (Stawikowski, 1989).

Habitat: Stawikowski *et al.* (1989) caught individuals of this species in a metre-wide bank zone with a sand and mud substrate. The water was somewhat turbid by virtue of this substrate, although the Rio Xingú is principally a clearwater river. *G.* sp. "Altamira" shares this habitat with a *Satanoperca* species (*jurupari*?) and an *Aequidens* species. The rocky sections of the river are avoided by *G.* sp. "Altamira", and instead those areas are home to *Geophagus argyrostictus* as well as the above-mentioned undetermined *Geophagus* and *Aequidens*.

Size: Males attain an eventual size of about 25 cm.

Characters of the species: The first thing to strike the eye is the greenish base coloration that covers the entire sides. No other colour patterns are obvious on the flanks, although, depending on the light, iridescent silvery flecks, arranged in longitudinal rows, may become visible.

The most typical character is, however, without doubt the lateral spot, which is 2-3 rows of scales wide and vertically intersected by a dark bar which is almost always clearly visible. There are in total seven vertical bars on the flanks, with the first running from directly in front of the dorsal insertion down barely as far as the operculum. The bars immediately in front of and behind the lateral spot are usually both rather bolder than the others, and often visible, while the remaining three bars, beneath the soft dorsal and on the caudal peduncle, are barely to be seen. The soft portions of the unpaired fins are covered with irregularly arranged, iridescent bluish spots on a yellow-reddish background. The fins are not particularly prolonged compared to those of *G. altifrons*.

Sexual dimorphism: Males grow to a few centimetres longer and have rather more prolonged unpaired fins.

Maintenance: The requirements of *G.* sp. "Altamira" do not differ from those of other *Geophagus*, and it can be maintained as for *G. altifrons*.

Breeding behaviour: This species has proved to be an ovophilous mouthbrooder, whose brood care by and large resembles that of *G. altifrons*.

Remarks: This species is also occasionally known and sold as *G. altifrons* "Altamira". I am of the opinion, however, that this is not just a local variant of *G. altifrons*, as the differences from that species are more than obvious. Particularly striking characters of this species are the large lateral spot and the almost always visible vertical band running through it.

Further reading: Stawikowski (1989a: 476-480).

Geophagus sp. "Rio Areões"

Distribution: Known from the drainage of the Rio Areões, and from the Rio das Mortes at BR 158 near Nova Xavantina (Werner *et al.*, 1990).

Habitat: The biotope inhabited by this species offers a variety of conditions. Werner (1990) describes the main stream, near the site of a former bridge, as having a strong current, while further downstream the river widens and there is calm water in the area around a bank of gravel. The fishes were caught over a muddy to sandy substrate in two large circular pools. The water was cloudy with sediment and the collectors sometimes sank up to their knees in mud. At 23° C the river water was rather cool, although that in the pools, being shallower, could rise to 25° C. The standing water of the pools had a relatively high pH of 7.5, and the conductivity was also rather higher than normal, at 75-80 µS/cm. Elsewhere in the area the pH was measured at 5.5 to 6.8, and the hardness was always well below 1° dGH and not measurable with normal drop reagents. Because of the powerful current of the main river the bottom was devoid of stones and wood.

Size: In contradiction to data given elsewhere, this species does not exceed the 20 cm mark. The largest male recorded to date measured 18 cm, while females remain somewhat smaller.

Characters of the species: The body shape by and large resembles that of other members of the genus. This species seems to be particularly close to *G. altifrons*, but when motivated it exhibits six diagonal double bands on the flanks. The most striking distinguishing character is the

1. *Geophagus* sp. "Altamira" has a high dorsal fin.
2. In earlier days the Rio Tapajós was a clearwater river; today, because of gold mining, it resembles more a whitewater river. Recent reports, however, suggest that visibility has increased in the last few years.
3. *Geophagus* sp. "Rio Areões" is characterised by the possession of two lateral spots, although there are many individuals that exhibit those two spots only on one side of the body.

clearly visible lateral spot, which is 2-3 rows of scales wide and lies on the middle of the body beneath the upper lateral line and on the third double band. In addition to this lateral spot the majority of specimens exhibit another, smaller spot on the second double band. Astonishingly, this second spot is not always present on both sides of the fish, but instead is more often present on one flank only. The upper lip is bluish. A bluish stripe runs from the corner of the mouth to the leading edge of the preoperculum. There is a vivid yellow on the breast region, while on the shoulder area the yellow become more of an orange shade. On the forehead, between the eye and the dorsal fin insertion, there is a pale yellow vertical stripe extending to the eye. Beneath the eye these fishes exhibit a pattern of bluish spots and stripes. The flanks are yellowish, and the centre of each scale iridescent bluish, giving the impression of rows of spots. Apart from the pectorals, which are colourless, all the fins have bluish spots and stripes on a reddish background. The upper part of the tail is noticeably more heavily spotted than the lower. In adults the tips of the ventrals and the unpaired fins are extended into white filaments.

Sexual dimorphism: Males grow larger than females. That apart, the only sure way to separate the sexes is by the blunted genital papilla in the female at spawning time.

Maintenance: This species is one of the more timid members of the genus, which unconditionally requires hiding places and muted lighting. A fine substrate and well-constructed decor (rocks and wood) will make for better health and help create separate territories. Active swimmers and aggressive species should always be avoided as tankmates. Even during the spawning phase this species is not well able to defend itself. But once these cichlids are settled, and provided they are not upset by tankmates, then they can become very tame and develop a healthy appetite. They will take all the usual foods, and vegetable food should not be omitted from the diet. They make no great demands as regards water parameters (hardness and pH), but will, of course do better, showing brighter colours and increased vitality, in soft acid water. It is important that levels of organic pollutants should not be too high.

Breeding behaviour: *G.* sp. "Areões" is a typical ovophilous mouthbrooder, in which pair formation takes place extremely peacefully. In general the aquarist will notice merely that the two fishes spend a lot of time together. Typical courtship behaviour is only seen immediately before the spawning. It is worth noting that the male positions himself at 45° to the female, with his head raised, all fins spread, and the floor of his mouth lowered. The females reacts to this behaviour by spreading her fins and shaking her head. The male then positions himself side to side and head to tail with the female in lateral display, with head-shaking and hefty tail-beating on the part of both fishes. A few males swim around their partner and spit sand towards her. This generally happens in the immediate vicinity of the chosen spawning substrate and usually results in a niche being created beneath it. Eventually both partners clean the spawning substrate, with the male guarding the territory as well. The cleaning of the substrate and the subsequent dummy spawning runs are always accompanied by quivering and lateral display.

The actual spawning is typical of a highly-specialised ovophilous mouthbrooder. Either fertilisation follows egg deposition immediately, or the female takes unfertilised eggs into her mouth and the male then emits his sperm across the substrate, to be taken in retroactively by the female. Werner (1994) reports that this species is a biparental mouthbrooder, with eggs first being transferred to the male after three or four days. During the transfer the parents position themselves face-to-face or at a slight angle, and their excitement is evident in their boldly expressed stripes. The larvae are next sat by the female into a little pit, and picked up immediately by the male. From this time on the pair alternate in their guarding of the brood. Depending on temperature, after about 9-11 days the fry are spat out for longer periods and can then be fed with freshly-hatched *Artemia*. The fry are not actively led by the parents, it is more a case of the parents swimming along behind the fry. If danger threatens the fry swim to the open mouth of one of the parents to seek shelter therein.

Werner (1994) noted that in the case of his fishes both parents invariably took the brood into their mouths. I have never seen this in my fishes, it has always been the female who performed the entire brood care and the male never played any further part. These variations may be related to individual behavioural patterns, or else occasioned by secondary influences such as decor, lighting, tankmates.

Further reading: Weidner (1994a: 39-42); Werner (1990b: 100-111; 1994: 62-67).

Geophagus argyrostictus Kullander, 1991

Original description: Cybium 15(2): 129-138.

Derivation of scientific name: *argyros* (Gr.) = silver; *stiktos* (Gr.) = spotted; referring to the silvery spots around the lateral spot.

Distribution: Endemic to the Rio Xingú and its drainage, with specific localities at Cachoeira do Espelho (Vanzolini, 1986); Balneario Pedral, some 8 km south of Altamira (Stawikoswki *et al.*, 1988); Cachoeira von Martius (Gosse & Léopold III, 1964); also reported from the mouth of the Rio Irm (Snethlage, 1909) and Belo Monte (Goulding, 1983).

Habitat: *G. argyrostictus* lives exclusively in the quieter zones of rapid-flowing water, as well as in residual pools separated from the main river. The bottom in these areas is often covered in large stones and rocks. In places there are also accumulations of driftwood. There is very fine sand between these accumulations of rock and wood, and it is these areas that are the actual habitat of the species.

The water of the Rio Xingú is clear and, in the areas of rapids, very rich in oxygen. While the temperature in the main river is 27-29° C all year round, the water in residual pools may reach almost 30° C. In general only juveniles are found in these residual pools, as adult specimens would very rapidly fall prey to birds on account of their size and the lack of cover. In the natural habitat (and in the aquarium) they give the impression of being extremely accomplished swimmers. To date the species has been considered endemic to the Rio Xingú and its tributaries, but very similarly marked species are also found in the Rio Trombetas, Rio Tapajós, Rio Arapiuns, and Rio Aripuana. The taxonomic status of these fishes has not yet been determined, but there is evidence to suggest that the fishes from the Rio Tapajós at least are a further population of *G. argyrostictus*.

Size: Males can grow to just over 20 cm, while females stop at 20 cm.

Characters of the species: Like all known *Geophagus*, *G. argyrostictus* is greatly compressed laterally and elongate in habitus. The body is slightly oval. The upper head profile rises gradually and the head appears triangular. The dorsal fin is moderately high. The ventral spines may be moderately prolonged in adults.

The base coloration is, depending on the light, bluish to greenish with a yellowish shimmer all over the body. Depending on their origin these fishes may also exhibit reddish areas, particularly around the lateral spot and behind the operculum. All the fins except the pectorals (which are transparent) are the same colour as the body, with the soft portions appearing reddish in some lights. The body and the soft parts of the unpaired fins may, again depending on the light, be strewn with shiny bluish flecks or spots, arranged in rows. The lateral spot, which encompasses only a few scales, is sited on the centre of the flank and surrounded by little silvery spots (hence the scientific name). On the cheek there is a narrow bluish stripe, which begins halfway up the eye and runs diagonally downwards to the mouth (a so-called lachrymal stripe). During brood-care coloration, or when in aggressive mood, these fishes exhibit seven vertical bars. The last lies on the caudal peduncle, the penultimate at the end of the dorsal fin base. Bars two to five lie below the dorsal, with the lateral spot on the third. The first begins level with the dorsal insertion and ends on the nape. Bars one and two may be forked from the mid-flank level downwards. Now and then there may also be a distinct longitudinal band, starting at the eye and ending at the lateral spot. A black streak runs from the anterior edge of the operculum upwards to the eye, continuing through the iris so that the pupil may appear split in two (mood-dependent).

Sexual dimorphism: Juvenile and semi-adult specimens cannot be sexed by secondary sexual characteristics. During the breeding season adult females look somewhat fuller-bodied and are paler in colour than males. In addition the dorsal, anal, and ventrals in males may be rather more prolonged. But the species can only be sexed definitely by the shape of the genital papilla — blunt in females and more pointed in males.

Maintenance: For long-term maintenance the water should have a hardness of less than 12° dGH and the pH should be around neutral. Maintenance is possible in rather harder water, but it must be borne in mind that the

1. *Geophagus argyrostictus* is sometimes known as "Tearstripe Eartheater".
2. *G. argyrostictus* exhibits many shiny spots on the flanks.
3. *G. argyrostictus* is usually an open brooder, but in this case the fishes spawned under this slab on a vertical wall.
4. *Geophagus* cf. *argyrostictus* "Tapajós" is also known as *Geophagus.* sp. "Tapajós III".

101

time the river bed lay in a deep trench, with stepped sand walls towering up to 5 metres above the water. There were often residual pools between these steps, sometimes on the verge of drying up. A few of these pools were only a few centimetres deep, others, mainly those at the edge of the river bed, were still up to 2 metres in depth. At this time of the year the main river is only about 30 metres (maximum) wide at the point visited, but it was obvious that at other times the river at this spot was far broader, about 300 metres from bank to bank. The river was this reduced to a tenth of its original width, and part of its bed was occupied by a huge sandbank covered with brush vegetation. A number of fist- to football-sized boulders were also to be seen.

Because of the lack of shade the water in the residual pools was sometimes heated to 35° C, but despite this the *G.* sp. cf. argyrostictus "Tapajós" did not exhibit any increase in respiratory rate and appeared to be in good health. The temperature in the Rio Tapajós itself measured 28-30° C. The hardness could not be measured using the usual reagent-drop test kit, and the pH was 6-6.5.

Size: Males barely exceed the 20 cm mark, and are 2-4 cm longer than females.

Characters of the species: There is no doubt that *G. argyrostictus* from the Rio Xingú is the closest relative of this species. Externally the two species can be differentiated by only a small number of characters. As in *G. argyrostictus* there is a bluish lachrymal stripe beneath the eye. There are a few bluish spots and streaks on the operculum. A dark bar runs from the eye to the anterior edge of the operculum. In contrast to *G. argyrostictus* the present species has a yellower base colour, on which there are bluish iridescent spots, arranged in lines (not the case in *G. argyrostictus*). There are no bluish spots around the lateral spot, which is very small and extends across only 2 rows of scales. The pectorals are colourless. The spinous parts of the ventrals and anal exhibit bluish stripes, while there are bluish spots on the caudal and anal. There is a reddish sheen on the soft portions of the unpaired fins. The edge of the dorsal is reddish brown.

As regards shape, there is very little difference from *G. argyrostictus* except that the head looks rather heavier and the lips fleshier.

Sexual dimorphism: Females have rounder fins than males and remain several centimetres smaller.

Maintenance: This species appears to be rather easier to maintain that *G. argyrostictus*, as so far no problems have been encountered. This species can be kept in harder water (up to a maximum of 20° dGH), but does not show such attractive coloration in such conditions.

These fishes do not seem particularly fussy when it comes to food. Any available aquarium food — frozen, dried, live — is taken greedily. Problems arising from dietary deficiency appear to be less common than in the better-known form from the Rio Xingú. This species does not harm plants.

1. *Geophagus* cf. *argyrostictus* "Arapiuns" has, in contrast to *Geophagus* cf. *argyrostictus* "Aripuana", a stronger coloration in the caudal fin.
2. *Geophagus* cf. *argyrostictus* "Aripuana".
3. A semi-adult *G.* cf. *argyrostictus* "Aripuana".

Although only a few specimens have so far been kept in captivity, it has been found that the aquarium should be of good size — no less than 150 cm long. The water should be warm (26° C or more), soft, and slightly acid. This species too appreciates cover and muted lighting.

This species should not be kept in pairs, as it too appreciates the company of conspecifics, even though it can be rather aggressive intraspecifically. However, serious biting is rare. As a rule there is just head-to-tail lateral threat with the combatants using beats of their tails to create waves and thus prove who is the strongest.

Breeding behaviour: This species has not yet been induced to spawn. In all probability the brood-care behaviour will turn out to be largely similar to that of *G. argyrostictus*.

Remarks: It remains to be seen if this species is identical to *G. argyrostictus*. Aquarists can help here, as the two forms may turn out to exhibit ethological differences which might support the view that they are distinct species.

Geophagus sp. cf. argyrostictus "Arapiuns"

Distribution: Klingner (pers. comm.) found specimens of this species in 1996 and 1998 in the vicinity of the village of Vila do Aruc downstream of the Cachoeira do Aruc. The species was previously found in the same place by Stawikowski *et al.* in 1992.

Habitat: To date this species has been reported only from the immediate vicinity of the rapids, in fast-flowing water. The water is brownish in colour, but clear. The substrate of the rapids is a sand-gravel mixture, while below the rapids Klingner was able to make out a slightly muddy bottom. Dead wood was also present, but was not used as cover by *G.* sp. cf. *argyrostictus* "Arapiuns". The shoreline was sand. The pH was very acid — 4.4 to 4.7.

Large *Leporinus*, *Crenicichla acutirostris*, and even *Satanoperca lilith* formed part of the sympatric ichthyofauna.

Size: This species appears to be full-grown at 25 cm.

Characters of the species: The body form resembles the *Geophagus* norm: high and moderately compressed laterally. The base coloration is blue-green. The lachrymal stripe is longer, but narrower, than in *G.* sp. cf. *argyrostictus* "Aripuana". There are a few bluish spots and lines on the operculum. No noteworthy markings on the nape. Reddish longitudinal lines alternate with iridescent blue rows of scales on the flanks. The base colour becomes rather lighter towards the underside. The lateral spot lies high on the body, encompassing three rows of scales, is practically bisected by the upper lateral line, and in contrast to that of *G. argyrostictus* is not surrounded by metallic spots. The unpaired fins and the ventrals are the same colour as the body base colour, with (ventrals and anal) a large number of bluish spots and lines, especially on the soft portions. By contrast to *G.* sp. cf. *argyrostictus* "Aripuana" the spots on the tail retain their full colour, rather than becoming paler, right to the edge of the fin. Moreover the tips of the ventrals are not such a gleaming white as in *G.* sp. cf. *argyrostictus* "Aripuana", but more of a rusty grey.

Sexual dimorphism: There are no secondary sexual characteristics in this species, so that once again one must look for a more compact habitus and blunter unpaired fins in females.

Maintenance: These eartheaters have proved to be rather tricky in the aquarium, and require a large aquarium (more than 600 litres) in keeping with their intraspecific aggression and expected eventual size. Provided attention is paid to water quality and a balanced diet, then they are generally hardy pets. Pollution of the water such as very commonly occurs through overfeeding and simultaneous inadequate water changes, will very rapidly manifest itself via an increased respiratory rate and washed-out colours. If these conditions last for too long then signs of deficiency diseases will quickly appear and are very difficult to cure. In addition the pH should not exceed 7.0 in the long term and the hardness should be maintained at less than 10° dGH. The maintenance temperature should not drop below 26° C.

As regards the aquarium decor, this species does not differ from other *Geophagus* in its requirements. Likewise it has no special dietary requirements, so no problems are likely in that respect.

Breeding behaviour: To date it has not been possible to observe this species during spawning preparations or brood care. It can be assumed, however, that it does not differ appreciably from other members of this group, i.e. in all probability it is an open-brooder with both parents guarding the fry.

Remarks: In external appearance this species particularly resembles the population from the Rio Aripuana, which, however, is less aggressive and grows larger. They are probably sibling species from the two separate river systems.

Further reading: Stawikowski (1997a: 53-58).

Geophagus sp. cf. *argyrostictus* "Aripuana"

Distribution: Klingner (pers. comm.) found this species in 1997, an hours voyage (about 10-15 km) upstream of Novo Aripuana, in the area where the Rio Aripuana widens into a lake at its mouth. But he was unable to find any eartheaters of this lachrymal-stripe group in the lake itself.

Habitat: In the area where the Rio Aripuana widens into a lake at its mouth, the river is branched during the dry season in September, as the river basin is dotted with tiny islets. Between these islets, where the water is also quite shallow, the current is usually found to be strong, while in wider, deeper areas the water flows rather sedately towards the river mouth. The bottom consists mainly of a sand-gravel mixture, with the sand giving way to coarser material towards the shore. There are often a number of large rocks between the islets. There is much driftwood and other dead wood on the shore, as well as in the main river, and this is used for cover. The distance between individuals is noticeably smaller than in *G.* sp. cf. *argyrostictus* "Arapiuns".

The water is clear, but in places small whitewater affluents join the main river, muddying the visibility somewhat. Unfortunately there are no published details of the water parameters.

Size: This species grows very large. Females of 25 cm have been caught, and males are somewhat larger.

Characters of the species: This species is very much like *G.* sp. cf. *argyrostictus* "Arapiuns" in outward appearance. The only differences are that in this species the bluish spots on the tail become paler towards the upper and lower edges. Further possible distinguishing characters are the shorter, but wider, lachrymal stripe and the white ventral fin tips. Individuals in aggressive mood exhibit six dark vertical bars on the flanks, with the lateral spot sited on the third.

Sexual dimorphism: No secondary sexual characteristics are discernible. But if the female is ripe then her ventral region appears rather more corpulent. Females also remain somewhat smaller.

Maintenance: Like other eartheaters of this lachrymal-stripe group, this species needs very good quality water. For long-term maintenance a pH of less than 7.0 is advisable, and the hardness should not exceed 10° dGH.

This species is appreciably less aggressive than *G.* sp. cf. *argyrostictus* "Arapiuns", such that it can readily be kept with conspecifics. Because of the size of these fishes an aquarium of 600 litres capacity should be regarded as the minimum.

This species poses no special demands as regards feeding, equipment, and decor, and these should

1. This individual of *G.* cf. *argyrostictus* "Curuá" has a total length of 15 cm. It almost completely lacks the shiny spots characteristic of *G. argyrostictus*.
2. Some eartheater biotopes seem to be taken from postcards and remind us of Caribbean beaches. A sandbank in middle Rio Tapajós near Boim.
3. *G.* cf. *argyrostictus* "Aripuana" has spawned in the aquarium as an open brooder. However, fry could not yet be raised.

be as for the other members of the group.

Breeding behaviour: Partial breeding success has already been achieved. According to Klingner (pers. comm.) the fishes spawned on a piece of wood. The clutch comprised 250-300 striking orange eggs. At 26.8° C the larvae hatched after 4 days and were moved around a series of pre-dug pits by both parents. Unfortunately it was not possible to rear the fry: the larvae were repeatedly decimated by the other residents, until after a few days there were no longer any to be seen.

By and large the spawning and brood care behaviour of this species resemble those of *G. argyrostictus*.

Remarks: It is probable that this species and *G.* sp. cf. *argyrostictus* "Arapiuns" are sibling species.

G. sp. cf. *argyrostictus* "Curuá"

Distribution: Warzel, Loew, and their companions caught this species in the Rio Curuá in 1997, near to the Cachoeira da Lontra.

Habitat: This species was found above the Cachoeira de Lontra in about 2 metres of rather slow-flowing water. The substrate was sandy but strewn with large boulders and pieces of basalt. Basalt terraces extended at right-angles to the current, protruding from the water (but still submerged in places) and covered in a rather hard moss (probably *Mourera fluviatilis*). The deeper areas between these terraces were the preferred habitat of *G.* sp. cf. *argyrostictus* "Curuá", as these offered plenty of cover. The species could be found only above the rapids, and shared its habitat with *Teleocichla* sp. "Curuá", *Crenicichla marmorata*, *Sartor respectus, Leporinus* spp and various other large characins that are often to be found in faster-flowing waters. Below the plateau the current was appreciably slower and here *G.* sp. Cf. *argyrostictus* "Curuá" was replaced by *G. altifrons*. The water was light red-brown, had a conductivity of 42 µS/cm at 32° C, and, with a pH of 4.8, was very acid.

G. sp. cf. *argyrostictus* "Curuá" is solitary even when juvenile, as no shoaling behaviour could be seen in specimens of 3 cm. Time and again just one individual was spotted and caught. A distance of 1-2 metres between individuals can be regarded as normal. Although one can slowly prowl around among juveniles this is not possible with adults, which have a very high flight distance.

Size: The specimens brought back by Warzel, Loew, and their companions in 1999 have attained a size of about 12 cm. One specimen with a total length of 15-18 cm was seen in the natural habitat.

Characteristics of the species: This species bears a very close similarity to *G.* sp. cf. *argyrostictus* "Trombetas" (see later), only in *G.* sp. cf. *argyrostictus* "Curuá" the lateral spot is somewhat smaller (only 3 rows of scales) and lies a long way from the dorsal, not right on the lateral line but somewhat beneath it. Both species lack metallic spots around the lateral spot that are typical of *G. argyrostictus*.

In contrast to *G.* sp. cf. *argyrostictus* "Trombetas", in *G.* sp. cf. *argyrostictus* "Curuá" the dorsum is overlain with a very light blue, while the ventral region is again bright yellow.

This species is very similar to *G.* sp. cf. *argyrostictus* "Trombetas" in body shape as well as markings.

Sexual dimorphism: So far no significant secondary sexual characteristics have been discerned. It is, however, to be expected that males will grow rather larger, be more slender-bodied, and have rather more prolonged fin tips than females.

Maintenance: This species is rather more tolerant than *G.* sp. cf. *argyrostictus* "Trombetas". However, it is a rather active species that requires a very large aquarium (500 litres or more), as it is prone to intraspecific squabbles which have no harmful consequences in a spacious aquarium. These cichlids can even be kept in a small group, and this is certainly better than keeping a pair or trio. There is essentially no barrier to keeping this Geophagus with other fishes provided the latter are able to look after themselves and/or are sufficiently accomplished swimmers to make a getaway.

There is no need to make a lot of fuss about the aquarium decor. A sandy substrate, a few hiding-places, and not too bright lighting, will suffice for successful maintenance. The water parameters should, of course, reflect those of the natural habitat, but these fishes can also be kept in moderately hard water with a neutral pH. It is important when keeping fishes which, like these, come from rapids, to keep levels of metabolic by-products as low as possible — i.e. a large regular water change at least once per week is obligatory (this applies to other fishes as well!). An generously-sized filter will otherwise ensure optimal water quality, as in the first instance it will have a greater capacity for breaking down metabolic waste products, and in addition it will improve water circulation in the aquarium, creating a stronger current which will be enjoyed by and benefit these cichlids. As regards diet, *G.* sp. cf. *argyrostictus* "Curuá" has no special requirements, and any food will be taken greedily.

Breeding behaviour: To date it has not been possible to make any observations of breeding behaviour.

Remarks: In all probability this species is identical with *G.* sp. cf. *argyrostictus* "Trombetas", even though they differ in their aggression potential and slight differences in coloration are apparent.

G. sp. cf. argyrostictus "Trombetas" (also known as *G.* sp. cf. argyrostictus "Cumina")

Distribution: Stawikowski caught this species in the Rio Trombetas in 1998, at the Cachoeira Porteira. Warzel, Loew, and their companions caught this species in the Cachoeira do Pancada in the Rio Cumina (also known as the Rio Erepecuru or Rio Paru de Oeste). It cannot be ruled out, and is actually highly probable, that this species can be found in other parts of these rivers.

Habitat: According to Loew (pers. comm.) the water is basically transparent to light brownish, with a pH of 6.25 and no measurable conductivity (!) at a temperature of 31.7° C. Close to the shore the current was only moderate, while in deeper water it was far more powerful. The substrate consisted of a gravel-rubble mix, and the individuals observed were seen to retreat under the larger rocks when danger threatened. Only juveniles of 3 to (maximum) 5 cm were observed in the natural habitat — it would appear that adults have a higher flight distance. On the other hand it was striking to note that individuals of just a few centimetres length were already solitary — at no time was more than one *G.* sp. cf. *argyrostictus* "Trombetas" seen or even caught at a single site.

G. sp. cf. *argyrostictus* "Trombetas" shares its habitat with various dwarf *Crenicichla, C. tigrina, C. marmorata,* plus suckermouth catfishes and members of the genus *Leporinus,* i.e. the sort of mixture normally found in rapids.

Stawikowski caught his specimens in the Cachoeira Porteira in rather deeper zones with less current, over a substrate of rock and sand (pers. comm.).

Size: The small number of individuals imported to date have so far attained a length of 15 cm and it can thus be assumed that they will not exceed the 20 cm mark.

Characters of the species: The lips are moderately thickened. The distance between the eye and the mouth is relatively small for a *Geophagus*. The upper head profile rises only moderately and the dorsal fin is low. The fins are only moderately prolonged. The body is more elongate than in other *Geophagus*.

A cheek stripe runs through the eye and then vertically downwards, ending between the lower jaw and the operculum. The lateral spot is sited in the middle of the upper lateral line,

1. Individuals of *Geophagus cf. argyrostictus* "Trombetas" from the Rio Cumina were, in the aquarium, very aggressive towards conspecifics. Specimens from the Rio Trombetas were much easier to keep in groups.
2. *Geophagus* sp. "Porto Franco" seems to be an intermediate between *G. argyrostictus* and *G.* sp. "Orange Head", because also this species possesses a "tear-stripe" but also a reddish forehead and thin vertical bars on the body, which are typical for *G.* sp. "Orange Head".

encompasses 4 rows of scales, and lies 3 rows of scales below the dorsal base. Individuals in aggressive mood may have an poorly-delineated dark band from behind the operculum to the caudal peduncle, interrupted in the region of the lateral spot. At the same time such individuals exhibit six distinct dark transverse bars on the flanks, each about as wide as the lateral spot.

The forehead is brownish, while the basic body colour is a beige-yellow. There is a narrow iridescent bluish stripe extending diagonally downwards from below the eye to the mouth (lachrymal stripe). The lips have a bluish sheen. There are light, iridescent spots, arranged in horizontal lines, on the flanks. The ventral spines are white, while the soft part has a yellowish-red base colour with iridescent bluish stripes. The anal has spots of a similar gleaming bluish shade, again on a reddish background. Numerous small roundish spots can be seen on the reddish caudal, visibly decreasing in size towards the centre of the fin. The dorsal spines are reddish, while the membranes between them are a bluish colour. The soft dorsal exhibits numerous small bluish dots on a reddish background.

Sexual dimorphism: To date no secondary sexual characters have been discerned.

Maintenance: From observations so far (Lowe, with regard to *G.* sp. cf. *argyrostictus* "Cumina") this species is extremely aggressive in the aquarium, not just towards conspecifics but also towards other species of quite different appearance. To date it has not been possible to keep conspecifics together for long, even in an aquarium 2.5 metres long. Even when ample hiding-places are provided they will seek out and fight opponents. Although these encounters do not last long, the next squabble begins within just a few minutes. This does not lead to serious injury, but fin damage may occur. Other species are invariably chased from within a radius of about 20 cm and bitten as they flee, with the assault always on the fins alone. Even 20 cm long *Crenicichla* are not exempt. By contrast the fishes from the Rio Trombetas are in general more peaceful than those from the Cumina (Stawikowski, pers. comm; pers. obs.).

Leaving aside the unusual aggressiveness and the aquarium size necessary as a result, *G.* sp. cf. *argyrostictus* "Trombetas" is an easy earth-eater to maintain, which will be happy with any type of food offered. Of course live food should figure high on the menu, but dried and frozen foods are readily taken. No particular aquarium arrangement is required apart from the need for plenty of swimming space for these agile and active cichlids. It goes without saying that adequate filtration producing a strong current is required, as these cichlids originate from rapids and prefer fast-flowing water.

Breeding behaviour: So far no information is available on breeding behaviour, but it is very probable that this species (population?) is also an open-brooder.

Remarks: As regards body markings, coloration, and external habitus, this species seems to lie morphologically between *G. argyrostictus* and *G. taeniopareius*. Whether or not this form belongs to one or other species, or is a separate taxon, cannot be determined at the present time.

Geophagus sp. "Porto Franco"

Distribution: Up to now this species has been imported to Germany from Porto Franco on the lower course of the Rio Tocantins.

Habitat: No definite details of the habitat are available at present. It is to be assumed, however, that the substrate of the biotope does not differ appreciably from that of other *Geophagus*.

Size: Imported specimens have so far attained 18 cm and will probably not appreciably exceed the 20 cm mark.

Characters of the species: The head of *Geophagus* sp. "Porto Franco" is relatively short, and the eye is not sited as high on the head as in, for example, *G.* sp. "Maicuru". The mouth is remarkably pointed. The upper head profile rises rather more steeply. Maximum body depth lies between the dorsal and ventral insertions. The upper body profile does not curve significantly towards the caudal peduncle until the beginning of the soft dorsal.

The lateral spot lies at approximately mid-height on the flank and its upper edge intersects the upper lateral line. Posterior to the operculum there are 12 narrow vertical bars on the flanks, with the lateral spot sited between the fifth and sixth of these stripes. The basic body colour is a light green, becoming darker on the back. The cheeks are yellowish, while a light reddish area is apparent on the forehead, extending down to the level of the eye and before yielding to the yellow of the cheeks. On the flanks light, iridescent, longitudinal lines alternate with bright yellow ditto. There is a distinct narrow lachrymal stripe beneath the eye. There are yellowish-white spots on the soft parts of the unpaired fins only, on a bluish (caudal and anal) or reddish (dorsal) background. On the upper and lower edges of the tail the spots are few in number, arranged in lines, and somewhat larger than those on the centre of the fin.

Sexual dimorphism: There are no discernible secondary sexual characteristics. Males may grow larger.

Maintenance: So far *Geophagus* sp. "Porto Franco" has proved very

1

territorial. The few observations available indicate that these fishes are best kept in a small group, as thus their intraspecific aggression is shared between several individuals. Because these are very active and agile cichlids, under no circumstances should aquarium length be less than 150 cm. Naturally these eartheaters also like soft, acid water, fine sand, as well as hiding-places in the form of bogwood or rocky structures. They are totally adaptable as regards food, and are content with any of the usual aquarium foods.

Breeding behaviour: Loew succeeded in breeding this species in 1999 (pers. comm.), and was unable to detect any noteworthy differences from *G. argyrostictus*. This is another open-brooder in which both parents guard the brood.

Remarks: In some respects *Geophagus* sp. "Porto Franco" resembles *G.* sp. "Orange Head" from the Rio Tocantins and the Rio Tapajós. From this it must be assumed that these forms constitute a species-complex of related species within the genus *Geophagus*, or which may in fact represent a single species. There may even be other similar species awaiting discovery in other river systems.

Further reading: Warzel (1998: 20). Stawikowski (1990c: 73-80) refers to a different species, whose status remains unclear, but, because it too is spoken of as *Geophagus* sp. "Tocantins", it is mentioned here for purposes of comparison.

Geophagus brachybranchus
Kullander & Nijssen, 1989

Original description: The Cichlids of Surinam. Brill, Leiden, Netherlands.: 48-56.

Derivation of scientific name: *brachys* (Gr.) = short; *branchia* (Gr.)

= gills. Referring to the narrowly exposed gill filaments.

Distribution: Kullander & Nijssen, 1989, cite the middle-lower Corantijn Drainage and the Nickerie River drainage in Surinam, and presume a distribution extending further west to the Essequibo drainage in Guyana. This may in turn imply a distribution as far as Venezuela (via the Rio Cuyuni drainage). In 1992 I was able to import a very similar form from the Rio Caroni in Venezuela, which I will designate as *G.* sp. cf. *brachybranchus* until its taxonomic status can be properly determined.

1. *Geophagus* sp. "Porto Franco".
2. The Río Caroni at Paso Caruachi in Venezuela. Locality of *G.* cf. *brachybranchus*.
3. This *Geophagus*, imported from Guyana, combines characters from *G. surinamensis* as well as from *G. brachybranchus*.
4. An adult male *G.* cf. *brachybranchus* from the Rio Caroni.

Habitat: No information is provided on the natural habitat in the original description. If, however, *G.* sp. cf. *brachybranchus* from the Guri reservoir and the Rio Caroni in Venezuela turns out to be identical with *G. brachbranchus*, then the species is found over sandy substrates with rocky deposits. The water is very clear, with visibility of up to 5 metres, and slow-flowing. Deeper water is the preferred habitat. Only at night are shallower regions sought out, where additional shelter is provided by rocky caves and accumulated wood. The pH, with values below 6.0, is rather low and the hardness is too low to be measured with the test kits available in the aquarium trade. The conductivity is about 15 µS/cm.

Size: A rather large species, with males attaining about 25 cm; females remain 2-4 cm smaller.

Characters of the species: Apart from the short gill filaments, which are of little help to the aquarist, *G. brachybranchus* possesses distinct characters which permit it to be differentiated from the other members of the genus. Specimens of 7 cm total length upwards have a dark preopercular stripe which is always present in adults. The stripe pattern on the flanks is an additional character. The first stripe is above the eye. The second begins at the dorsal insertion and ends at a not always visible, incomplete, lateral band that starts behind the eye and ends at the level of the lateral spot. The third likewise begins beneath the spinous dorsal, and again ends at the level of the lateral band, sometimes ending in a small, isolated, not always visible lateral spot. The 4th stripe is not always completely apparent and ends in the large roundish lateral spot. In aggressively-minded specimens the lateral spot becomes pale. Further back, still beneath the spinous dorsal and at the base of the fin, there is a smaller, slightly rounded, lateral spot. The 6th stripe begins below the first soft dorsal rays, runs vertically down, and ends 1-2 scales beneath the lower lateral line. The seventh stripe lies at the end of the dorsal and likewise ends 1-2 scales beneath the lower lateral line. The eighth and last stripe lies on the caudal peduncle. Between the second and third stripe the upper lateral line kinks slightly upward. There is no appreciable difference in body shape between *G. brachybranchus* and the more familiar species *G. altifrons* and *G. surinamensis*.

Sexual dimorphism: As well as the fact that males grow larger than females, the latter have more rounded unpaired fins and are somewhat more rotund in the ventral region once they have reached a length of 15 cm.

Maintenance: This species does not differ markedly from other species in its maintenance requirements. *G. brachybranchus* can be regarded as easily pleased, as it will take every type of dry, frozen, live, and vegetable food, hence a generously proportioned filtration system is absolutely necessary. These eartheaters make no special demands as regards water parameters, and will even do very well in relatively hard water (20° dGH), although unfortunately they will not breed. Skin lesions, such as may occur in a number of other species, do not affect *G. brachybranchus*. Bear in mind, however, that the aquarium must be of adequate dimensions. Because these fishes do best in large groups, and grow rather large, then no aquarium with a capacity of less than 500 litres should be considered. It should go without saying that the aquarium should be decorated with fine sand, plus bogwood and stones.

Breeding behaviour: While maintenance in hard water is problem-free, only water with a hardness of less than 10° dGH should be used for breeding and at the same time the pH should be significantly lower than 7.0. Unfortunately the species is not sexually mature until 2 years old.

Courtship and disputes between rivals are comparable with those of other species in this closely-related group. In both instances there is lateral display with spread fins, plus tail beating, by virtue of which the intended partner or rival is impressed or frightened away, respectively. In addition the opercula are slightly expanded. During this phase the body may be quivered slightly. Circling takes place only rarely. If the partner or rival fails to be suitably impressed, then occasionally there may be mouth-fighting, with the opponents facing each other and pushing each other more or less "gently" across the aquarium. This never leads to injury. Once the pair has formed then both fishes together select the intended spawning substrate. This involves experimentally testing — by brief cleaning — practically every item of decor and equipment for suitability as the future nursery. My fishes have always chosen a piece of slate lying flat on the substrate and protected from above by bogwood. The slate is then partially excavated and cleaned intensively, mainly by the female.

After 3-4 days of preliminary cleaning the genital papillae appear, but another 1-3 days may pass before spawning occurs. This follows the typical *Geophagus* procedure. The female lays the L-type eggs in a straight line on the substrate. Next the male glides over them, again in a straight line. If the male is occupied with defending the territory then the eggs are fertilised later. Clutch size is about 250 eggs. *G. brachybranchus* is a larvophilous mouthbrooder, in which both sexes free the larvae from the egg-shells about 48 hours after spawning and then take them into their mouths. In the period that follows the parents repeatedly dig new pits in the aquarium, in which the fry are deposited for a short time.

The parents take turns to brood all of the fry while the other digs pits. This division of labour can also be observed at feeding time, i.e. while one parent feeds, the other takes over the brood care. At night both parents brood the larvae. Some eight days after spawning the larvae can be fed with newly-hatched *Artemia*. The subsequent rearing can be described as problem-free. After about 6 weeks the fry will have attained a length of 2-3 cm and after three months this will have exceeded the 5 cm mark. By now the black opercular spot is clearly visible.

1. A male *Geophagus proximus* from Santarém.
2. A female *G. proximus* of the same population.

Remarks: This species could perhaps be confused with *G. proximus*, but the latter has a reddish zone, particularly behind the operculum, which *G. brachybranchus* lacks. That aside, the lateral spot is appreciably larger in *G. proximus*.

Further reading: Kullander & Nijssen (1989: 48-56); Weidner (1998c: 502-505).

Geophagus proximus (Castelnau, 1855)

Original description: Animaux nouveaux ou rares de l'Amerique du Sud. Poissons. Paris. pp: 14-15.

Derivation of scientific name: proximus (lat.) = nearest; in the sense of the relationship to another species. Which other species Castelnau meant is unclear from the original description. Perhaps *G. brasiliensis* (*Chromys unimaculata* Castelnau, 1855), as this species is compared with *G. proximus* in the text. According to current wisdom, however, *G. megasema* and *G. brachybranchus* are the closest relatives.

Distribution: From the Rio Ucayali at Sarayacu (the type locality (Castelnau, 1855)) in Peru to round about Santarém (pers. obs., 1996); Werner, 1988) in Brazil. Additional confirmed localities in Brazil are: Rio Tefé (Stawikowski, 1993; Goulding, 1979) plus Lago Amaná (Kullander, 1986); Rio Trombetas (Kullander, 1986); near Alenquer (pers. obs., 1996); as well as Lago Janauaca (Kullander *et al.*, 1980). Although there have been no recent imports of *G. proximus* from Peru, it is in fact the species with the most westerly distribution.

Habitat: *G. proximus* does not appear to prefer any particular type of water. There is no evidence for the hypothesis that it is a blackwater fish, and new discoveries from the Santarém area in fact disprove the idea. The species has never been found in large groups. Stawikowski (1993) was able to catch only single individuals in the Rio Tefé. Likewise in the vicinity of Santarém only single

- G. brachybranchus
- G. proximus
- G. sp. "Rio Negro"

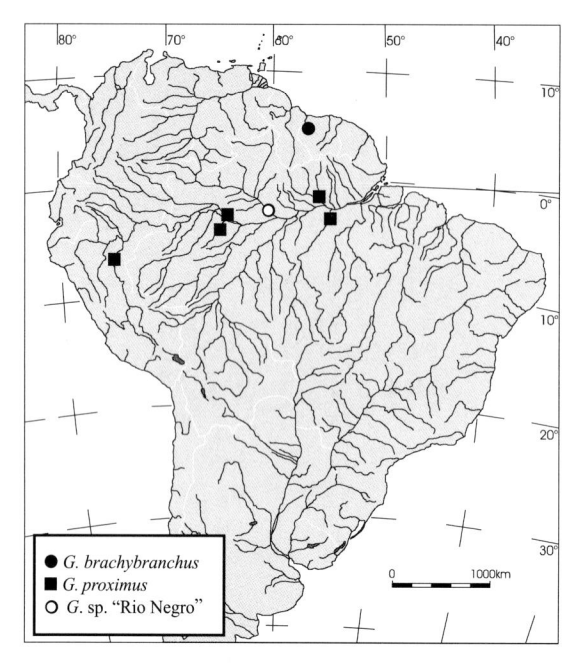

individuals of *G. proximus* could be caught with the cast-net, although other species evidently had a greater population density. The species apparently thrives over leaf litter as well as sandy substrates. Root tangles complete the picture of the habitat. The water temperature generally lies between 25 and 29° C. The water is soft and slightly acid.

Size: Males probably do not exceed the 25 cm mark, while females remain appreciably smaller (20 cm).

Characters of the species: If only the *Geophagus* species of the Brazilian Amazon are under consideration then identification is relatively easy. Adult *G. proximus* have a very high body for a *Geophagus*, and males have a pronounced nuchal gibbosity. In addition there is a dark stripe on the lower part of the anterior operculum. The most striking feature is, however, the large, almost rhombic, lateral spot, which extends significantly either side of the upper lateral line (cf. *Geophagus* sp. "Rio Negro I"/ "Stripetail"). This lateral spot is always visible but may pale depending on mood, and is then visible as a light spot (negative coloration). *G. megasema* has a lateral spot of comparable size, but lacks the opercular stripe. *G. proximus* exhibits a red-orange zone between the operculum and the lateral spot (again cf. *G.* sp. "Rio Negro I"/"Stripetail"). There are orange and bluish horizontal stripes all over the body. The unpaired fins as well as the ventrals exhibit blue stripes on a reddish background.

Sexual dimorphism: Males have more pointed extensions to the unpaired and ventral fins, while females remain smaller and always look plumper in the ventral region. In addition males exhibit a marked nuchal hump, although this characteristic does not develop clearly until a length of more than 10 cm has been attained.

Maintenance: *G. proximus* makes no great demands as regards water parameters. A hardness of less than 20° dGH and a pH below 8.0 are ad-

122

equate for normal maintenance, and possibly also for breeding. However, lower hardness and pH value will improve the colours and activity levels of the fishes enormously. *G. proximus* also exhibits a greater tolerance of nitrogenous compounds than do other geophagine cichlids, but even so the maxim "the lower the better" applies. Although *G. proximus* is encountered only very sparingly in the natural habitat, in the aquarium it enjoys the company of its own kind. A group of 5-8 individuals is appropriate, and this means, of course, given the eventual size of these fishes, that aquaria less than 150 cm long are unsuitable. Likewise the filtration should be suited to the active metabolisms of these fishes. Feeding poses no difficulties, as they will eat practically anything that comes within reach of their mouths. It matters not whether it is dried food or frozen. Vegetable food should always be offered as well, in the form of fruit, salad greens, and vegetables. A little experimentation may be required as these fishes do exhibit individual preferences. As long as tankmates are not too small or aggressive there is no barrier to a community setup, although the decor must be suited to the requirements of the eartheaters, i.e. no coarse gravel or bright lighting.

Breeding behaviour: Courtship is similar to that of other eartheaters that are ovophilous mouthbrooders and require a spawning substrate. After pair formation the parents clean the chosen substrate. The eggs are always deposited in a straight line, and, as usual, in batches of 4-10 per pass. At this point individual variations may appear. Thus it may be that after each spawning pass the eggs are immediately picked up by one of the two parents, or that all the eggs are laid and both parents then finally take them into their mouths. And there are all types of variation in between. In general the male performs the bulk of the brood care during the early days, though once again there are individual variations, such that sometimes the female carries the brood right from the start and the male guards the territory, as is known from other species. Normally, however, the female takes on the brooding of eggs/larvae increasingly as time passes, although the growth of the young, which may number up to 250, may oblige the parents to split them between their two mouths when they will no longer fit into one. Once the fry are free-swimming and released from the mouth, then the male mainly guards the territory, while when danger threatens the female endeavours to pick up as many fry as possible in as short a time as possible. When the male returns, the young are immediately guarded by both parents in the shelter of a pit in the sand or a rock. Although both parents share equally in the brooding, taking turns in protecting the eggs/larvae/fry during the breeding phase, the pair bond dissolves after breeding. Thus it is quite normal for each of the former partners to seek a new mate for the next spawning. This makes optimal use of the genetic potential of the population as a whole.

Remarks: Because of the huge distribution area it cannot be entirely excluded that different spawning and brood-care strategies may exist, depending on the habitat. It should also be briefly mentioned here that there may be geographical varieties of *G. proximus*, or very similar species (see, for example, *G.* sp. "Rio Negro I"/"Stripetail").

Further reading: Castelnau (1855: 13-19); Kullander (1986: 147-154); Stawikowski (1994a: 222-228); Weidner (1994c: 228-229).

Geophagus sp. "Rio Negro I"
also known as
Geophagus sp. "Stripetail"

Distribution: So far these cichlids have always been imported singly from the Rio Negro basin. As most specimens come in via the trade, detailed data are not available.

Habitat: Stawikowski (pers. comm.) found this species in the lower Rio Negro in the Anavilhanas region, in an area of flooded *igapó* (seasonally flooded forest) in the immediate vicinity of the river bank. In this area the substrate consisted of sand and leaf litter.

Size: This species barely exceeds 20 cm.

Characters of the species: At a casual glance *G.* sp. "Rio Negro I" resembles *G. proximus*, but on closer examination there are a number of visible differences. In *G.* sp. "Rio Negro I" the lateral spot is nothing like as large and lies somewhat beneath the upper lateral line, but the most obvious difference is that the lower part of the tail is spotted instead of striped. There are a few bluish longitudinal lines on the upper part. In general these fishes exhibit five broad vertical bars on the flanks; in

1. The stripe on the gill cover and the large lateral blotch of *Geophagus* sp. "Columbia" resembles those of *G. proximus*, only the species from Colombia has a slenderer body.
2. A male *Geophagus proximus* from Santarém.
3. At first glance *Geophagus* sp. "Rio Negro I" resembles *G. proximus* in many details; nevertheless it is distinguished from that species by the position and size of the lateral spot and by the colour pattern in the tail.

fact *G. proximus* may also exhibit such bars, but usually only during courtship.

Otherwise these two species are very similar. *G.* sp. "Rio Negro I" also has an opercular stripe, and there are no other markings on the head apart from an iridescent bluish band which can sometimes be seen running from the corner of the mouth to the opercular spot. The head is basically green-blue. Behind the operculum there are five to six red-orange horizontal stripes, alternating with bluish, running towards the tail. The *G. proximus*-typical orange area behind the operculum is absent in *G.* sp. "Rio Negro I". Apart from the pectorals, which are colourless, all the fins have a reddish base colour on which there are bluish lines and spots. The tips of the anterior dorsal spines are black.

Sexual dimorphism: There is no 100% certain way of sexing, particularly in sub-adult specimens. Once adult, males can be identified by their slenderer form. In addition females usually remain three to four cm smaller.

Maintenance: This species can be kept in the same way as *G. proximus*. It should merely be noted that this species is more prone to deficiency diseases and should therefore be kept in rather softer water and always fed a diet which includes vegetable matter. If vegetables, salad greens, and fruit are refused, then either vegetable flake must be offered or a good vitamin supplement added to frozen food in order to provide for the vitamin requirements of these cichlids. Alternatively it is possible fall back on the already-supplemented frozen food mixes available in the trade.

Breeding behaviour: According to Stawikowski (pers. comm.) these fishes have proved to be larvophilous mouthbrooders. He was able to observe that, after the larvae had been picked up, a jelly-like mass of eggshells remained on the spawning substrate (a flat horizontally-positioned stone). During brooding Stawikowski was even able to observe conflict between the parents as to who was going to brood the larvae. Now and then it happened that both parents brooded alone until the fry were free-swimming and then maintained separate territories in which to guard their personal brood! (Stawikowski, 1994).

By and large these observations match those of Neumann (pers. comm.), who likewise found these fishes to be biparental larvophilous mouthbrooders. Neumann observed that it was always the female who initiated pair formation, but he also found that the actual pairing was variable in nature: while in one pair it took place very peacefully and only a small amount of mutual flank-nudging occurred, another pair behaved very aggressively while "getting acquainted", continually driving other fishes from the immediate vicinity and threatening each other with expanded throats. By the next day, however, it was all sorted out and the pair were tolerant of each other.

Neumann was also able to observe that the female chivvied the male into guarding the territory while she herself cleaned the spawning substrate. The preparations for spawning took up to a week. Usually a small pit was dug around the spawning substrate, so that the eggs were laid on a stone or piece of wood in the middle of a "nest". Once the pair were synchronised spawning took place in typical open-brooder fashion, i.e. the female laid batches of eggs on the spawning substrate, and these were then fertilised by the male. Even after the female had finished spawning, the male glided over the spawn a few more times in order retroactively to fertilise as many unfertilised eggs as possible. After 36-48 hours the larvae were freed from their shells by the female, and handed over to the male in the hours that followed. From this point on the larvae were exchanged between the partners several times per day, so that both parents had the chance to feed. No territory was defended during the mouthbrooding stage. Later on, when the fry became free-swimming after 8 days, a small territory was established. Brood care lasted for 3-4 weeks, and after 2 weeks the female no longer brooded the fry. The male allowed them into the shelter of his mouth for a longer period. During brood care Neumann observed that the parents fed their fry by sifting through the substrate and spitting it out into the shoal of fry, or by using their pectoral fins to stir up small particles of food upon which the fry then eagerly descended. Basically rearing is no problem, as the fry can manage *Artemia* nauplii as soon as they first leave the mouth.

Neumann also indicates that with *G.* sp. "Rio Negro I" it is immensely important to establish a compatible pair. The number of fry is then significantly higher, as losses through "squabbling" over the fry are then minimal. A compatible pair, once formed, will remain extremely monogamous.

Remarks: By and large this species is strikingly similar to *G. proximus*, except for the characteristic barring and smaller lateral spot in *G.* sp. "Rio Negro I".

Further reading: Neumann (pers. comm.); Stawikowski 1994a: 222-228).

Geophagus camopiensis
Pellegrin, 1903

Original description: Bull. Mus. Hist. Nat. 9: 123.

Derivation of scientific name: named after the Camopi River in French Guiana, the home of these cichlids.

Distribution: The Camopi River and the Oyapock River drainage (von Drachenfels, 1987); Kullander & Fang, 1994), the river that forms the border between French Guiana and Brazil. *G. camopiensis* is also reported from the Rio Pantanari, Amapá State, Brazil (Stawikowski *et al.*, 1989 — pers. comm.) and in the drainage of the Approuague River, French Guiana (Le Bail, 1983; Planquette, 1986; Boujard *et al.*, 1988; von Drachenfels, pers. comm.; pers. obs., 1999)

Habitat: This species is found in fast-flowing waters, usually clear and whitewater rivers, in which smooth-surfaced but fissured rocks alternate with sandy areas, forming rapids (von Drachenfels, pers. comm., and pers. obs., 1999). The species can,

1. A freshly caught *Geophagus camopiensis* from the Approuague-River near Saut Mapaou.
2. Saut Mapaou at the Approuague river — the rapids are visible in the background. *G. camopiensis*, however, was mainly found over soft bottoms and therefore most specimens were caught in the immediate vicinity of the boat.
3. *G. camopiensis* is characterised by a slender body.
4. *G. camopiensis* in the aquarium making preparations for spawning. Photo: Ernst-Otto von Drachenfels.

however, also be found in smaller streams and calmer reaches, where the bottom is often covered with leaf litter which gives the water a tea-coloured look. At Saut Maripa, von Drachenfels found the species in very warm, shallow water in a bay somewhat sheltered from the main river — and hence from the current — by large rocks. The water was only waist-deep and slightly brown, over a sandy bottom. In 1998 von Drachenfels found *G. camopiensis* in a similar area of water in the Approuague River near Sauts Mapaou.

At the same site in 1999 *G. camopiensis* was found actually in the rapids as well as in the calmer peripheral areas (Frank, Neumann, & Weidner). While the sandy substrate in the rapids was littered with numerous large stones, near the banks the bottom was sandy to muddy. Numerous branches dipped into the water, and these supplemented the few stones as additional cover. Interestingly the majority of specimens were caught in the morning in the bank zone, in the immediate vicinity of a small affluent. The water was rather murky, with a visibility of at most 30 cm. The water temperature measured 30° C. *G. camopiensis* shares this habitat with *Guianacara geayi*, which is almost always caught with the same cast of the cast net, with *Guianacara* significantly in the majority. Naturally there were numerous loricariid catfishes and headstanders (family Anostomidae) in the same section of river.

Size: The largest specimen measured by Gosse (1975) had a standard length of 15 cm, so a total length of about 20 cm can be assumed.

Characters of the species: The upper head profile of *G. camopiensis* rises appreciably more gently than in many other members of the genus. The body is slimmer and more elongate. The dorsal fin is relatively low. The pectorals are almost as long as the head and extend to the anal insertion. The lateral spot, which is in the centre of the flank, is relatively large and extends only half a scale-width above the upper lateral line, but downward to the level of the lower lateral line. There are longitudinal rows of iridescent bluish dots on the olive-coloured flanks. The unpaired fins likewise exhibit iridescent bluish dots and stripes, particularly clearly expressed on the anal.

Sexual dimorphism: The sexes can be differentiated only during spawning, as males have a more pointed genital papilla than females, in which the papilla is blunter and rather larger. No secondary sexual characteristics have been discerned in this species. It is very difficult to distinguish the sexes even on the basis of eventual size and finnage.

Maintenance: Only a few details of maintenance in captivity have been reported. On the basis of observations with *G. argyrostictus*, which also inhabits fast-flowing waters, powerful filtration will be required to provide adequate water movement and to keep ammonia, nitrite, and if possible nitrate, concentrations at minimal levels. In addition high temperatures (28-30° C) and a varied diet are necessary.

Breeding behaviour: This species has spawned a number of times in the aquarium, and in each case the eggs were laid on a smooth horizontal stone and fanned by the female (?). After 2 days the parents could be seen to be mouthbrooding. Unfortunately it has not been possible to establish whether this is an ovophilous or larvophilous mouthbrooder. Further observations are required, as the fishes stopped brooding after 3 days and ate the brood (von Drachenfels and Stawikowski, pers. comm.)

On the basis of observations of other mouthbrooders it seems likely that *G. camopiensis* is a larvophilous mouthbrooder, as it is unlikely that the eggs would be picked up at such a late stage.

Remarks: Two additional very slim-bodied *Geophagus* have now been imported from the Rio Xingú and the Rio Negro (only single individuals with no exact locality data), but these are probably not forms of *G. camopiensis*.

Further reading: Bitter (1998: 39); Gosse (1975: 71-76); Pellegrin (1903: 120-125); Regan (1906: 49-66).

Geophagus sp. "Rio Negro II"

Distribution: This species has always been imported as single individuals from the Rio Negro drainage, but so far the actual collecting locality remains unknown. It may have been this species that Gottwald, Seva, and Sucker (pers. comm.) caught in the Rio Branco drainage on the border with Guyana, near to Bonfim on the Brazilian shore. But whether or not it was the same species remains a mystery, as the captured specimens were very small and unfortunately did not survive the journey.

● *G. camopiensis*
■ *G.* sp. "Rio Negro II"
◆ *G. grammepareius*
○ *G. taeniopareius*
□ *G. harreri*

Habitat: No data are available on the habitat of this rare commercially imported by-catch. Gottwald, Seva, and Zucker (pers. comm.) caught their fishes in a typical *Geophagus* biotope. The bottom consisted in large part of fine sand, with occasional patches of coarser gravel. In places there were accumulations of dead wood near the bank, and these served as cover for the cichlids. The bank zone was only moderately vegetated, and submerse vegetation was completely absent — the very turbid water made plant growth impossible.

Size: To date only specimens of up to 12 cm have been collected and maintained. It is to be expected, however, that *G.* sp. "Rio Negro II" will grow somewhat larger.

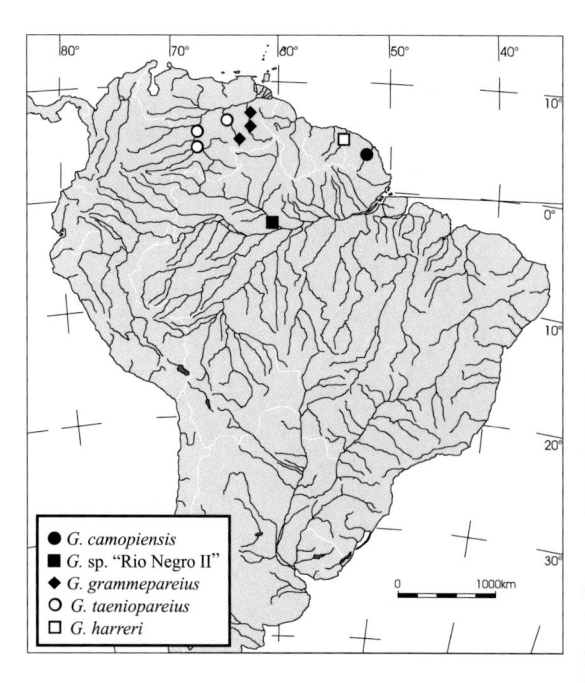

Characters of the species: *G.* sp. "Rio Negro II" differs from the typical habitus of *Geophagus* species, particularly in its body shape, which is rather reminiscent of *G. camopiensis*. The elongate body, the narrow caudal peduncle, the low dorsal, and the relatively short head with the eyes set very high all serve to reinforce this impression. The upper head profile is not straight, but curves slightly above the eyes.

The lateral spot encompasses two rows of scales, is clearly visible, and lies above the upper lateral line. A special character is provided by two narrow, light areas in front of and behind the lateral spot, which make the latter appear more prominent. *G.* sp. "Rio Negro II" also possesses a prominent opercular spot which, depending on mood, may continue to just below the eye, while the stripe

1. A juvenile wild-caught *Geophagus* sp. "Negro II". Photo: Frank Warzel.
2. This individual could also be *Geophagus* sp. "Negro II". It was caught in 1998, by Gottwald, Seva and Zucker, near Bonfim at the Brazil-Guyana border in the Rio Branco drainage. Photo: Antoine Seva.
3. This species closely resembles *G.* sp: "Rio Negro II". It was collected at an unknown location but came accompanied with fishes from the Rio Xingú.
4. A freshly caught *Geophagus grammepareius*. Unfortunately this species has not yet reached hobbyists' aquaria. Photo: Uwe Werner

on the cheek is only faintly marked.

All the fins are virtually without markings, appearing transparent with at most a few spots on a yellow-blue background. The body colour is rather undistinguished — a few iridescent longitudinal lines on a blue-grey background. Depending on the light, there may be a yellowish or golden sheen on the back.

Sexual dimorphism: Because only a few specimens have been imported to date, no secondary sexual characteristics have been identified.

Maintenance: No detailed data have been reported yet. The few specimens which have reached the aquaria of enthusiasts have survived well in soft, slightly acid, water and not presented any special requirements as regards feeding. Decor and other maintenance conditions have been as for other *Geophagus*.

Breeding behaviour: Thus far no breeding has been reported, quite simply because too few individuals have been imported.

Remarks: Unfortunately there have been no bulk imports of this species to date. Whether this is because the species is intrinsically rare, or whether the collecting site is away from the main population, is not as yet known. If the species caught on the Guyana border by Zucker and Seva should actually turn out to be *G.* sp. "Rio Negro II", then we will probably have a long wait for bulk imports, as the locality is quite simply too far from civilisation and collecting uneconomic.

It would appear that there are similar species in other river systems. A consignment supposedly collected in the Rio Xingú included a single specimen of a very elongate *Geophagus* with a low dorsal fin, which likewise exhibited an opercular spot and whose coloration had features in common with that of *G.* sp. "Rio Negro II". One obvious difference, however, was in the light edging to the lateral spot, present in *G.* sp. "Rio Negro II" but not in the possible sibling species from the Rio Xingú. Moreover the lateral spot is larger in the Xingú form and extends either side of the upper lateral line.

form the caudal peduncle looks proportionately stouter than in many other *Geophagus*. A characteristic feature of this species is the suborbital stripe, which connects the eye with the lower end of the anterior part of the operculum; likewise the relatively large lateral spot on the middle of the flank.

Depending on mood there may be a broad black horizontal band from the rear of the operculum to the lateral spot. The base colour is a bright yellow on which there are rows of iridescent bluish dots, the intensity of which depends, however, on the spectrum and angle of the light. The lips are bluish. The unpaired fins exhibit the base colour of the body or may even display an orange tinge. The soft parts are covered in innumerable iridescent bluish spots or stripes.

Sexual dimorphism: In juveniles and semi-adult specimens no secondary sexual characteristics are discernible. Adult males grow larger and have rather more prolonged dorsal and anal fins than females.

Maintenance: Despite its small size, *G. taeniopareius* can look after itself. In particular its swimming agility allows it to hold its own even against larger fishes. Minor attacks on conspecifics and other members of the genus are the order of the day, but serious battles do not occur. There is often intraspecific mouth-fighting, which does not result in in-

1. A group half-grown *Geophagus taeniopareius*.
2. A spawning female *G. taeniopareius*. The spawning substrate is usually horizontal, but under circumstances also vertical surfaces are chosen.
3. In open brooders, such as *G. taeniopareius*, the eggs are deposited by the female in small batches and are immediately fertilised by the male, who usually waits near the egg-laying female.

jury, and status within the group can alter on a day-to-day basis. By contrast they are neutral in their behaviour towards other fishes and can thus be kept with almost any other fish. This is one of those cichlid species that is never timid, is always curious about its surroundings, and has its nose into everything.

The aquarium should be no less than 120 cm long, as otherwise these active cichlids will be too constricted and this may lead to intraspecific fighting. Apropos of which, it should be borne in mind that *G. taeniopareius* prefer to move around in a group, and this too dictates a large aquarium.

As for other eartheaters, the decor should, of course, include fine sand which the fishes can sift at will. Large and small stones, as well as cover in the form of bogwood, should also be provided. The light intensity plays a subordinate role, as these fish are not timid even under bright light. There is no need to dispense totally with plants, as although these fishes are interested in vegetable food, they can make no impression on tough leaves. Vegetable food should always be offered, but one can always fall back on dried food with a vegetable component, or scalded spinach/lettuce. Cooked peas or Brussels sprouts will also be picked at. That apart, any type of frozen or, of course, live food, will be taken as long as it will fit into their mouths.

Although *G. taeniopareius* lives in very soft water, this eartheater is very easy to habituate to harder water. It does well even at a hardness of up to 20° dGH and a pH of up to 8.0, and will even breed under such conditions.

Breeding behaviour: The courtship behaviour of *G. taeniopareius* is particularly noteworthy. The male flutters around the female like a butterfly. He positions himself in front of the female, head down and fins spread, and quivers, before darting up to 30 cm away, swimming in a semi-circle around the female, and then displaying in front of her again. This ritual is repeated until she follows him. Next they choose and clean a spawning site (a stone) together, in the process removing large amounts of sand from around the stone so that there are cavities beneath it, in which the larvae, once hatched, can be guarded. Nearby stones are also involved in this procedure, so that the larvae, and subsequently the fry, can be moved around frequently. It is mainly horizontal rather than vertical stones that are preferred as sites for the L-type eggs. The female lays batches of 2-8 (maximum) eggs in a line, and the male them fertilises them. The spawning process continues for about 90 minutes, and the clutch comprises up to a maximum of 150 eggs, usually close-packed. Once all the eggs have been laid the female spits sand over them for camouflage; she then positions herself a short distance away and fans fresh water over the spawn with her pectoral fins. The male defends the territory and can be rather aggressive in so doing.

Depending on water temperature, the larvae hatch after 70-80 hours and in my experience escape unaided from the eggs, although Darda (1997) reports that the females free the larvae from the eggs. The now wriggling larvae are transported by the mother (less frequently the father) to one of the pre-dug holes under a rock, and subsequently moved around frequently. The eggs/larvae are never kept in the mouth for long except during transportation. After 8 days in total the fry become free-swimming and are able to follow their mother. They will also accept their father as leader, as most of the time one or other parent will be busy chasing away intruding fishes. Feeding with *Artemia* nauplii can begin as soon as the fry are free-swimming. They grow relatively slowly and take three months to attain a length of 3-4 cm.

Darda (1997) reports that the day after a brood was lost the male courted another female in order to make a further breeding attempt.

Further reading: Darda (1997b: 52-54); Kullander, Royero, & Taphorn (1992: 359-375); Staeck (1990: 8-10); Stawikowski (1981a: 184-189); Weidner (1993: 687-688; 1994b: 136-142; 1997b); Werner (1992b: 7-8; 1996: 19-23).

Geophagus harreri Gosse, 1976

Original description: Acad. roy. Sci. d'Outre-Mer, Cl. Sci. Nat. Med., Nouv. Série XIX-3: 88-94.

Derivation of scientific name: In honour of the Austrian Professor Heinrich Harrer, Gosse's faithful companion on his collecting trips to Surinam and French Guiana.

Distribution: The distribution of *G. harreri* extends along the Maroni River, in both Surinam (Gosse 1966; 1969) and in French Guiana at St. Laurent du Maroni (Kullander & Fang, 1994), at Saut Gostou (Planquette, 1979), and at Maripasoula (Lamp, 1997, pers, comm.). Additional documented localities are given in the original description, for example the drainages of the Ouaqui, Marouini, and Inini (Gosse *et al.*, 1969), the Lawa and Paloemeu rivers (Gosse *et al.*, 1966), and the Tapanahoni (Mees, G. F., 1965).

Habitat: From the original description it can be assumed that the species is also found in rapids. Gosse (1976) cites the Anapaikekondre and Paloemeu rapids in the Maroni Basin. In 1998 Stalsberg (pers. comm.) looked for this species at Albina on the Maroni; unfortunately he was unable to catch *G. harreri*, but he described the river at this site as very murky with a substrate of fine sand with a few rocks.

In 1997 Lamp succeeded in catching *G. harreri* in the Maroni, about 2 km above the rapids at Maripasoula. Because of the muddy bottom the water was very murky and visibility only a few centimetres. Between the sections of flat water it was possible to make out piles of hardened clay in the river bed. The fishes were caught exclusively with a drag-net, and were generally of variable size (4-12 cm); frequently *G. surinamensis*, *Guianacara* sp., and *Crenicichla multispinosa* were caught at the same time. The water was not particularly fast-flowing, and rather deep at 180 cm. No cover was discernible. The time when Lamp caught the fishes was just before the rainy season, and probably for that reason the water was rather cool (26-28° C).

Size: The largest of the paratypes designated by Gosse (1976) measured 225 mm (SL).

Characters of the species: *Geophagus harreri* is a species whose external appearance suggests that it may not fit too well into this genus. Kullander & Nijssen (1989) detail similarities to *Retroculus* and *Satanoperca* as regards the dentition and gill arches, and it is a fact that juveniles and semi-adults look like deep-bodied *Satanoperca*. The upper head profile rises at a rather shallower angle and this gives the body a more elongate appearance than in many *Geophagus*. Adults apparently develop a nuchal hump.

The colour pattern is very striking. There are three vertical bars on the head and anterior half of the body. The first of these runs through the eye and ends on the cheek. The second begins immediately below the dorsal insertion and ends at the level of the pectorals. The third and most prominent bar runs from the back, between the fourth and tenth dorsal spines, down to the belly, becoming progressively narrower as it does so. Further back there are hints of two additional bars on the upper body, ending at the level of the lower lateral line. An additional positive identification character is a dark spot on the back, between the end of the dorsal fin base and the caudal insertion.

Juveniles have a yellow-bluish base colour with metallic scales, sometimes arranged in rows. This pattern is noticeably less regular on the caudal peduncle. While the pectorals are colourless, all the other fins are patterned with almost circular spots. The dorsal and the upper part of the caudal have a bluish base colour, while the lower part of the caudal, the anal, and the ventrals are basically yellow. Depending on mood, elements of the spotting described above may be visible on the flanks. In freshly caught specimens there is a striking bluish line running beneath the eye, and this, together with the base colour, is similar to that found in *G. argyrostictus*.

Sexual dimorphism: Probably only males develop a nuchal hump (see Characters of the species, above).

Maintenance: Apparently these fishes, like many other eartheaters, are not very demanding as regards maintenance, and will be happy with whatever water happens to be in the aquarium; likewise they have no special feeding requirements. First observations indicate that these agile and active fishes are rather aggressive towards conspecifics. Unfortunately no further data are available at present, as too few individuals have been imported to date.

1. It is difficult to assign *Geophagus harreri* to one of the groups withing the eartheaters. It has affinities with *G. camopiensis* as well as with *G. argyrostictus*. However, the position of the lateral spots is unique among *Geophagus* species. Photo: Ulrich Minde.
2. Such "postcard" sandbanks are home to *Geophagus surinamensis*. Gobaya Soula near Maripasoula in Surinam, close to the border with French Guiana.

Breeding behaviour: Not yet observed.

Remarks: *G. harreri* and *Guianacara owroewefi* are commonly collected together and Kullander & Nijssen (1989) suggest that "a mimicry situation appears fairly evident as the wedge-shaped contrasting dark bar over the side is unique to these fishes among cichlids. The similarity is strongest at small sizes, when the major superficial differences are in the more elongate shape of *G. harreri* and the dark spot below the end of the dorsal fin. Large *G. harreri* have a less contrasting pattern of dark markings."
Kullander & Nijssen (1989) further suggest tentatively that "*G. harreri* is the mimic and *G. owroewefi* (or its ancestral form) the model, because the colour pattern is more widespread (geographically and in taxa) in *Guianacara* than in *Geophagus*, but above all we recommend field work to investigate the actual ecological relationships of these species, that may elucidate their possible coevolutionary history. This is the first strong case of potential mimicry involving particular species in South American cichlids."

Further reading: Gosse (1976: 88-94); Gottwald (1999: 6); Kullander & Nijssen (1989: 56-65).

Geophagus surinamensis (Bloch, 1791)

Original description: Naturgeschichte ausländischer Fische 5. Berlin.: 112-113.

Derivation of scientific name: The name refers to the distribution as assumed by the describer: *surinamensis* = from Surinam.

Distribution: In their work "The Cichlids of Surinam", Kullander & Nijssen (1989) cite as Surinam localities for this species the Sarramacca, the Maroni, and the Surinam River, and mention that the Species occasionally lives sympatrically with *G. harreri*. Stalsberg (pers. comm.) found his specimens in the Surinam River. The species is also found in French Guiana: Sinnamary River near Cayenne (Planquette, 1979) and the Maroni in the vicinity of Maripasoula (pers. obs., 1999). Moreover specimens from the Lago Janauacá on the Rio Solimões and at Aveiro on the Rio Tapajós (Kullander *et al.*, 1980), and from the area around Belém, Pará State, Brazil (Thayer Expedition, 1865) have also been identified as *G. surinamensis*. But whether the last-mentioned specimens are truly *G. surinamensis* cannot be confirmed here, as the material is not exactly recent and needs to be re-investigated on the basis of current knowledge.
It can be assumed that *G. surinamensis* may also occur in the Mana

drainage in French Guiana, being replaced by another, undescribed, species (with an opercular spot) further east in the Sinnamary drainage.

Habitat: In the Surinam River these cichlids live in calm, pool-like, widenings offset from the main stream. The water is warm (26° C or more), soft, and rather acid (Mayland, 1995). This species too prefers sandy substrates with areas of wood and rocks. Stalsberg (pers. comm.) observed *G. surinamensis* over fine sand in the Surinam River near the township of Brokopondo. There were no plants, but leaves from the trees littered the surface of the water as well as the substrate.

In 1999 we (Dotzer, Neumann, & Weidner) had an opportunity to observe *G. surinamensis* in its natural habitat in the area around Maripasoula. At the end of October the water was very murky and extremely warm (32° C). In the Gobaya Soula (rapids) there was an area of very shallow and rather clearer water over a large sandbank, and in this area *G. surinamensis* was found to have a very high flight distance — it was not possible to approach the fishes closer than 3 metres before they streaked away through the water. Attempts to catch them with the cast net were also singularly unsuccessful, as they saw the net coming, and its size (5 metres) was too small for such fast-moving fishes. Further downstream towards Maripasoula we had much better luck, and were able to capture numerous half-grown specimens using both cast and drag nets in the murky water of a small bay on the Surinam side of the river. The water was at half its maximum depth, and the bottom extremely muddy, so that we sank up to our knees in the mire. Because the water was very warm it was extremely tiring working with the drag net. In addition branches extending into the water made fishing far from easy. Even we netted 12 specimens in a very short time. We also found a few *Guianacara owroewefi*, *Krobia* sp., plus various characins of the genera *Astyanax* and *Moenkhausia*, and an approximately 40 cm long *Hoplias aimara*, syntopically. Further downstream, almost to Mankassiaba Soula, we repeatedly encountered more *G. surinamensis*, which does not seem to be particularly uncommon in the Maroni River, and noted that the larger specimens were generally to be found swimming in pairs.

Size: *G. surinamensis* attains a maximum length of approximately 25 cm.

Characters of the species: The most important criterion for identifying *G. surinamensis* is not so much the body form and coloration, but the locality, as current wisdom is that only specimens from Surinam and French Guiana should be assigned to this species. Fishes that closely resemble this species are also found in Brazil, but these should not be regarded as *G. surinamensis* (see Distribution, above). For this reason the locality data for tankbreds, as well as wild fishes, which resemble *G. surinamensis*, should always be cited.

From the aquarist's viewpoint, characters which can be used to differentiate this species from other members of the genus include the absence of dark markings on the head (contrast *G. proximus, G. argyrostictus, G. brachybranchus, G. harreri, G. taeniopareius, G. grammepareius*); the always visible lateral spot encompassing several scales, which in adults and/or depending on mood may become pale but is still clearly visible as a light spot (contrast *G. megasema* and *G. proximus*, which exhibit an obviously larger lateral spot, and *G. altifrons*, which has no lateral spot or only a very small one);

1. Freshly caught *Geophagus* cf. *surinamensis* from (man-made) Lake Sinnamary. It is not yet certain that this is indeed *G. surinamensis*.
2. *G. surinamenensis* from Mana, French Guiana. Photo: Jens Gottwald.
3. Lake Sinnamary. All cichlids we caught in this man-made lake were wounded and needed to be treated with antibiotics immediately else they would develop skin fungus.

the irregular spotting of the central part of the caudal (contrast *G. brokopondo*, with spots arranged in vertical rows, and *G. megasema*, with a horizontal stripe pattern on the tail); plus the deep-bodied shape (contrast *G. camopiensis, G. harreri*).

Sexual dimorphism: No clear secondary sexual characteristics can be discerned in either juvenile or adult specimens, but in males the points of the unpaired fins are rather more prolonged than in the females. After a large feed it is sometimes possible to see the broad genital papilla of the female.

Maintenance: *G. surinamensis* does not differ appreciably from other members of the genus as regards maintenance requirements. A soft, sandy substrate, cover in the form of wood and scattered smooth round stones, will ensure the wellbeing of these fishes. As usual *G. surinamensis* prefers rather muted lighting. If greenery is required, then the more robust species of plants should be chosen as these will withstand nibbling by the fishes and not be completely shredded in the long term. Vegetable food should form part of the diet, together with live, frozen, and/or dried food. The pieces offered can be of reasonable size, and mussel flesh, raw fish, and krill will not be rejected. The water should be as soft as possible and slightly acid. *G. surinamensis* can be kept in harder

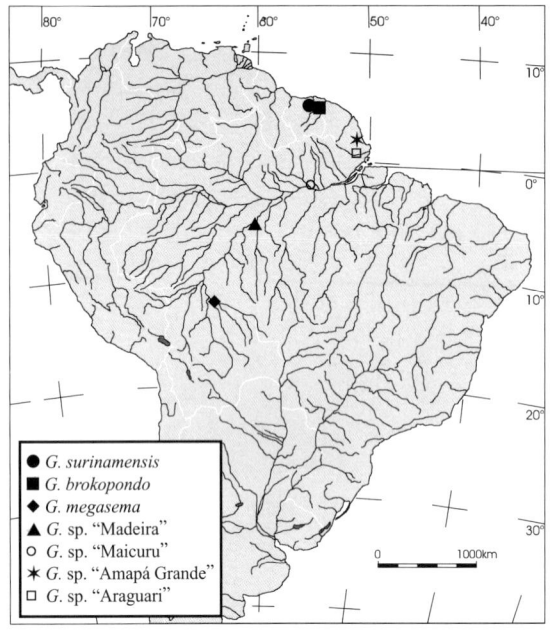

- G. surinamensis
- G. brokopondo
- G. megasema
- G. sp. "Madeira"
- G. sp. "Maicuru"
- G. sp. "Amapá Grande"
- G. sp. "Araguari"

water, but its colours then gradually fade. If one intends keeping these cichlids then their eventual size must be taken into consideration: aquaria of less than 300 litres are out of the question, as this species enjoys the company of its own kind, and significantly larger quarters are required for a group.

Breeding behaviour: All the available reports on the breeding of this species were published during the 1980s (see Further reading, below) and all describe the brood care of a biparental larvophilous mouthbrooder. A more or less extended courtship ritual precedes the actual spawning. As well as the usual lateral threat, the male butts the female noticeably frequently in the flank. Now and then the female reciprocates in kind, but far less often. This often takes place immediately above the intended spawning substrate and appears to strengthen the pair bond. Once the preliminaries are out of the way, the female lays her eggs, long side up, on the horizontal substrate, which has previously been cleaned by both parents. The loosely arranged clutch of up to 600 (?) eggs may be spread over several different substrates. Depending on the diet of the parents the eggs may be either colourless or reddish in colour. Pits are dug around the spawning substrate, and the larvae are subsequently "shunted around" these.

Both parents share equally in the care of the spawn and the subsequent brood care. Interestingly the parents conceal the spawn with sand and do not swim directly over the eggs and fan fresh water over them, but usually position themselves 20-30 cm away. After about 72 hours both parents pick up the already-hatched larvae and transport them to one of the pits. The eggshells remain on the spawning substrate. The larvae are moved around from pit to pit several times, and at night both parents take them into the protection of their mouths. By day they are often left in the pits for quite a long time. Depending on water temperature the fry are free-swimming after 7-12 days and must then be fed with newly-hatched Artemia. For a long time subsequently the parents take the young into their mouths at the least disturbance, until they are too large to fit in — if they are well fed then after only a few days they will no longer be able to take refuge in the sheltering mouths of their progenitors.

Remarks: At least 80% of all the *Geophagus* in the trade are identified as *G. surinamensis*, but probably fewer than 20% actually are that species. This problem originates in the fact that at the beginning of the 1980s there were numerous importations from Surinam to Germany of the "real surinamensis", but after these importations ceased in the mid 80s numerous export stations sprang up in other South American countries, and these exported practically all eartheaters as *G. surinamensis*. When these consignments reached their destination they caused all sorts of confusion, and everything was labelled "*G. surinamensis*" out of force of habit.

Aquarists too must shoulder some of the blame, as many cannot be bothered to learn new names and would rather there were "just" *G. surinamensis*. Importers and dealers are equally guilty, and despite knowing otherwise label the majority of *Geophagus* as this species. This is quite legitimate, as ultimately nobody wants to deal with fishes that no one knows and therefore can clog up shop aquaria and reduce turnover.

Further reading: Elias (1982: 139-142); Kullander & Nijssen (1989: 31-41); Mayland (1995); Werner (1981); 1983a: (14-18); 1983b: 74-80; 1983c: 118-123); Wollenweber (1971: 152-155).

Geophagus brokopondo Kullander & Nijssen, 1989

Original description: The Cichlids of Surinam. Brill, Leiden, Netherlands: 41-48.

Derivation of scientific name: Referring to Lake Brokopondo, an artificial lake in Surinam, the only known locality for the species.

Distribution: The material used for the description was collected exclusively along the northern shore of the Brokopondomeer near Afobaka in Surinam. It is not known how widely the species is distributed in the lake or neighbouring waters.

Habitat: Stalsberg (pers. comm.) describes the type locality near Afobaka as rocky and with fallen tree-trunks extending into the water, sometimes protruding above the surface. In this part of the lake the flooded landscape, with dead trees protruding from the water, can still clearly be seen. Stalsberg was able to observe a large number of fishes in this shore zone, including characins, *Geophagus*, and *Guianacara*, but they were all very timid. He describes collecting as exceptionally difficult, as the fishes had a high flight distance so that he could not work with small nets. Meanwhile large drag nets repeatedly snagged on dead wood underwater. In the event he managed to catch only two *G. brokopondo* using the cast net, and

1. Also Venezuela is home to *Geophagus* which strongly resemble *G. surinamensis*.
2. A semi-adult *Geophagus surinamensis* from Maripasoula.
3. Collecting eartheaters is only possible during the dry season because there is a much easier access to sandbanks. The Rio Guarico in the *llanós* of Venzuela at dusk.

these did not survive the journey back to Norway.

Size: No definite data are available as to the actual eventual size of these fishes. Of the 37 paratypes, the largest specimen had a standard length of 123 mm, which should equate to a total length of about 16 cm.

Characters of the species: It is difficult to suggest any characters of use to aquarists, as this is a typical representative of its genus with no special external characteristics. *G. brokopondo* has a large lateral spot and no opercular spot. The upper head profile runs in an almost straight line to the dorsal origin. The dorsal profile starts to descend again from the 9th dorsal spine. As in *G. surinamensis* the lateral spot lies on the fourth vertical bar. A possible difference between the two species, perhaps of use to aquarists, lies in the coloration of the caudal fin. The description of *G. brokopondo* mentions a large number of whitish spots, arranged in 4 vertical rows, on the central part of the caudal, while for *G. surinamensis* only light spots all over the caudal are cited. Kullander and Nijssen (1989) distinguish this species from all other Surinamese *Geophagus* on the basis of its different gill-arch morphology.

Sexual dimorphism: No data available to date.

Maintenance: Because the species has not been imported alive no details are available. It is, however, quite possible that this species may have been imported in the past as *G. surinamensis*, as in the final analysis the differences between the two species are extremely slight.

Breeding behaviour: No details — see Maintenance, above.

Further reading: Kullander & Nijssen (1989): 30-48.

Geophagus megasema
Heckel, 1840

Original description: Ann. Wiener Mus. 2(1): 388-389.

Derivation of scientific name: *mega* (Gr.) = large; *sema* (Gr.) = mark; not explained, but probably with reference to the large lateral spot cited as a character of the species.

Distribution: The species is probably restricted to the Rio Guaporé drainage (Loubens, 1984), the river which forms the border between Brazil and Bolivia. The original description cites as type locality a large lake, called Juquia, near Matogrosso on the Rio Guaporé, where the species was discovered by the collector, J. Natterer. It cannot, however, be ruled out that the species may also inhabit the Rio Mamoré and the upper Rio Madeira drainage.

Habitat: According to Mayland (1995), the river contains much vegetation, the water is very soft (total hardness 0.02° dGH, carbonate hardness 0.9° dKH.), very low in nitrate (less than 1 mg/l) and moderately acid (pH 6.4).

Size: Heckel cites sizes (in obsolete units) approximating to about 20 cm.

Characters of the species: *G. megasema* is characterised by a very large lateral spot, which, in contrast to that of *G. proximus*, is more round than rhombic, and its upper third intersects the upper lateral line from its 9th to its 14th scale. It also lacks the opercular spot typical of *G. proximus*. There is little difference in the body proportions of this species and *G. altifrons*, only in *G. megasema* the eye is rather larger and set rather lower than in *G. altifrons*. This more posterior positioning of the eye means that the gill opening, as well as the pectoral and ventral insertions, and even the dorsal and anal fins, are also somewhat further back. The pectoral fins are, in contrast to those of *G. altifrons*, strikingly short. The caudal fin is rounded and incurved on both sides, such that the outer rays protrude somewhat and form a point.

Preserved specimens have a pattern of 7-8 horizontal black stripes on the tail, which may join to form a very irregular reticulated pattern which may sometimes even manifest as serpentine cross bars at the base of the fin, and only further back give way to straight or slanting longitudinal bands. Heckel (1840) describes the live coloration of *G. megasema* (but only from a drawing) as very beautiful. Blue-green and grey-green shades are the predominant base colours, with yellow longitudinal lines all over the body. Apart from the pectorals (which are colourless), the fins are dominated by reddish and blue-white shades. The entire dorsal ash grey, darker at the base, with the lappets of the spines and the edge of the soft portion bright red. Ventrals turquoise with red stripes along their length, except that posteriorly and towards the tips the lovely blue turns to white. Anal similar, only paler. Tail pale bluish-green, reddish towards the end, and the reticulation dark violet.

Sexual dimorphism: Males probably grow larger and have more pointed and prolonged unpaired fins. According to Heckel (1840) females have a more gently sloping upper head profile, much shorter ventral fins and shorter soft dorsal rays, as well as a noticeably stockier body.

Maintenance: Because it can be assumed that this species has, through oversight or lack of knowledge, already been imported and kept as *G. surinamensis*, successful maintenance should be possible under identical conditions.

Breeding: At present no data are available regarding the breeding behaviour of *G. megasema*, for the reasons detailed under Maintenance, above.

Further reading: Heckel (1840: 388-389; Mayland (1995: 510).

Geophagus sp. "Madeira"

Distribution: So far this species has only been imported (by Uwe Werner) from Rio Madeira drainage in the general area of Porto Velho, Brazil. Werner (pers. comm.) has found this species in the Rio Matupi drainage, the Rio Aripuana, the Rio Jaciparana, the Rio Caracol, the Rio Nathanael (Rio Magangana drainage), plus the Rio Preto and the Rio Jarz.

Habitat: Werner and his companions found this species in very variable biotopes, usually rivers with a moderate current and also in a lake to the north of the BR 230 road. This lake was fed by a small stream, and Werner describes the bottom as pebbly (metallic red stones) to sandy. While snorkelling in the clear water of one 300 metre wide stretch of the Rio Aripuana it was possible to observe the species over light-coloured sandbanks dotted with rocks. The Rio Caracol was also described as extremely clear with a sandy bottom, but in this case a lot of wood had accumulated and the water was a light yellowish colour. In the Rio Preto *G.* sp. "Madeira" was found over sand near a *cachoeira* (rapids), while in the Rio Jarz it was again seen in clear water although the river was rather turbid; here the substrate was black sand and the *Geophagus* were caught among stones and wood. Werner and his companions were also able to capture this species in a clear nameless stream which emptied into the Rio Matupi, while another stream in the Matupi drainage was turbid. The Rio Jaciparana was so murky that snorkelling was out of the question, and instead a few specimens of this eartheater were caught with the drag net.

Klingner & Seidel caught this species in the lower course of the Rio Aripuana, along with *G.* sp. cf. *argyrostictus* "Aripuana" (see there for description of biotope).

Size: No reliable data are available at present regarding eventual size, but it is thought that these fishes may attain 20-25 cm.

Characters of the species: *G.* sp. "Madeira" can be regarded as one of the "lachrymal stripe eartheaters" in the broadest sense, as this species also possesses a light blue stripe below the eye, beginning at the level of the posterior edge of the eye and ending on the cheek about halfway to the mouth opening. There are several additional light blue spots on the operculum, on a yellowish background which also covers the flanks, where there are a number of iridescent bluish scales arranged in lines. The tail is orange-reddish with light blue, irregularly distributed, spots. The pectorals are colourless. The ventrals and anal exhibit bluish lines on a yellow-orange background. The dorsal is the same colour as the body with a number of light blue spots on the soft part. The large lateral spot lies very high on the back and is practically bisected by the upper lateral line.

In the specimens that Klingner brought back the lateral spot was not so high on the back and the coloration was very different (see photos) to that of those Werner imported.

Sexual dimorphism: There are no secondary sexual characteristics, hence adult males can be recognised only by their more slender shape and more prolonged fins.

Maintenance: To date there is no detailed information on the maintenance of this species, but the observations made by Werner in the natural habitat should be used as a starting point. Without doubt soft acid water will be beneficial, and given that this species is a member of the lachrymal stripe group, then the water should be as free of organic wastes as possible, as members of the group are prone to deficiency diseases and skin lesions at high nitrate levels. Because these are very active swimmers the aquarium should be of adequate size, i.e. never less than 150 cm in length.

1. *Geophagus* sp. "Madeira". The lateral spot of this species has a higher position on the flanks than that of *Geophagus surinamensis*. Photo: Uwe Werner.
The following three species were collected in the same area as *G.* sp. "Madeira".
2. *Geophagus* cf. *altifrons* "Aripuana I" has, in contrast to the variant "Aripuana II", a somewhat deeper body and a vividly patterned caudal fin.
3. *G.* cf. *altifrons* "Aripuana II" has not yet been bred in the aquarium.
4. *Geophagus* cf. *argyrostictus* "Aripuana".

Breeding behaviour: No information is as yet available on breeding behaviour, so there is much scope for interested aquarists to get involved.

Remarks: Although the distribution of this species overlaps that of *G. megasema*, it must be a different species, as, according to its original description *G. megasema* has a dark violet reticulation in the caudal fin.

Geophagus sp. "Maicuru"

Distribution: Warzel and Loew found this species in the Cachoeira da Fartura in the Rio Maicuru, Brazil. Stawikowski *et al.* found it at the Cachoeira Pancada and near the Cachoeira Alagacco in 1996.

Habitat: The water in the Cachoeira da Fartura was slightly tea-coloured and, with a visibility of only about 80 cm, rather murky. The bottom consisted of a mixture of gravel and rocks. The fishes could not be hunted visually in the cloudy water, so Warzel and Loew were able to catch only 4 specimens, by luck, using the gill net. No large specimens were seen. This typical *Geophagus* water (pH 5.7, conductivity 42 µS/cm, 29° C) proved to be home to loricariid catfishes, *Crenicichla saxatilis, C. reticulata, Caquetaia spectabilis*, and *Acestrorhynchus* sp.

Stawikowski *et al.* (1996) found *G.* sp. "Maicuru" in rather clear water over a sandy, in part rocky, substrate at the cachoeiras Pancada and Alagacco. The river ran over much-fissured rocks of volcanic origin, so that, in the dry season at least, calmer areas separated from the main stream were fairly commonplace. Otherwise the preferred habitat of *G.* sp. "Maicuru" was among the rocks above the rapids, where the accompanying ichthyofauna included loricariid catfishes, and various large characins such as pacus, *Leporinus*, and *Pygocentrus*.

Size: *G.* sp. "Maicuru" grows rather large — maximum length 25 cm.

Characters of the species: The upper head profile rises in a straight line to shortly before the dorsal origin. The eye lies high on the head. The mouth is terminal and relatively small, with somewhat fleshy lips. The dorsal fin appears very high and the body is extremely deep at the ventral insertion, posterior to which the dorsal profile runs in a gentle curve to the caudal peduncle. The ventral profile is very flat as far as the anal insertion. All in all, *G.* sp. "Maicuru" appears more deep-bodied and compact than *G. surinamensis*, although as regards coloration and markings there is a resemblance. The lateral spot encompasses two to three rows of scales and lies somewhat below the upper lateral line, with the upper edge of the spot intersecting the upper lateral line. There is no opercular spot. Aggressively-motivated individuals may exhibit numerous narrow, dark stripes on the flanks, and these are then particularly boldly expressed on the lower belly region, and sometimes reminiscent of double bands. The caudal is completely covered with small light blue spots, significantly larger on the upper part of the fin and almost forming a reticulated pattern. The spots on the lower half of the caudal are noticeably smaller. In adults the caudal spines are elongated into threads. There are bluish lines on the ventrals, and here too the spines in adult specimens are prolonged and extend back over the anal. There are bluish lines on the anal spines, while the soft part of the fin is covered in spots of the same colour. There are numerous light blue spots on the dorsal, arranged almost in longitudinal rows. The soft parts of the unpaired fins have a reddish tinge. The pectorals are colourless. The body base colour is yellowish, but depending on the light the back may appear more greenish or bluish. There are numerous red-orange longitudinal lines on the flanks, broader on the centre of the flank. The head is an intense yellow apart from a few light blue vertical lines on the operculum. The iris is red.

Sexual dimorphism: In this species too the males grow somewhat larger, have the more pointed, prolonged fins, and are more slender than females.

Maintenance: As regards maintenance requirements (water conditions, feeding, decor) there are no great differences between G. sp. "Maicuru" and other members of the genus. However, because this is a rather large species the aquarium should be of proportionate size, i.e. no less than 500 litres capacity. With regard to the fact that this species comes from fast-flowing waters, the filtration should have sufficient capacity, as metabolic wastes will be poorly tolerated and the oxygen requirement is rather high.

Breeding behaviour: There are no detailed data available on brood care. These fishes have proved to be mouthbrooders, but it is unclear whether they are ovophilous or larvophilous, as it was not possible to observe them during the spawning or the following eight days. After this period Loew (pers. comm.) stripped the brooding parent of the young, nine already rather well-developed larvae. The majority of the eggs were unfertilised but were still being brooded at this stage.

Geophagus sp. "Amapá Grande"

Distribution: Stawikowski (1989) found this species in the Rio Amapá Grande, Amapá, Brazil, over a sandbank immediately below a section of rapids. Thus it would appear the species prefers faster-flowing water.

1. *Geophagus* sp. "Maicuru" is a beautiful eartheater, but attains a rather large size. The first breeding reports suggest that this species is a maternal, ovophilous mouthbrooder.
2. *Geophagus* sp. "Amapá Grande" resembles *G. surinamensis* in body shape and position and size of the lateral spot. Only the colour pattern in the tail differs. Photo: Rainer Stawikowski.

Habitat: Nothing is known of the habitat except as indicated under Distribution, above.

Size: The specimens captured so far measure about 20 cm.

Characters of the species: The body is deep and moderately compressed laterally. The base colour of this eartheater is a deep yellow, changing to orange immediately behind the operculum. Blue longitudinal stripes alternate with the yellow background on the flanks. There are a few bluish markings on the operculum, but otherwise the head is the base colour. The iris is red. The lateral spot is relatively small, lies below the upper lateral line, and encompasses only two rows of scales. Depending on mood there may be five vertical double bands. All the fins have a yellowish base colour, although the pectorals are very pale, and all parts of the fins are covered in bluish spots and lines, although there are only a few spots in the uppermost part of the caudal, and its lower part is striped.

Sexual dimorphism: No secondary sexual characteristics present.

Maintenance: No aquarium observations to date, as the species has not yet been imported.

Breeding behaviour: No aquarium observations (see Maintenance, above), but Stawikowski (1989) managed to catch a mouthbrooding female. Because the larvae in this female's mouth (and between her gill rakers) were incapable of swimming, and because of the amount of yolk remaining, we can conclude that this is an ovophilous mouthbrooder, as larvophilous mouthbrooders produce larger eggs.

Further reading: Stawikowski (1995b).

Geophagus sp. "Araguari"

Distribution: In 1989 Stawikowski *et al.* caught this species in the vicinity of Porto Grande in the Rio Araguari, Amapá, Brazil.

Habitat: The substrate over which *G.* sp. "Araguari" was living was muddy and soft. The river at the collecting locality was so slow-flowing that it could almost be called still. Because it was the beginning of the dry season the water level was still rather high and many bushes and trees were standing in water. The water was turbid with sediment. *G.*

sp. "Araguari" was eventually captured with a drag net over a bare sandy surface. A little further upstream Stawikowski *et al.* also found the same species singly in areas with driftwood.

Size: No reliable data are available regarding eventual size, as the individuals caught to date were not adult, and the species has not been imported.

Characters of the species: *G.* sp. "Araguari" has a bluish-green background with an intense orange zone behind the operculum. Also behind the operculum there are alternating blue and yellow-orange longitudinal lines. The lateral spot is relatively large, lies on the upper lateral line, and encompasses three rows of scales. The unpaired fins have a reddish base colour with a number of irregularly positioned bluish spots. There are a few bluish lines on the ventrals, whose spines are white. There are no markings on the head, and the iris is red.

Sexual dimorphism: No secondary sexual characteristics present.

Maintenance: Unfortunately this species has not yet been imported alive.

Breeding behaviour: No observations available to date, but Stawikowski (1991) suggests it may be a larvophile mouthbrooder.

Further reading: Stawikowski (1991b: 56-69).

Geophagus sp. "Pindaré" and *Geophagus* sp. "Parnaíba"

Distribution: In 1988 A. Werner imported some *Geophagus* from the Rio Parnaíba, and these were introduced into the hobby as *Geophagus* sp. "Parnaíba". Additional specimens of the same variant were imported in 1993 and 1994. Also in 1994, an extremely similar *Geophagus* species from the Rio Pindaré, which empties into the Atlantic a little further northwest than the Rio Parnaíba, was imported by Uwe Werner and his companions. Detailed morphometric study by Schindler (1999) indicates that these are two populations of a single species, and they are therefore treated as such here.

At present *G.* sp. "Pindaré" is known only from the Rio Pindaré in the Federal State of Maranhão, Brazil. Uwe Werner caught his specimens about 250 km up-river near the villages of Santa Ines and Buriticupu.

Schindler caught *G.* sp. "Parnaíba" near the villages Monsinhor Gil and Barras, Piaui, Brazil, near Esperantina on the Rio Longa, and in a stream called the Riacho Ponti to the west of the town of Timon, Maranhão, Brazil.

Habitat: Werner describes the habitat as fast-flowing and extremely clear. The bottom was largely fine sand. The shore was densely vegetated. Accumulations of wood and submerse plants provided the fishes with adequate cover and hiding-places. At 28° C the water was relatively warm.

Schindler found *G.* sp. "Parnaíba" in water with a gentle to moderately strong current, in rivers and bays over bottoms of coarse and fine sand. While adult specimens lived in deep water, juveniles were found in the shore zone where they enjoyed adequate protection from predators. Schindler also states that over the course of the year these eartheaters experience considerable fluctuations in water level. A river near Monsinhor Gil, Piaui, Brazil consisted a number of unconnected pools of muddy water in September (dry season), but in April (rainy season) the very same river was fast-flowing and extremely clear. The water parameters were also very different. April 1994 (rainy season): pH 7.4, conductivity 140 µS/cm, temperature 27° C; September 1993 (dry season): pH 7.6, 350 µS/cm, 31° C. Schindler also reported pH 6.9, 20 µS/cm, 31° C in the vicinity of Barras, while near the town of Timon the conductivity was 20µS/cm at a mere 27° C, and the pH was rather low at 6.7.

Size: This species appears not to grow particularly large. Werner first observed spawning when the male measured 13 cm and the female 11 cm, and postulated that they would make no more than about 17 cm. This has since been confirmed.

Characters of the species: In spite of their small size these fishes look deep-bodied. The head is short and the upper head profile rises relatively steeply. The lateral spot lies approximately on the centre of the body and intersecting the upper lateral line, extending downwards from it in a circle and encompassing about 3 rows of scales. Depending on mood, the lateral spot may become pale leaving just a circular light spot (negative coloration). The pectorals are colourless. Depending on the angle of the light, the ventrals and the unpaired fins have a reddish or yellowish base colour with a large number of iridescent bluish spots and stripes, with the caudal patterning particularly striking. There are roundish to slightly oval spots on the top and bottom edges, as well as at the base of the fin, while the centre of the fin is covered in horizontal stripes. The body pattern consists of horizontal reddish stripes, alternating with yellow or bluish iridescent bands depending on the angle and spectrum of the light.

The two variants can be differentiated only by the coloration of the head: there are no markings, or only hints of markings, on the cheeks of *G.* sp. "Pindaré", such that depending on the light the head looks yellowish or light bluish. By contrast the form from the Rio Parnaíba drainage has iridescent bluish spots, sometimes joined together, below the eye from the corner of the mouth to the operculum.

Sexual dimorphism: Apart from the difference in size between the sexes, males have more elongate fins and are rather more slender-bodied. But because there is no sexual dichromatism it is extremely difficult to sex half-grown specimens and adults that are not yet sexually ripe.

160

Maintenance: This species appears to have no special requirements as regards water chemistry, and will spawn in hard water (18° dGH) with a decidedly alkaline pH of 7.5 as well as in prepared water with a pH of 6.8 and a hardness of only 6° dGH. It can thus be regarded as one of the hardier members of its genus. The quality of the water appears to be more important: at high levels of nitrate the colours vanish and even tiny amounts of nitrite will cause an increase in respiratory rate and visible discomfort. The species appears to be relatively insusceptible to skin lesions and swellings.

These *Geophagus* are omnivores that require a balanced diet. They will eat practically anything that drops in front of their mouths and will fit inside, but because of their small size the morsels should not be too large as they can easily "choke". The best foods are the various different types of frozen foods (assuming live food is not available) plus a good quality dried food with adequate supplementary vitamins. In addition green food should be offered, in the form of scalded lettuce or spinach, cooked Brussels sprouts, and various fruits (apple, strawberries). The only limits are those of your imagination. But when feeding green foods

1. *Geophagus* sp. "Araguari" has, like *Geophagus surinamensis*, a spotted caudal fin and a large lateral spot. Photo: Rainer Stawikowski
2. *Geophagus* sp. "Pindaré" or *G.* sp. "Parnaíba" from the state of Maranhão in Brazil, is a small and easy to keep *Geophagus*.
3. and 4. *Geophagus* sp. "Pindaré" is a biparental larvophilous mouthbrooder, which frees its larvae from the eggs already after 24 hours.

remember that they should be very soft, as hard foods will be ignored.

In 1994 Schindler dissected a 6.5 cm specimen of *G.* sp. "Parnaíba" in the field, and found that the digestive tract contained 80% plant material, plus some sand, detritus, and insect larvae. In the digestive tract of a smaller specimen he found insect larvae, sand, and detritus, but no vegetable matter.

On account of their small size an aquarium of 200-250 litres will be adequate for maintenance and breeding. This container should be set up with fine sand and a good choice of hiding-places in the form of rock structures and/or bogwood. A few separate, flat stones will serve as spawning sites. Any species that display a peaceful temperament will do as tankmates, but these *Geophagus* are unable to cope with rough fishes or those of significantly larger size, and under such circumstances they will always become retiring and waste away. Particularly suitable tankmates include loricariid catfishes (those that do not grow too big) and various peaceful characins, but they can also be kept with other earth-eaters and/or other large peaceful cichlids such as, for example, *Mesonauta* and *Uaru* as long as these prove indifferent towards the *Geophagus*.

Breeding behaviour: Pairing takes place after a short period of "getting acquainted" and is not particularly spectacular; it follows a common pattern of frontal and lateral display. *G.* sp. "Pindaré" are larvophilous mouthbrooders which lay their eggs on a flat stone, previously cleaned by both partners, lying on the bottom. In the aquarium the chosen site is often very difficult to see, so that the species could almost be described as an "undercover" brooder.

After spawning is completed the eggs are covered with sand to conceal them; the amount of sand used is variable. In order to avoid alerting potential egg-predators to the presence of the spawn, the parents remain at some distance from the eggs and only occasionally approach them. The female, who plays the major role in the care of the eggs, remains about 20-30 cm away while the male chiefly busies himself with defending the territory. It may happen, however, depending on the population density of the aquarium, that the parents stand guard in the immediate vicinity of the spawn. Because both parents are capable of guarding the spawn it is possible for the division of labour to differ.

Depending on water temperature, the larvae are picked up at the earliest possible moment, i.e. when the yolk is completely surrounded by the periblast. At 27° C this may be just 24 hours. For this reason the eggs are relatively small and not very yolk-rich, as larger eggs would require a longer developmental period. After 24 hours the larvae are only slightly differentiated and the fact that it is time to pick them up is signalled only by the presence of a little dark tail. At this point the parents free the larvae from the eggshells and take them into the shelter of their mouths. The eggshells remain on the spawning substrate as a whitish mass.

The parents share the subsequent brood care. Each day the larvae are several times exchanged between the parents so that each has an opportunity to feed during the brooding period. The exchange of the larvae usually involves the digging of a small pit into which the brooding parent spits the larvae, making it easier for the accepting parent to "field" possible wanderers and to make sure all of the increasingly more strongly wriggling larvae are picked up. By and large both parents again play equal parts in this stage of the brood care, but if circumstances dictate either the male or the female can assume the main burden of the brooding, or one parent can care for the brood alone.

After 9-12 days the fry are released from the sheltering mouth for the first time, and are led by both parents. At night and if danger threatens both parents pick them up again. As time passes first the female loses interest in mouthbrooding, and thus it is the male alone who collects up the fry in the event of danger, as long as the rapidly-growing young will still fit into his mouth. At this stage, however, the female shows no further interest in the brood. The young can be fed as soon as they are free-swimming; at this stage they can already manage newly-hatched Artemia, so there are no problems in this respect.

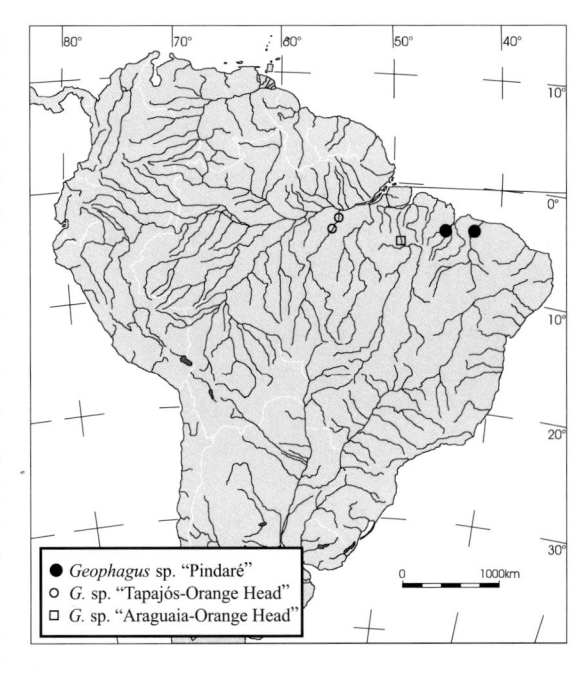

To date no breeding observations on *G.* sp. "Parnaíba" have been published, but there is no reason to expect that the two forms will differ in their brood care.

Further reading: Schindler (1999: 61-57); Weidner (1998d: 150-155); Werner (1997: 4-8).

● *Geophagus* sp. "Pindaré"
○ *G.* sp. "Tapajós-Orange Head"
□ *G.* sp. "Araguaia-Orange Head"

Geophagus sp.
"Tapajós Orange Head"
also known as
Geophagus sp.
"Tapajós Red Cheek"

Distribution: In 1991 Christoph Seidel and Rainer Harnoss discovered this species in the Tapajós downstream of Itaituba and at Alter do Chao. In Alter do Chao (the lake at the river's mouth) the species appears to occur at only low population densities, while it is commoner further upstream.

Habitat: During the low water season the river bottom at the edge of the lake at the mouth of the Tapajós consists largely of sand, with mud in places. However, at the time of maximum precipitation the water level rises by up to 12 metres and the tree-clad shore zones are flooded, so that while sandy zones must be regarded as the preferred habitat, inundated areas with accumulations of wood are also frequented. There are, of course, also accumulations of wood (sunken driftwood) and large stones in the main river, which never runs dry, and in places rocks are present, providing shelter. There are no permanently submerse plants in the Rio Tapajós, as the murkiness of the water does not permit of plant growth. The water has only a moderate current. The pH is always well within the acid range (6.2-6.8), there is no

1. *Geophagus* sp. "Tapajós - Orange Head" are attractive and relatively small eartheaters.
2. *G.* sp. "Tapajós - Orange Head" are larvophilous mouthbrooders which free their larvae from the egg-shells 2 to 4 days after spawning. The photo shows a spawning female.
3. This species is known as *Geophagus* sp. "Tapajós" and is found syntopically with *Geophagus altifrons* and *G.* sp. "Tapajós - Orange Head".
4. The copper-coloured back of *G.* sp. "Tapajós" is readily apparent under subdued lighting conditions.

measurable hardness, and the conductivity is significantly less than 50 µS/cm. In the middle of the year the temperature is about 28° C, and fluctuates by a maximum of 12° C.

Size: This species barely exceeds the 20 cm mark.

Characters of the species: The most characteristic feature of this species is without doubt the orange forehead, although an eartheater from the Rio Araguaia has a similar coloration. But these two cichlids can be differentiated by the form and position of the lateral spot and the basic flank pattern. *G.* sp. "Tapajós Orange Head" has a roundish lateral spot which lies below the upper lateral line and ends at the level of the fish's horizontal axis. Moreover this species does not have any up to 1 cm wide horizontal band running along the lateral line. *G.* sp. "Tapajós Orange Head" has a fine pattern of vertical bands on the flanks, very close to one another and running down from the back to the belly, sometimes splitting at the level of the lateral line to form an inverted V. The Tapajós variant appears rather more deep-bodied. The fins are reddish with iridescent bluish horizontal stripes. The body base colour is yellow, but when the light strikes the fish at the right angle, a green-bluish shimmer may be seen.

Sexual dimorphism: Differentiating the sexes is possible only with great difficulty in this monomorphic species. It was originally assumed that the females had a brighter-coloured forehead, but the subsequent importation of greater numbers has shown this formula to be in need of revision. In fact the vividness of the orange area appears to depend on social rank, state of health, and mood. Individuals that today have a brightly coloured forehead and are perhaps in breeding condition may in a few weeks time exhibit only a pale tinge on their forehead. A more reliable method of sexing is the degree of development of the fins and the body structure. Males as a rule have more prolonged, pointed fins and grow somewhat larger. Females fairly quickly become corpulent in the ventral region. The genital papilla of the female is blunt and rounded, while that of the male is longer and more pointed.

Maintenance: These cichlids do not differ appreciably from other closely related species in their requirements. It should, however, be noted that this species has a very outgoing demeanour and is very active, such that in the long term they should be kept in an aquarium with a length of at least 150 cm. In particular, during the breeding phase they can be very aggressive towards conspecifics and it is therefore necessary to provide other fishes with safe refuges to which they can retire.

A hardness of up to 20° dGH and alkaline water (up to pH 8.0) will not prevent *G*. sp. "Tapajós Orange Head" from breeding successfully, and this species does not seem to be particularly susceptible to the skin lesions that commonly occur in *Geophagus* in harder water. It should, however, be borne in mind that softer water is more akin to the conditions encountered in nature and in addition will intensify the colours of the fishes.

These eartheaters do not seem to be upset by brighter light than usual, which means a larger selection of plants can be introduced. It should be noted, however, that the plants should be well-rooted in advance, as otherwise you may end up with a surface layer of floating plants! Hiding-places in the form of wood or rocky structures should be provided, but not restrict swimming space unnecessarily. A few isolated stones will complete the picture and subsequently serve as spawning sites.

Breeding behaviour: *G.* sp. "Tapajós Orange Head" is a larvophilous mouthbrooder which chooses a flat stone lying on the substrate, usually away from other decor, as a spawning site. If no suitable substrate is available then they will also spawn on a sloping surface. These fishes also seem to be capable of learning to some degree, as after my pair failed to breed successfully near the bottom, they subsequently spawned on a horizontal surface on a root only 5 cm below the water's surface.

The spawning substrate is thoroughly cleaned, mainly by the female, And little pits are dug all around it, which are not, however, used until the fry are free-swimming. Spawning takes place in typical open-brooder manner, i.e. the female first lays a batch of eggs in a straight line and the male then fertilises them, again moving in a straight line. There is no circling during the spawning. In fact in this species the male is more likely to fertilise the eggs as soon as they are laid by swimming parallel to the female, and often both sexes swim side-by-side over the substrate. The eggs measure 1-2 mm and are whitish to pink, with an overall opaque effect. After 2 (current author) to 4 (Müller, 1997) days the larvae are freed from the eggshells and immediately taken into the protecting mouths of both parents. They are subsequently exchanged now and then so that both parents have an opportunity to feed. The exchange generally takes place via the abovementioned shallow pits. When after 8-10 days the fry swim free, feeding with *Artemia* nauplii can be commenced immediately. The parents endeavour to keep the shoal of fry together in the previously-mentioned pits for a few days longer, picking them up at night as well as when danger threatens. But with every passing day the up to 200 fry become more active and after about 10 days brood care ceases. By this time at the latest some of the fry should have been siphoned out for separate rearing. The fry do not grow particularly rapidly, but nevertheless after about 3 weeks they can take lobster eggs and/or Bosmina.

Remarks: This species shares its habitat with *G. altifrons*.

Further reading: Müller (1997: 9-10); Stawiskoswki (1998b: 41-48).

Geophagus sp. "Araguaia Orange Head"

Distribution: Exact details are unknown, as the species has been imported only via the trade and more exact data have not been made available.

Habitat: Likewise no details of the biotope are available.

Size: At 18 cm maximum, this is a rather small species.

Characters of the species: The closest species to *G.* sp. "Araguaia Orange Head" is *G.* sp. "Tapajós Orange Head" (see above) but there are a number of distinct characteristics by which *G.* sp. "Araguaia Orange Head" can easily be distinguished. Thus this species has a somewhat longer lateral spot which again lies below the upper lateral line but a scale-width above the lower lateral line. This form is rather slimmer than its close cousin from the Tapajós. The upper head profile is more rounded and the orange area above the eyes is nothing like as bold. Like its relative from the Tapajós *G.* sp. "Araguaia Orange Head" has a pattern of fine stripes on the flanks. The tail has a pattern of bluish streaks on a yellow background. The lower half of the head and the base colour of the flanks are also yellowish.

Sexual dimorphism: In this species the sexes can be differentiated only on the basis of secondary sexual characteristics. Thus here too females remain smaller and have rounder fins. There are no differences in coloration.

Maintenance: This species is far more peaceful than its relative from the Tapajós and can easily be dominated by other larger species. It is happiest and will "blossom" in the company of quiet and peace-loving tankmates. In other respects maintenance is as for *G.* sp. "Tapajós Orange Head".

Breeding behaviour: This is another larvophilous mouthbrooder whose behaviour is directly comparable to that of *G.* sp. "Tapajós Orange Head".

According to Albering (pers. comm.) this is a monogamous larvophilous mouthbrooder. He was able to observe two breeding pairs in a 2 metre (500 litre) aquarium. Except during brood care both pairs sought the company of their conspecifics. When they spawned their territories were in the immediate vicinity of each other (30-40 cm) although the aquarium offered plenty of space. Albering was unable to observe the actual courtship, but 2-3 days before the spawning the

1. Sunset over the bridge over the Orinoco river in Ciudad Bolivar, Venezuela.
2. Also *Geophagus* sp. "Araguaia - Orange Head" is a monogamous, larvophilous mouthbrooder.

female's genital papilla was already visible. Over the following days the spawning substrate was cleaned by both parents, and as time went by the fishes became territorial and more aggressive. Intruders were driven away by lateral threat, expanded opercula, and beats of the tail. In extremis the flanks of the opponent were bitten.

The preferred spawning substrate has to date always been a flat stone lying on the substrate. Movable substrates – e.g. leaves — are not accepted.

According to Albering his fishes have always spawned between 1600 and 1800 hours. The larvae hatch after 36-38 hours at 27° C and are taken into the sheltering mouths of both parents. The black tails of the larvae, which are vigorously waved, may serve to stimulate the parents to pick them up. Eventually all that is left on the spawning substrate is a whitish gelatinous mass.

In the course of the next 8 days the parents repeatedly dug little pits into which they spat the larvae so that the other parent could then pick them up. Them while one parent continued brooding the other could busy itself with constructing pits or go searching for food.

Albering also observed that his fishes stole larvae from other brooding parents. The two pairs of *G.* sp. "Araguaia Orange Head" carried on a remarkable little "war" in this respect.

Remarks: *G.* sp. "Araguaia Orange Head" is, in my opinion, identical with *G.* sp. "Tapajós Orange Head" (sibling population of one and the same species).

Further reading: Stawikowski (1999: 56-59).

'Geophagus' crassilabris Complex
"Red-hump Eartheaters"

Derivation of scientific name: *geos* (Gr.) = earth; *phagein* (Gr.) = eat; thus eartheater, with reference to their behaviour, taking food from the substrate. For *crassilabris* see under *'G.' crassilabris*, below.

Note: The common name of this group, the "Red-hump Eartheaters" refers to the fact that males may develop a nuchal hump. In the event that the *Geophagus* genus is revised, then the three red-hump species will probably be assigned to a new genus. The complex is named after the first species described, *'Geophagus' crassilabris*.

Distribution: The distribution of the three known Red-hump Eartheaters is restricted to Colombia and southern Panama. The distribution of *'G.' crassilabris* encompasses the canal zone and Darién, *'G.' pellegrini* is found in the Chocó province of Colombia, while *'G.' steindachneri* inhabits the Rio Magdalena and its drainage, again in Colombia. Because of their distribution the three species are well separated and there are no intermediate forms to create nomenclatural difficulties. A possible exception is the transition between *'G.' pellegrini* and *'G.' crassilabris*, as the former has apparently been reported from the distribution region of the latter.

Characters of the group: Although male Red-hump Eartheaters are noted above all for their imposing nuchal humps, females also differ from the true *Geophagus* in having only a moderately ascending upper head profile, being thus more reminiscent of *Satanoperca*. The body is only moderately compressed laterally. The eye is sited rather high on the head. The mouth is terminal and horizontal, and the lips are sometimes rather fleshy. The anterior half of the cheek is scaleless. Depending on mood the body may exhibit a pattern of numerous broken horizontal and vertical, such that the flanks have a more or less blotched pattern along the median line. Females often have a lateral spot on the central flank, but on the other hand there is no peduncular spot (or only a hint of one). Females have a beige base colour. The dorsal is relatively low and the ventrals are short by comparison with those of *Geophagus sensu stricto*, as the spinous rays are not prolonged.

Ecology: While *Geophagus sensu stricto* prefer sandy substrates to a greater or lesser extent, the Red-hump Eartheaters can also be found over coarse pebbly bottoms, although sandy or muddy terrain forms a major component of the habitat. The rivers of the natural habitat are moderately fast-flowing,

1. A young male *Geophagus* steindachneri. The red hump is clearly visible but not yet fully expanded.
2. Sunset over the Amazon river near Alenquer.

but juveniles generally prefer the stiller zones out of the main current. These zones are often created by the accumulation of wood, and offer not just juveniles but also brooding individuals shelter from predators.

Ethology: Within the *'Geophagus' crassilabris* complex the usual rule applies — where you find one you will find several — as Red-hump Eartheaters are sociable creatures. Adults may be solitary to some extent, but these cichlids appear generally to form schools. That is to say, Red-hump Eartheaters should not be kept in pairs, but do best in a small group of, say, 3 males and 3 females. With the exception of *'G.' steindachneri* they are not well able to look after themselves against other (larger) species, although naturally this may be relative during the breeding season. Squabbles among themselves are usually decided by lateral threat, with the combatants swimming side by side and head to tail; or frontally with opercula spread. Only exceptionally does mouth-fighting occur, and serious battles leading to injury are rare.

Because all three species are maternal mouthbrooders, pairing is limited to the spawning act, after which the female broods the eggs alone and the male goes on his way.

Additional peculiarities of mating, described by Jacobi (1981) as shaking and snapping, should be mentioned here. These initiate pair formation and play an important role in the laying and fertilisation of the eggs. When a dominant male encounters a ripe female then he generally begins to shake his head, with movements of the head from side to side being the most striking. He simultaneously spreads his fins to their full extent. As his excitement increases he curves his body in an S-shape. Next he raises his lower jaw and at the same time extends the premaxillary (upper jaw) forwards. All this behaviour is termed shaking by Jacobi. Snapping often develops from shaking. The mouth is now closed while extended, and the jaws, which are now one above the other, are moved very rapidly and rhythmically. While doing this the male often touches the substrate. Snapping is associated with slowly swimming backwards.

Remarks: The mouthbrooding method of these cichlids is remarkable, as they do not brood their eggs and larvae in a buccal sac, as is known for most mouthbrooding cichlids, but in the mouth cavity. In the process the preoperculum is expanded and the upper lip protruded far forwards, considerably expanding the oral cavity. This brooding mechanism is related to the feeding method of these eartheaters, which are able to extend the preoperculum independent of the posterior operculum and simultaneously extend the premaxillary far forwards with the mouth closed. This enables the Redhump Eartheaters to take up a large quantity of substrate and then use the close-packed gill rakers to sort out the edible from the inedible. This provides ideal conditions for mouthbrooding, as there is adequate space in the oral cavity and the close-packed gill-rakers prevent the eggs from being swallowed, and the opercula, which can be moved independently of each other, prevent any eggs from being lost via the gills.

Also worthy of mention is the physiology and function of the nuchal hump in males. The hump is not, as once assumed, used for the storage of nutrients, and in fact it contains only very little in the way of fat and nutrients. The hump region does, however, have very dense connective tissue with elastic blood vessels (arterioles) which may be responsible for regulating the fluid content of the hypodermal tissue such that the hump develops when the fish is motivated. Jacobi observed that males who had to contend with not only higher rank but also lower rank conspecifics developed enormous humps. Moreover he observed that breeding males developed a large hump only during spawning, and that this disappeared again fairly soon afterwards. Jacobi speaks of "magnification through conflict", as both the alpha male (highest ranking) and the lowest-ranking male had only weakly developed humps, and only those individuals who had to contend for their rank against opponents of both higher and lower rank developed significantly larger humps. The reason being that the strongest and weakest individuals had to fight fewer battles to maintain their rank. Individuals with a strongly developed hump appear appreciably more imposing and impress their opponent with their stature. The highest-ranking individual no longer needs such a hump as its ranking within a group remains stable for longer, while the beta male, for example, must deal with both stronger and weaker individuals in order to improve or maintain his status. The lowest-ranking male endeavours to camouflage himself by looking like a female, and thus develops no hump and adopts female coloration.

Further reading: Jacobi (1981).

'Geophagus' crassilabris Steindachner, 1877

Original description: Sitzber. Kais. Akad. Wiss. Math. Naturw. 74 (1): 65-67.

Derivation of scientific name: *crassus* (Lat.) = thick; *labrus* (Lat.) = lip; "with thick lips", with reference to the fleshy lips.

Distribution: This species is found in the eastern part of Panama where it is found in both Atlantic and Pacific coast drainages. The type material originated from the vicinity of the town of Candelaria. In 1911 Meek & Hildebrand found this species in the Rio Missimbi, in Limon Creek, in the Rio Mandingo, at Trinidad and at Chagres, in the Rio Frijoles, the Rio Calobre, the Rio Indio, and the Rio Boqueron, as well as in the Rio Aruza and the Rio Cupe in 1912 (all localities in southern Panama). In 1932 Shattuck found the species in the Bayano River, while in 1935 Hildebrand again went looking for this species and caught it in Lago Miraflores, the Rio Chagres, and Lago Gatun.

Hofer (pers. comm.) found specimens in the Rio Parti, Rio Ipeti, and Rio Santa Rosa, in eastern Panama. In February 1989 Kullander and Silfvergrip caught *'G.' crassilabris* in the Rio Baudá, Colombia, though this may be a case of confusion with *'G.' pellegrini*.

Habitat: This species is found in both clear and white water, as well as in mixtures of the two. The biotope is similar to that of the other members of the group. Stones, roots, and leaf litter alternate to produce a very varied habitat. Hofer (pers. comm.) always found *'G.' crassilabris* over muddy bottoms with large amounts of detritus and in the immediate vicinity of emerse vegetation close to the bank. There were usually the remains of clumps of reeds providing additional cover. Hofer found brood-tending *'G.' crassilabris* in a residual pool with no proper connection with the main river (the Rio Ipeti). The bottom was muddy and covered in detritus. The adults measured at least 15 cm and without exception were swimming in pairs, leading their fry. He noted considerable aggression on the part of the species towards other cichlids such as *Aequidens coeruleopunctatus*, which were allowed no closer to the brood than 50 cm. In a side-arm of the Rio Parti he saw juvenile *'G.' crassilabris* in the reed-clad bank zone during the day, while at night he found adults in about 1.5 metres of depth in the main stream. In the Rio Santa Rosa juveniles were found only in very warm shallow water, which was very murky and full of algae.

The water in the natural habitat is relatively soft (up to 4° dGH) and usually slightly alkaline (pH 7.0-7.6). The temperature can vary between

75.2 – 89.6 (82.4)

24 and 32° C. Thus this species can be regarded as easy to keep as regards water parameters.

Size: Males can attain the 20 cm mark or even exceed it by a few centimetres. Females remain smaller as a rule.

176

Characters of the species: Juvenile specimens can easily be confused with *'G.' steindachneri*. Only adults exhibit the noticeably more swollen lips that give the species its name. In adults the lower lip may even protrude laterally over the lower jaw. The blue-black lips are characteristic. There is almost always a visible dark spot on the centre of the back, above a poorly marked, interrupted, lateral band. Whiel females are usually plain beige, sexually mature males have vivid red shades on the posterior dorsal and the anal. The ventrals are also reddish. Depending on the spectrum of the light, reddish, bluish, or just brass-

1. A semi-adult male of *'Geophagus' crassilabris*. The lips of this species seem to be thicker as those of the other two species of the complex.
2. *'Geophagus' crassilabris* in its natural habitat, Rio Ipeti, Panama. Photo: Xaver Hofer.
3. A semi-adult female *'G.' crassilabris*. Photo: Ad Konings.
4. The Rio Ipeti in Panama. Habitat of *'G.' crassilabris*. Photo: Xaver Hofer.

coloured shades may predominate on the body. The head of adult males exhibits a brassy sheen.

Sexual dimorphism: Males grow larger and may have the typical Redhump Eartheater hump on the forehead. Moreover from about 5 cm the sexes can be differentiated on the basis of coloration — in this sexually dichromatic species the males are more brightly coloured.

Maintenance: *'G.' crassilabris* should present the aquarist with no serious problems as regards water parameters (see Habitat, above). Decor likewise poses no difficulties, as a few pieces of wood and rock are virtually indispensable in any aquarium and will provide these fishes with shelter and hiding places. Plants need not be neglected either, as they will be neither grubbed up nor nibbled, although fine-leaved plants are best avoided as they will soon become dirty and unsightly as a result of the constant sifting. When it comes to food there are likewise no special requirements, as both dried food and all sorts of frozen foods are greedily taken.

'G.' crassilabris should be kept only with peaceful species, as they can tend to shyness. They are best kept in a small group with other peaceful fishes, as only in the company of their own kind can the entire behavioural repertoire of these very interesting cichlids be seen.

Because of their size the aquarium should have a capacity of at least 300 litres, proportionately larger if a bigger group is required or other cichlids are to be included as tank-mates.

Breeding behaviour: When a ripe male and female meet then the male commences courtship by rapidly opening and shutting his mouth in front of the female while simultaneously spreading his unpaired fins and extending his preopercula slightly. This behaviour is accompanied by violent head-shaking. This ritual is generally conducted over a spawning substrate and the male repeatedly lowers his head towards this substrate. The female reacts to this courtship by cleaning the substrate, although she is not particularly meticulous about the task. Once both partners are ready they circle each other with widespread fins. Once this preliminary pairing is complete the female begins to clean the spawning site thoroughly while the male keeps intruders at bay. After a few "dummy runs" the female lays up to 5 large orange-yellow eggs at each pass and immediately takes them into her mouth. Next the male emits his milt in the same spot and encourages the female to pick up the sperm by making "snapping" movements with his mouth while swimming backwards. Next the female snaps at the substrate as if trying to pick up eggs. It may also happen now and then that the male fertilises the eggs while they are still on the substrate, but snapping remains a normal feature of the breeding behaviour and is performed in every case.

'G.' crassilabris is a highly-specialised ovophilous maternal mouthbrooder, i.e. only females practise broodcare. Under aquarium conditions I have been unable to perceive any bond between the pair after spawning, and males have immediately spawned again with other females (assuming other ripe females were available). However, this is contradicted by observations made by Hofer (pers. comm.) in the Rio Ipeti, where he saw males and females performing brood care together.

Once spawning is over, the female retires to a quiet corner of the aquarium to brood her eggs and not yet free-swimming larvae for a period of 16-18 days. The fry, by now free-swimming, are then released from the mouth, and are immediately capable to taking newly-hatched Artemia. For a period of several days the fry are taken into the protection of the mother's mouth at night, and when danger threatens. But after about 6 days the female refuses to pick them up and from then on they are left to fend for themselves. Given several feeds per day they grow on rapidly, and rearing them poses no difficulties.

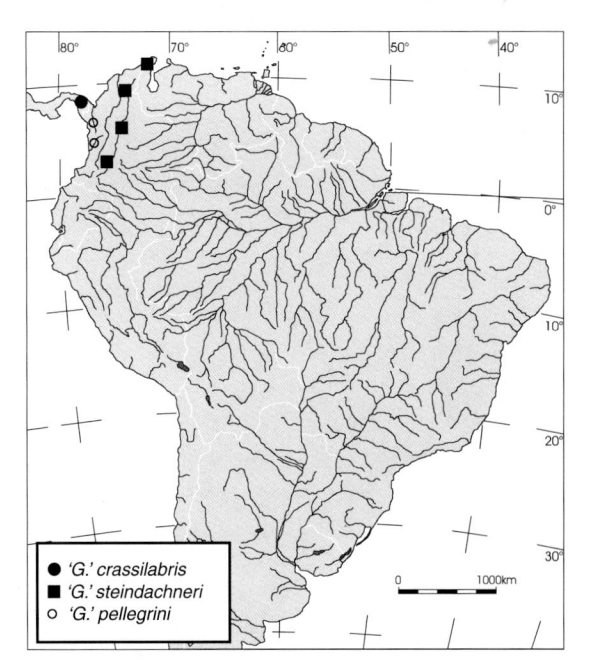

● 'G.' crassilabris
■ 'G.' steindachneri
○ 'G.' pellegrini

Remarks: Strictly speaking 'G.' crassilabris is found only on the land bridge between North and South America and is thus not a South American eartheater. However, the fact that its closest relatives are inhabitants of the South American continent, and it is the only mouthbrooding cichlid in Central America, justify its inclusion here.

Further reading: Gosse (1975: 71-76); Werner (1998a; 1998b: 212-214).

'Geophagus' pellegrini
Regan, 1912

Original description: Ann. Mag. nat. Hist. (8) 9: 505-506.

Derivation of scientific name: In honour of the French ichthyologist Dr. Jacques Pellegrin.

Distribution: The distribution of *'G.' pellegrini* is apparently restricted to the Chocó province of Colombia, to the west of the Andes and bordered by the Serranía de Baudó and the cordilleras. Recorded localities are the Rio Baudó (Fowler, 1944) and the Rio San Juan (Palmer, 1909), both of which empty into the Pacific Ocean, as well as the Rio Atrato (Stalsberg, 1991), which empties into the Gulf of Darién. The type specimen originated from the town of Tadó on the Rio San Juan (Palmer, 1909; Regan, 1912). Additional, smaller, streams in which *G. pellegrini* occurs are the Rio Quito (Stalsberg, 1991), Rio Condoto (Stalsberg, 1991; Regan, 1913), Rio Jurubida (Fowler, 1944), and Rio Juradó (Loftin, 1963). Gosse (1975, citing Fowler, 1945) mentions as an additional locality the drainage of the Rio Caquetá, but it must be assumed that this is an error as that river is in the Amazon drainage, on the other side of the Andes.

In addition Gosse (1975) lists specimens found by Loftin in Panama in a creek emptying into the Rio Armila. These must almost certainly have been *'G.' crassilabris* as there is no direct link between this locality and the northernmost (confirmed!) site for *'G.' pellegrini*.

1. Aquarium individuals of 'Geophagus' pellegrini do usually not possess the large humps as seen in some wild specimens.
2. A spawning pair of young adult 'G.' pellegrini. The male has not yet attained full breeding coloration. The female has already eggs in her mouth.

Habitat: 'G.' pellegrini is an adaptable cichlid, as the species is found in slow- as well as fast-flowing waters; this is a function partially of the topography of the landscape but also depends on the time of year. The clarity of the water also varies considerably, as during the rainy season more sediment is washed into the rivers, and this clouds the water. These fishes are omnivores and for this reason do not need to occupy any particular ecological niche. They are generally found near the bank, where sand and leaf litter alternate. The natural habitat of 'G.' pellegrini is often shaded by primary forest. The species is also found in smaller streams and rivulets where the bottom is usually covered with coarse shingle, but these cichlids can also be found over rocky substrates and in places with accumulated wood. Stalsberg (1991) reports the following water measurements: pH about 7.0, nitrite not measurable, water temperature 28° C, conductivity 24 µS/cm, hardness up to 2 dGH.

Size: 'G.' pellegrini is the largest of the Red-hump Eartheaters. Males can exceed the 25 cm mark. Females remain somewhat smaller, but they too can exceed 20 cm.

Characters of the species: The most typical character of *'G.' pellegrini* is the orange-red body colour which sexually mature males exhibit all over the body. Females are far more inconspicuously coloured, and in addition to their beige base colour possess only the irregular pattern of spots on the flanks that is typical of both sexes, and which can, depending on mood, disappear completely or be visible as a faint pattern of vertical and horizontal bands. A dark spot is almost always visible on the centre of the flank, above the faint longitudinal band. Vertically above this spot, in the dorsal, there is another dark spot of irregular shape, and in males in particular this can extend over almost all of the spinous part of the fin. The upper head profile is not as steep as in *'G.' steindachneri* and even adult males develop only a vestige of a hump which does not differ from the body in colour. If the light is right then the lips may appear bluish.

Sexual dimorphism: As already mentioned for *'G.' crassilabris* above, males begin to exhibit greater colour at only 5 cm, in this case an orange tinge on the flanks, which intensifies with increasing age. The body colour in males is at first visible mainly on the head and the unpaired fins. Females remain somewhat smaller and have no hump on the forehead. In *'G.' pellegrini* the hump does not develop until a very late stage and in the aquarium single males usually exhibit only a hint of a hump. Only if several males are kept together will some show significantly larger humps than others (see Remarks for the Red-hump group, above).

Maintenance: Despite its size *'G.' pellegrini* is one of the shyest of the eartheaters, and quite unable to cope with the presence of lively or aggressive species — they will in fact continue to feed, but their natural behaviour will not be observed. If, however, *'G.' pellegrini* are kept with other similarly "quiet" fishes then they will become almost tame and can then be fed optimally, as they are rather slow feeders. They often appear rather clumsy when they snap at the food and have to make several attempts at capturing something to eat. The species is best kept in small groups of, say, 3 males and 3 females.

This eartheater is relatively easy to please as regards decor and water parameters. It should go without saying that hiding-places in the form of bogwood and rocks should be provided, as brooding females like to retire to such retreats in order to brood in peace and quiet. Fine-grained sand should not be forgotten so that the fishes can feed in their natural manner. Plants can be included, as they will be virtually ignored.

The best diet for these fishes will offer a balance between variety and nutritiousness. Being omnivores, they will take all the usual foods. However, vegetable material must be almost at the decomposing stage before *'G.' pellegrini* will eat it.

Breeding behaviour: *'G.' pellegrini* is another polygynous cichlid, in which the pair bond lasts only for the duration of the spawning. The male then goes on his way, and thus it may happen that one and the same male spawns with a number of different females in rapid succession. The similarity to the behaviour of many cichlids of the East African rift valley is obvious. There too there is no permanent pair bond and the male plays no further role after spawning. The female is thus left to her own devices after spawning and straightaway retires to a quiet spot where she carries out the brooding process in the typical ovophilous maternal mouthbrooder fashion.

A somewhat raised stone is usually selected as the spawning substrate. This substrate is then cleaned, but only insofar as is necessary, with the female performing the bulk of the chore. Meanwhile the male guards the territory, albeit not particularly vigorously — potential intruders are driven only a short distance away. Courtship involves not only lateral but also frontal display, the latter involving the lowering of the mouth region while simultaneously quivering the entire body. Once both partners are ready there is only a short time to wait before spawning begins. As soon as the first eggs have been laid the male glides over them and fertilises them. Next he drops his lower jaw and "snaps" in front of the female, encouraging her to pick up the fertilised eggs. Sometimes the eggs are picked up as soon as they are laid and then fertilised in the mouth, with the male emitting his milt over the substrate and then again "snapping" in front of the female. The eggs are slightly oval and yellow to orange in colour.

The actual brooding time in *'G.' pellegrini* is only 10-12 days at 26° C, in contrast to *'G.' steindachneri* which broods for 16-20 days. The now free-swimming fry still have a relatively large yolk sac, which is absorbed within two days at most. Once the fry have been released from their mother's mouth they will take freshly-hatched Artemia even though their yolk sac is not yet completely absorbed. The female is able to take all of her rapidly-growing offspring into her mouth for only 5 days thereafter, and after this time an increasing number remain outside the closed lips of their mother, as there simply isn't room for them all inside. After 21 days the fry will have attained a size of 13 mm. Up to this point, however, the fry retain their shoaling behaviour, and except at feeding time gather together in a group only 3-4 cm across. Only from the 23rd day onward do they disperse all over the aquarium, and their greed for food continually increases such that they can soon be seen foraging in the upper levels of the aquarium.

Further reading: Andersen (1993: 88-90); Gosse (1975: 76-81); Stalsberg (1991: 687; 1993: 556-558); Weidner (1995c: 54-57).

'Geophagus' steindachneri
Eigenmann & Hildebrand, 1910

Original description: Rep. Princeton Univ. Patagonia, Vol 3 (1), Zoology: 317.

1. A male *'Geophagus' steindachneri* with "swollen" hump. Photo: Hans-J. Mayland.
2. *'Geophagus' steindachneri* was responsible for the name "Red-hump Eartheater" for the members of the complex.
3. Red to orange spots are sometimes found on the end of the lower lip at the corner of the mouth. Photo: Ad Konings.
4. A mouthbrooding female of *'G.' steindachneri*.
5. A fry-guarding female of *'G.' steindachneri*. A few days after first release the fry are allowed entrance to the mouth only in case of danger.
6. The fry of *'G.' steindachneri* grow quickly and are abandoned after about two weeks.

Derivation of scientific name: In honour of the Austrian ichthyologist Dr. Franz Steindachner.

Distribution: *'G.' steindachneri* has a relatively restricted distribution limited largely to the Magdalena drainage in Colombia (Gosse, 1975) as well as the Rio Magdalena itself, recorded localities include the Rio Sinu (Gosse, 1975; Anka, 1996; Sneidern, 1949), the Rio Cauca, the Rio Seco, and the Rio Guali (Gosse, 1975), as well as other small tributaries in these drainages. Ploeger (1999) indicates that *'G.' steindachneri* is also found in the Maracaibo basin in Venezuela, where he found it in the Rio Limon on the Guajira peninsula. Whether or not this is part of the natural distribution or the result of an introduction is unclear.

Habitat: Because the habitat of *'G.' steindachneri* is reported as extremely varied, it is difficult to make any valid generalisations. The species is found over stony substrates as well as extensive sandy areas. The current varies fairly rapidly because of variations in the topography. The water parameters depend on the area in question, and/or the time of the year, as during the rainy season the rivers acquire a heavy sediment burden and the water parameters may be influenced thereby. Beck (in Jacobi, 1981) reports pH measurements between 5.8 and 6.8

in the natural habitat from 1970-78, as well as conductivity readings between 10 and 160 µS/cm, at temperatures ranging from 26-34° C.

Size: In the aquarium *'G.' steindachneri* rarely exceeds 15 cm, while females remain a few centimetres smaller. In exceptional cases lengths of up to 20 cm may be attained (See Remarks, below). These fishes are sexually mature at only 8 cm.

Characters of the species: The body shape by and large resembles that of the other Red-hump Eartheaters: while the ventral profile is generally straight, the upper body profile is strongly curved. The upper head profile rises appreciably more steeply in males than in females. Depending on the light the nuchal hump may appear reddish or brownish. In adult males with a very well developed nuchal hump the lower part may be transparent and the supra-orbital blood vessels visible within the hump. The mouth is slightly sub-terminal and there are yellow-orange spots at the corners of the mouth; it has several times been suggested that these may be egg dummies (Schmettkamp, 1998).

Juveniles, plus females and subordinate males, usually exhibit a highly variable pattern on their flanks, generally dependent on mood. It is usually possible to see a broken longitudinal band on the flank, running from the eye to the caudal peduncle, and becoming paler towards the peduncle. Subordinate or aggressively motivated individuals have vertical bands running from the back to the belly, with those between the eye and the middle of the body extending down only as far as the mid-lateral band, while those further back are full length. Subordinate individuals have a paler base colour than aggressive specimens, and the latter are also darker on the throat region. This dark coloration may extend back to the anal fin. Neutrally-coloured and dominant males are very difficult to describe, as various populations are known, which vary in their base colour. Thus reddish, orange, or yellowish metallic spots, or variable prominence, may be seen on a whitish, yellowish, or greenish background. These metallic spots are usually arranged in lines. Very old specimens may lose their colour and then often have just a pale reddish area behind the operculum.

Sexual dimorphism: Like all the red-hump Eartheaters the most reliable secondary sexual characteristic is the development of an orange to brown-reddish nuchal hump in males, which increases in size from a length of 6 cm on and may already be coloured reddish at that size. Juveniles of less than 6 cm are difficult to differentiate as females too have a reddish area on the forehead.

On close examination, however, males generally already have a more intense body colour even at this size, although this depends on the population. Adult females are significantly less colourful than males.

Maintenance: *'G.' steindachneri* is undoubtedly one of the hardiest eartheaters known. It makes only trivial demands as regards water parameters: thus a hardness of up to 30° dGH is generally acceptable and any pH between 6 and 8 is tolerated without any signs of ill-health. Temperatures between 25 and 32° C are acceptable. In order to be able to observe the exceptionally large behavioural repertoire, several males and females should be kept together. A group of three of each will be fine. This will require an aquarium of appropriate size, i.e. with a capacity of more than 300 litres. *'G.' steindachneri* are easy-to-please omnivores which will take any of the usual foods without any acclimatisation phase. Vegetable food should not be omitted. A little care is required as regards choice of tankmates, as under certain circumstances this species can be rather rough or even aggressive. Normally, however, they are indifferent towards other fishes.

In order to allow the fishes to feed in the natural manner, the substrate should be as fine-grained as possible. The aquarium should be arranged so as to permit individual territories to be created, and hiding-places in the form of bogwood should be provided. In addition a number of large flat stones should be laid on the substrate, as such stones are preferred spawning sites.

Breeding behaviour: When a dominant male and a ripe female meet, then the male will start by "shaking" and "snapping". A short time later the pair will position themselves side by side and head to tail, often with lateral threatening as well. Next comes leading behaviour, with the male leading the female to the intended spawning site, and the "snapping" is repeated over the spawning site, accompanied by slow circling of the partner. From time to time the male picks up some sand in his mouth. While the female cleans the spawning substrate the male displays and continually repeats the "snapping" behaviour, which apparently has a stimulating effect on the female. After a few "dummy runs" the female lays her relatively large yellow eggs in batches of one to eight on the previously roughly cleaned substrate. Fertilisation by the male sometimes follows immediately, i.e. the eggs may be fertilised while still on the substrate or later in the mouth of the female. In the latter case the male glides repeatedly over the substrate even though there are no longer any eggs there as the female has already picked them up in her mouth immediately after they were laid. The female next snaps gently at the substrate several times, swimming head-down, thus collecting sperm retroactively. In this way fertilisation takes place in the mother's mouth. Schmettkamp (1998) mentions that the orange-coloured prominences at the corners of the male's mouth may be egg dummies; supposedly, while the male glides backwards after emitting sperm he displays these dummies to the female and she is thus encouraged to snap up sperm. But as there are populations of *'G.' steindachneri* that lack these "egg dummies", as do also *'G.' crassilabris* and *'G.' pellegrini*, then this hypothesis is rather questionable as regards its general validity.

Once the female's egg supply is exhausted the pair bond dissolves. The female withdraws and for the 3 weeks that follow broods the up to a hundred offspring by herself. Young females do not feed during brooding. Adult and/or experienced can often be seen to take food, although this involves hesitantly picking up smaller particles and then "chewing" these very carefully. After about 20 days the fry leave their mother's mouth for the first time; they already measure 4 mm and can take newly-hatched Artemia. The female continues brood care for about two weeks, and during this period the fry find refuge in the shelter of her mouth at night and when danger threatens. Thereafter the maternal urge disappears and the fry are no longer taken into the mother's mouth, although they still try to get in when danger threatens. The mother does not herself pose a threat to her offspring.

Newman (1993) kept males and females in separate aquaria, but with the two sexes able to see each other through the glasses of the adjacent tanks. If one or more females was ripe with eggs, he put a male with the female. After only a short settling-in phase the male would court the female and a short time afterwards spawning took place. Newman was unable to observe and deviation from the spawning behaviour described above. His method — keeping males and females separate — could be useful where a very aggressive male is involved or if the space available is too limited for both sexes, as *'G.' steindachneri* males

1. Waterfall in the *igarapé* Ambroso near Alenquer.
2. The airstrip at Santarém is in itself worth the journey.

1. A male '*Geophagus*' cf. *brasiliensis* "Pernambuco" from the Rio Capibaribe. Photo: Frank Warzel.
2. A male '*G.*' cf. *brasiliensis* "Pernambuco".
3. Female '*G.*' cf. *brasiliensis* "Pernambuco" (from the Rio Capibaribe) are pale coloured compared to males.
4. A male of an undescribed '*Geophagus*' sp. aff. *brasiliensis*. This specimen was caught in the drainage area of the Rio Turvo in the Brazilian state of Rio Grande do Súl. This form is characterised by a large lateral spot. Photo: Wolfgang Staeck

also develop a nuchal hump. Males have longer finnage and a metallic sheen on the flanks, while females sometimes have attractive black markings.

Maintenance: Because of their size and their ability to look after themselves, these eartheaters should not be kept in aquaria less than 150 cm in length, especially if they are to be kept with other cichlids. It matters not in the least whether fine sand or a coarser substrate is used. These eartheaters will not mind at all. Except during the breeding phase they pay little attention to the substrate, as, in contrast to *Geophagus sensu stricto* and *Satanoperca* they search only its surface for edible material. However, it is best to dispense with plants, as although these will not be eaten, during brood care the brasiliensis group are inclined to rearrange the aquarium to their own liking. This may involve major excavations which will not be survived by many plants. If an element of greenery is required then plants can be added in pots and/or their root balls covered with large stones. Because these cichlids prefer rather muted lighting the surface can be covered with floating plants.

The remaining aquarium decor should consist of rocks and bogwood, arranged to provide caves and other hiding places that will comfortably accommodate fishes of this size. Although they prefer to swim in the open, they do appreciate places to which they can retire when necessary.

When it comes to feeding these cichlids have proved undemanding, but prefer larger foods such as mussels, raw fish, and coarse krill. But dried foods and any sort of frozen food will also be consumed in large quantities.

Because these cichlids are found in nature in practically every type of water, water parameters play a subordinate role. Thus temperatures ranging from 16 to 30° C are tolerated without harm, although the optimum range is between 22 and 26° C. The hardness should not exceed 30 dGH. Because these fishes are salt-tolerant to some degree, the conductivity can be up to 3000 µS/cm for short periods, but in the longer term the hardness should be between 5 and 15° dGH. A pH between 5.0 and 8.0 is likewise tolerated. Because these large cichlids produce large amounts of metabolic wastes, at least 1/3 of the aquarium water should be changed weekly and the filter should be of appropriate dimensions (turnover of twice aquarium volume per hour).

Ethology: 'G.' brasiliensis and its relatives are far from retiring in temperament, and under certain circumstances this may have unfortunate consequences in the restricted environment of the aquarium. It is virtually impossible to stop these cichlids breeding, and when they are about to spawn they are more than capable of demanding respect. For this reason they should have as much space as possible, and this will at the same time afford tankmates greater scope for evasion. But it would be unfair to regard these eartheaters as rough or aggressive. Yes, they are well able to deal with other eartheaters, but they are like lambs in the face of many large Central American cichlids or other large cichlids. Having won the respect of tankmates, these are generally ignored, such that serious injuries and deaths are rare.

Some members of the *'G.' brasiliensis* complex have been kept in captivity for the past 100 years, and because they are relatively easy to keep, their breeding no longer holds any secrets. The only difficulty is in trying to generalise as regards their breeding behaviour. The older literature describes them as open brooders, but this is not strictly correct. It is true that members of this complex prefer to spawn on smooth, usually horizontal, substrates. But they actually prefer places that are protected on several sides, and thus it may happen that they spawn in narrow cracks and crevices and even open caves (van den Niewenhuizen, 1977; Stawikowski, 1981, 1983; Werner, 1987).

F. Schäfer (pers. comm.) has seen a pair spawn and guard their eggs in a drainpipe.

I have kept a pair of *'G.' brasiliensis* of unknown origin which repeatedly spawned in the same, barely visible, spot, an open cave with large branches, built from rocks and wood and occupying the entire right-hand corner of the aquarium. The eggs were laid on the bottom glass (previously cleared of sand). Prior to spawning the pit was repeatedly altered at the whim of the parents, with large heaps of sand being piled at both main entrances.

The location of the spawning site may depend on the population of the aquarium and the rank of the breeding fishes vis-a-vis their tankmates. The individuals kept by Grad (1987) in a thinly populated 1100 litre aquarium spawned on a vertical piece of slate which was also in full view.

Before spawning can take place the parents-to-be must select and clean a spawning substrate. This is done in stages. First the potential spawning substrates are tested for suitability by the parents. This involves mouthing the substrate. If one parent is of the opinion that this is a good spot, then he/she shows it to the partner to the accompaniment of spread fins, lateral display, and leading (to the chosen site) behaviour. If the substrate is in sight then the "exhibiting" parent swims to it and mouths it again. Usually the other parent tests it too, again by mouthing.

Once the parents have agreed on a site, then the female begins the systematic cleaning of the substrate, while the male defends the territory. But the male also repeatedly returns to the spawning site and shares, albeit only briefly, in the work. When spawning is imminent large pits are excavated round the spawning site, chiefly by the male, with the sand generally being heaped up to provide extra shelter. Once the spawning site is prepared to the satisfaction of the pair, then the spawning begins immediately. The female attaches rows of eggs to the substrate and the male fertilises them over again. Both parents glide repeatedly in a straight line over the substrate until up to 1000 eggs have been laid in loose formation and fertilised. The eggs are small, white-grey to yellowish, and at the same time slightly transparent.

Once the spawning is ended, the female always remains in the immediate vicinity of the spawn, while the male guards the territory. If the male comes near the eggs then he is generally driven away by the female and encouraged to return to guarding the territory by gentle biting of his flanks. Depending on temperature the larvae hatch after 3-4 days and the female then moves them, in batches, to one of the pre-dug pits and subsequently from pit to pit. From now on the male is allowed nearer to the brood, although territorial defence remains his chief role. The larvae, which are not yet free-swimming, are repeatedly moved around during the days that follow, being carried from one pit to another. After a further four to five days (a total of 7-9 days after the spawning) the larvae become free-swimming and after another 24 hours take food for the first time. During this period the parents are especially aggressive and drive any intruder away with particular zeal. The female now becomes noticeably paler in colour and the black markings on her sides (lateral spot, eye-stripe, and the now more intensely black anterior dorsal spines) are particularly striking. It may be that these markings assist orientation by the fry, as in many other cichlid species.

During their first days the

- ● '*G.*' *brasiliensis*
- ★ '*G.*' cf. *brasiliensis* "Pernambuco"
- ■ '*G.*' *iporangenis*
- ○ '*G.*' *itapicuruensis*
- □ '*G.*' sp. "Bahia Red"
- ◆ '*G.*' *obscurus*

jerks her body, whereupon the fry drop to the bottom and remain their motionless. Once the female ceases jerking then after a little while they rise up again. At night the fry are gathered together by their mother and put to bed in a pit. The male repeatedly takes a share in the leading of the fry and now plays an equal role with the female in the brood care.

fry remain in a close-packed group and rarely stray away from their siblings. With increasing age they wander further afield and brood care becomes harder work for the parents. For up to three weeks the female in particular concentrates on ensuring that none of the fry wander too far from the shoal. If danger threatens she spreads her unpaired fins and

After the yolk sac has been absorbed the young can immediately be fed with freshly-hatched live *Artemia*, and after a few weeks they can take frozen lobster eggs, *Daphnia, Cyclops,* and *Bosmina*. Dried food can now be offered. The little ones grow rather rapidly, and may measure 2-3 cm after only two months. After 6-8 months the juveniles will have attained about 8 cm and be already sexually mature.

Remarks: Staeck (1999) found cichlids belonging to this complex in the Rio Turvo, a tributary of the Rio Uruguay (Rio Grande do Sul State, Brazil), between the towns of Tenente Portela and Crissiumal. Whether these were *'G.' brasiliensis* is doubtful. It is far more likely that they were a new species or *'G.' iporangensis*, as this species too has a large lateral spot and a pointed head profile.

Further reading: Boguth (1975); Grad (1987: 12-15); van den Niewenhuizen (1977: 194-199); Staeck (1999: 180); Stawikowski (1981c: 190-199; 1983: 454-461); Stawikowski & Werner (1988); Werner (1987b: 298-304); Winkelmann (1975: 99-100).

1. *'Geophagus' brasiliensis* (female?) from the Rio Paraiba do Súl. Photo: Frank Warzel.
2. A male *'G.' brasiliensis* from the Rio Itapemirim. Photo: Frank Warzel.
3. A male of a population of *'G.' brasiliensis* from the Rio Tiête, São Paulo, Brazil. Photo: Frank Warzel.
4. A fry-guarding male *'Geophagus'* sp. of the *'G.' brasiliensis* complex from an unknown locality.

1. In particular females of the *'Geophagus' brasiliensis* complex (a female of unknown locality is shown) are devoted parents.
2. *'Geophagus'* sp. of the *'Geophagus' brasiliensis* complex of unknown providence.
3. *'Geophagus' itapicuruensis* from the Rio Jacuipe north of Salvador, Bahia, Brazil. The characteristic vertical bars are clearly visible. Photo: M. T. C. Lacerda.
4. *'Geophagus' iporangensis* from the Rio Ribeiro de Iguapé. Photo: Frank Warzel.

laterally, with maximum body depth at the dorsal origin. The upper head profile generally rises in a straight line. Old males may, however, develop a distinct nuchal hump.

For Size/ Sexual dimorphism/ Maintenance/ Breeding behaviour see introductory material under *'G.' brasiliensis* species complex, above.

Further reading: Castelnau (1855: 13-19); Eigenmann & Bray (1894: 607-624); Gosse (1975: 71-76); Günther (1862: 278-315); Haseman (1911: 329-373); Quoy & Gaimard (1824: 286-287); Stawikowski (1999: 20-21); Warzel (1999: 18-19).

'Geophagus' iporangensis
Haseman, 1911

Original description: Ann. Carneg. Mus. Vol. 7: 364-365.

Derivation of scientific name: Originally described as a subspecies of *'G.' brasiliensis*, *G. b. iporangensis*, and named by Haseman after the type locality, the village of Iporanga, São Paulo, Brazil.

Distribution: According to Haseman this species originated from a mountain stream near the village of Iporanga, São Paulo, Brazil, a tributary of the Rio Ribeiro de Iguapi. Unfortunately in the same work Haseman mentions two localities for *'G.' brasiliensis*, the villages or Xiririca and Iguapi, both likewise on the Rio Ribeiro de Iguapi, which must be presumed to in fact be locations for *'G.' iporangensis*.

Habitat: No details of the natural habitat are available to date.

Characters of the species: This species is more elongate compared to *'G.' brasiliensis*. The head is longer and appears rather more pointed. The body and the caudal peduncle are less deep. According to Haseman (1911) the fins of preserved specimens are virtually without spots, dark at the base, and edged in black. There is a dark spot at the base of the caudal, a lateral spot on the centre of the flank, and no, or only a few, blue dots on the body.

For **Size / Sexual dimorphism / Maintenance / Breeding behaviour** see introductory material under *'G.' brasiliensis* species complex, above. No specific details available, as *'G.' iporangensis* was for a long time synonymised with *'G.' brasiliensis*.

Further reading: Haseman (1911: 329-373); Warzel (1999: 18-19).

Characters of the species: In contrast to 'G.' brasiliensis, 'G.' sp. "Bahia Red" has rather more fleshy and more strongly developed lips. The upper head profile rises visibly more gently, as in 'G.' obscurus, and the head thus appears rather more pointed.

This species can be differentiated from all other known species of the brasiliensis complex by the reddish zone on the operculum, which is equally pronounced in both sexes. The unpaired fins exhibit no notable spot or stripe markings and their soft parts appear transparent. In this species the lateral spot is, as in 'G.' brasiliensis, not clearly delineated and is extended somewhat vertically, and is thus a good differentiating character from 'G.' obscurus.

For Size/ Sexual dimorphism/ Maintenance/ Breeding behaviour see introductory material under 'G.' brasiliensis species complex, above.

Remarks: It is at present unclear whether 'G.' sp. "Bahia Red" is a good species or merely a population of 'G.' brasiliensis or 'G.' obscurus. In fact 'G.' sp. "Bahia Red" appears to combine characters of both those species (see Characters of the species).

Further reading: Eigenmann & Bray (1894: 607-624); Knopf (1996: 73-78); Stawikowski (1999: 20-21); Warzel (1999: 18-19).

1. 'Geophagus' obscurus from the Rio Paraguassu. Note the pointed snout. Photo: Frank Warzel.
2. A young couple of 'Geophagus' sp. "Bahia Red" guarding their offspring. Photo: Rainer Stawikowski.
3. The red-coloured, pointed snout is the most prominent character of 'Geophagus' sp. "Bahia Red". Photo: Rainer Stawikowski.

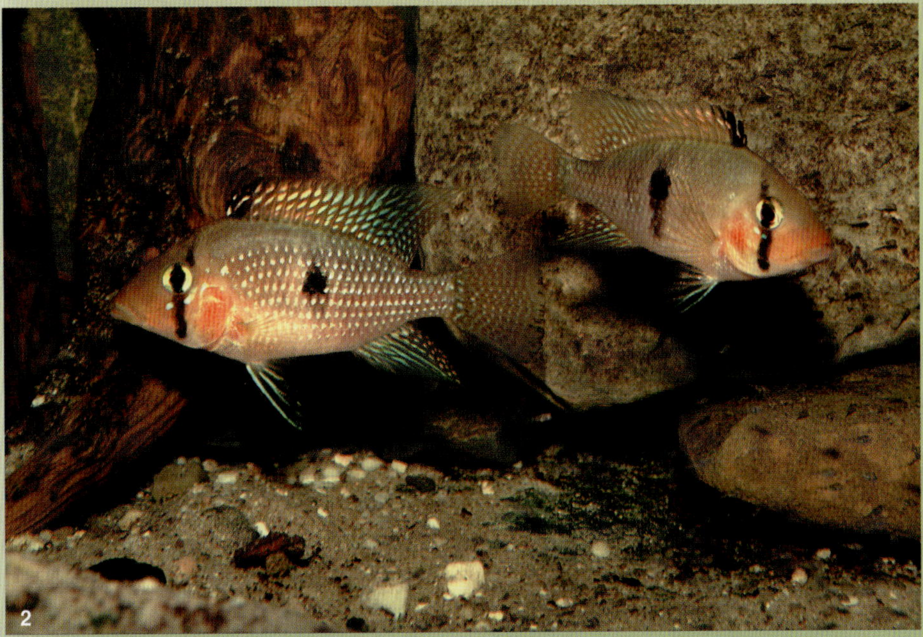

2

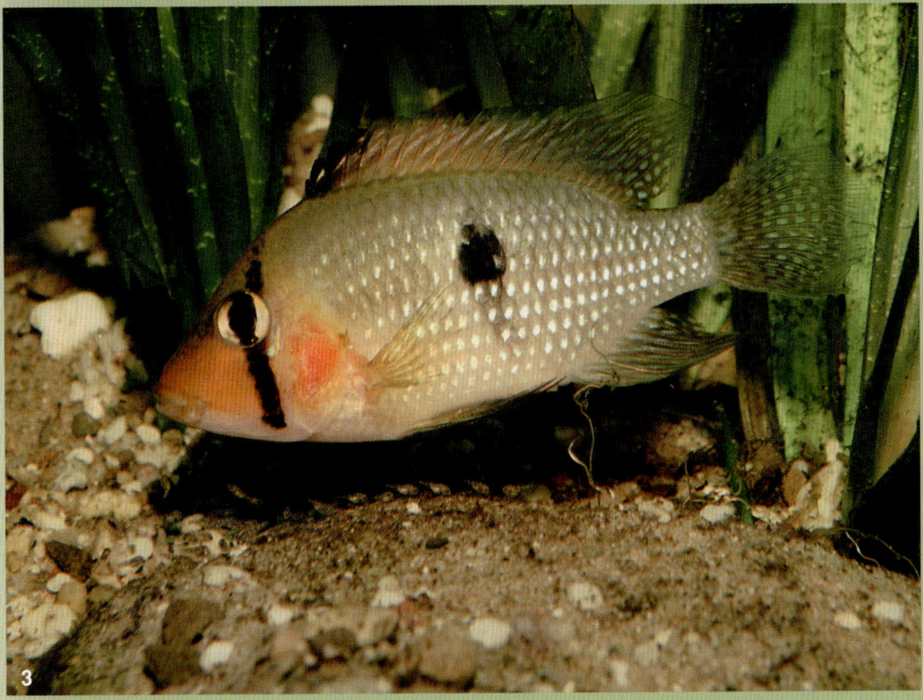

3

Satanoperca Günther, 1862

Derivation of scientific name: *Satan* (Lat.) = the devil; *perca* (Lat.) = perch; = Devil's perch.

Distribution: *Satanoperca* species are throughout almost all of northern South America. Its range is limited by the natural barriers of the Mato Grosso watershed in southern Brazil and the Andean cordilleras in the west.

Ecology: *Satanoperca* species can be considered classic eartheaters, as they are at home anywhere that there is a substrate of fine sand or mud and slow-flowing water. While a number of *Geophagus* species enjoy fast-slowing rivers with coarser substrates, *Satanoperca* are rarely found in such biotopes. All species far prefer almost still zones with plenty of cover provided by roots and branches as well as leaf litter, although open sand constitutes the primary habitat. Naturally the waters that are home to *Satanoperca* are extremely soft with a slight acid pH, and a number of species require a much lower pH of about 4.5-5.0, especially during the breeding phase (in order to ensure egg development), although such low values are not necessary all year round. The members of the genus do not prefer any particular type of river and are thus found in black, white, and clear waters. They have a basic preference for larger river systems and their environs, where relatively constant and high temperatures (27-30° C) prevail for most of the year.

Characters of the genus: All the species of the genus have a gently ascending upper head profile. The mouth is terminal and the lips only moderately thickened. The head is almost an isosceles triangle. All species have a spot on the caudal peduncle, but in some populations/species this occupies only a few scales. This peduncular spot is often surrounded by light metallic reflective scales. While three species have one (*S. lilith*) to four (*S. acuticeps*) lateral spots, the members of the *G. jurupari* complex have no lateral spot but may, depending on mood, exhibit a lateral band or faint traces of vertical barring beneath the dorsal fin. And while the members of the *S. jurupari* complex have an only moderately prolonged dorsal fin, the species with lateral spots may have threadlike elongations to the first soft rays of the fin. *S. jurupari* complex members have a facial mask of dark transverse stripes running between the eye and the lips. The position, form, and expression of this facial mask, together with the position of the vertical flank stripes relative to one another and the colour of the flanks and fins, are differentiating characters within the *S. jurupari* complex. Kullander (1986) and Kullander & Nijssen (1989) were unable to find any morphological distinction between *S. leucosticta*, *S. jurupari*, and *S. pappaterra*, and within this complex the mode of brood care can be just as important a distinguishing character as those of classical ichthyology used throughout the aquarium hobby.

Ethology: In contradiction of the genus name *Satanoperca* are very shy cichlids. The "Devil" part of the generic name refers exclusively to the names given to these fishes by the natives: *jurupari pampé* means "Devil's claw" and *jurupari pinda* denotes "Devil's angel". Both relate to the mode of reproduction, as the indians were frightened by the fact that the young of these fishes were born from their mouths, as in the past they did not understand all the intricacies of mouthbrooding and thus regarded it as the work of the Devil. In addition these fishes were not eaten. Science has put this situation to good use and hence several scientific names (*daemon, jurupari,* and *lilith*), including the genus name, refer to it. The mode of brood care is extremely variable within the genus and hence is detailed separately for each species.

Satanoperca species are essentially very sociable creatures which are usually seen moving around in groups in nature. Solitary individuals are rarely seen. This should be taken into account in the aquarium, and at least four individuals per species should always be kept. It is true that they can be kept in pairs, but this does not reflect their natural inclinations. On the other hand keeping a trio is pointless — one individual will be dominated to such an extent that it will eventually succumb. Only a few species (*S. daemon, S. lilith, S. acuticeps*) require a territory — these species can be regarded as concealed brooders in the widest sense (see species descriptions), while the mouthbrooders need to hold territory only during spawning and until the eggs are picked up.

In the natural habitat *Satanoperca* species spend almost the entire day searching through the substrate for food. This should be borne in mind in when maintaining them captivity.

Remarks: All *Satanoperca* are exceptionally timid fishes which require special attention during maintenance; this includes feeding and water quality, as some species are prone to skin lesions on the head region under inadequate maintenance conditions. Moreover these fishes need to be able to feed constantly (!) in order to grow into top quality specimens. They feed very slowly and for this reason greedy or rapid-feeding species are not ideal tankmates. Under such circumstances the *Satanoperca* may quite simply not receive enough nourishment, as although they will take large morsels they then take a correspondingly long time to swallow these. It is thus appropriate to offer repeated small feeds so that food intake is accomplished over as long a period as possible.

The members of the *S. jurupari* complex are at present the cause of much confusion among ichthyologists and aquarists, as new species, which cannot be identified as any known taxon, are forever appearing in the trade or being brought back by travelling aquarists. Thus individuals of a number of populations have been imported that clearly differ from known species by virtue of their manner of brood care, eventual size, colour, and/or general habitus. It is at present unclear to what extent this is indicative of new species or simply populations of one species, and promises plenty of work for the ichthyologists. But dedicated aquarists can also make a significant contribution in this respect, as observations of brood care can provide definitive answers to questions of species identity within this species complex (see Characters of the genus, above). To date it has been established that the Amazonian species are maternal mouthbrooders which pick their eggs up immediately at the conclusion of spawning or in batches during the spawning; while the species of the Guianan Shield (in this case just *S. leucosticta* and perhaps *S. mapiritensis*) are biparental mouthbrooders which take their eggs into the protection of their mouths 24 hours after spawning at the very earliest. Additional problems are presented by the fact that no morphological differences exist and species differentiation by means of markings is extremely haphazard, plus there are species in the Amazonian lowlands which are highly reminiscent

of *S. leucosticta*. Unfortunately no observations on the brood care of these fishes have been reported which might answer these questions or at least provide a partial solution to the problems.

Satanoperca acuticeps (Heckel, 1840)

Original description: Ann. Wien. Mus. 2(1): 395-395.

Derivation of scientific name: *acutus* (Lat.) = sharp, pointed; *ceps* (Lat.) = headed; referring to the rather more pointed head distinguishing this species from its closest relatives.

1. The bank of Rio Tauari, an effluent of the Rio Tapajós and locality of *Satanoperca acuticeps*.
2. The four spots and the high dorsal are some of the typical characters of *Satanoperca acuticeps*.

Distribution: This species has a very wide distribution within the Amazon drainage. Thus it has been found in the Rio Negro at Manaus and in the Amazon downstream to Santarém, as well as in areas of calm water in the larger and smaller tributaries. Documented localities include the Rio Negro and the Rio Solimões (Melin & Vilars, 1923); Lago Janauaca (Soarez, 1979; Staeck, 1986); Lago Janauari (Kullander *et al.*; Rio Tefé (Agassiz *et al.*, 1865; Stawikowski, 1993); Rio Tapajós at Santarém (Kilian & Seidel, 1991) and near

209

- Satanoperca acuticeps
- Satanoperca daemon
- Satanoperca lilith

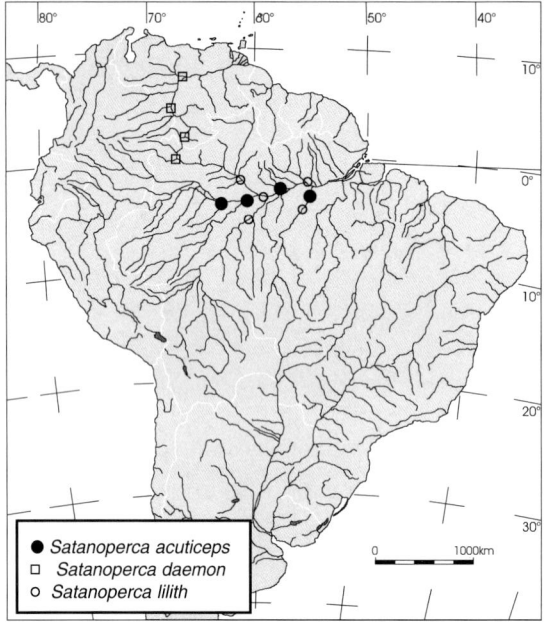

Aveiro (Kullander, 1980; Stawikowski et al., 1992, own obs., 1996), as well as in the Igarapé Tauari (Warzel, 1992, own obs., 1996). *S. acuticeps* appears to prefer clear- and blackwater biotopes, although the whitewater of the Amazon presents no insuperable barrier.

Habitat: *S. acuticeps* inhabits only peaceful shore zones and by preference lives over open sandy surfaces of muddy bottoms. Vegetated areas are also inhabited where there are plenty of open sandy areas among the stands of plants (Igarapé Tauari). Roots and leaf litter are also used as cover, with smaller individuals in particular being aware of the value of leaves for protection. The water is as a rule very soft with a hardness not exceeding 4° dGH and a pH no higher than 6.8. *S. acuticeps* requires warmth and will not tolerate temperatures below 26° C in the long term.

S. acuticeps are basically sociable creatures which seek the company of conspecifics. Usually small groups of up to 10 individuals move together across the sand, always on the search for food. Only during the breeding season do pairs split away from the group, and at such times become very aggressive towards conspecifics.

Size: Although specimens measuring a good 25 cm have been caught in the natural habitat, this species only exceptionally exceeds 20 cm in the aquarium.

Characters of the species: The four lateral spots on the flanks (the fourth and last on the caudal peduncle) are an unmistakable character. Depending on the angle of the light, the base colour of *S. acuticeps* is grey-green to golden. The flank scales all exhibit an iridescent greenish spot. Two iridescent green stripes run diagonally from the upper lip towards the eye, with the upper ending at the eye and the lower continuing below it to the operculum. Depending on mood the 4 spots on the flank may unite into a longitudinal band running from the operculum to the caudal peduncle. There may also be seven transverse bars on the back, extending from the dorsal to just below the lateral spots. Three of these bars intersect the lateral spots while four run between them. The iris is mainly reddish.

The tips of the dorsal and anal spines are grey-black with a slightly reflective submarginal zone below. This colour gives way to an orange area extending to the end of both dorsal and anal. The membranes between the rays are grey-green. In adult specimens the third to the fifth soft dorsal rays are prolonged into threadlike extensions and orange. The soft parts of the unpaired fins have greenish spots on a yellow to reddish background. The caudal spines have a slight orange sheen. The ventral spines are orange with a submarginal band below. The soft ventral rays are likewise yellowish-orange.

However, because *S. acuticeps* has a very wide distribution the shade and extent of the various colours may vary geographically. Moreover it should be remembered that the base colour of this species may also be dependent on its current basic diet. Thus *S. acuticeps* fed largely on green food may have a generally greenish colour, while those fed a diet rich in carotene (e.g. planktonic crustaceans such as *Cyclops* and *Mysis*) may exhibit a more reddish coloration.

The mouth is more terminal than in *S. daemon* and *S. lilith*. In addition this species has the most pointed snout (see photos) and is the only member of the genus to have the fold of the lower lip uninterrupted.

Sexual dimorphism: It is very difficult to tell the sexes apart, except that in adult males the third, fourth, and fifth soft dorsal rays and the ventral spines are generally more prolonged than in females. Adult females look more rounded than male conspecifics.

Maintenance: Basically, *S. acuticeps* should be kept in soft to medium hard (up to 10° dGH) water with a pH of between 5.0 and 7.0. In my view acid (pH 5) and very soft water (up to 150 µS/cm) water is mandatory for breeding.

S. acuticeps will live along time under these maintenance conditions. But it should be mentioned that problems may arise during the acclimatisation period, with individuals dying without warning as soon as they enter captivity. For this reason one should acquire a largish group from which pairs may subsequently form. Moreover maintaining a small group more closely corresponds to natural conditions.

S. acuticeps should be fed as varied a diet as possible, with a high value placed on vegetable food. It is advisable to feed up to four times per day (see Remarks, below), but with the occasional fast day. If the intention is to bring the fishes into spawning condition then these fast days should be omitted. A careful eye should be kept on these fishes when feeding them frozen foods, as some types (*Artemia*, glassworm, *Daphnia*, and the like) may be taken in but not eaten, and sometimes ejected via the gills. Even so these foods should not be omitted from the diet as they are an important component of a balanced diet.

Suitable tankmates are other earth-eaters and/or dwarf cichlids of the genera *Nannacara*, *Dicrossus*, *Laetacara*, and *Apistogramma*. However characins can be the optimal companion fishes for *S. acuticeps*. The aquarium should be decorated with fine sand and hiding-places created from wood and rocks, in order to simulate the natural habitat. Fairly muted lighting will allow the fishes to be more relaxed. Plants should not be forgotten, but make sure they are well-rooted as otherwise they may be dug up, although the "quarrying" is not of any major concern as sand is picked up and spat out again only a few centimetres away.

Breeding behaviour: To date there are no reports of successful breeding. I have, however, been able to observe spawning and initial brood care, although I was not able to rear the fry. The aquarium in which spawning took place has a conductivity of 150 µS/cm and a pH of 6.0, with a temperature of 28° C. The nitrate reading was less than 30 mg/l and the nitrite at 10 mg/l. No carbonate hardness was measurable and the total hardness was about 2° dGH.

When they spawned the fishes measures 12 cm. *S. acuticeps* is an open- or pit-brooder, which digs a pit some 5-10 cm deep and about 20 cm in diameter in open sand. Both parents excavate this pit, in which up to 200 eggs are subsequently laid. The eggs are green-yellowish and moderately adhesive, such that finer particles of sand adhere to them. At this stage the normal shyness of the parents is no longer in evidence, and they are quite capable of showing appreciably larger and sturdier species the door. Both parents take turns at the brood care, although the male is more involved in territorial defence while the female remains close to the pit. Unfortunately I was unable to observe the spawning. Immediately after spawning the eggs were sporadically covered with various "objects" such as empty mussel shells, coarse gravel, bits of wood, and dead leaves. From this point on the parents no longer hovered over the spawn but guarded the brood from a distance. This offered

1. Depending on mood the four lateral spots of *Satanoperca acuticeps* can pale or totally disappear.
2. Breeding pit of *S. acuticeps*. The spawn is located in the centre of the pit and is camouflaged with pebbles or empty snails shells.
3. *S. acuticeps* belong to the open brooders. They spawn on the sand but cover the eggs with sand, pebbles, or leaves when spawning is over.

the advantage that possible spawn-predators were not shown the exact location of the nest while the parents could still keep it in view.

Although I did not see the eggs/fry being transported from pit to pit, I assume this did in fact take place as I was forever discovering new, freshly-dug, pits, although I could not see the brood in them. Probably the brood was again camouflaged with sand or the like. The parents usually positioned themselves at a distance of about 10-20 cm and fanned with their pectoral fins. Now and then they would swim to the pit without my being able to see exactly what they did there.

48 hours after spawning the larvae hatched, at a temperature of 28° C. The larval attachment apparatus was clearly visible and again sand stuck to the larvae. The yolk sac was greenish and slightly marbled.

After 72 hours the head was visible, and after 96 hours the larval attachment apparatus had lost its function. The eye was not clearly visible. On the 5th day the larvae attempted to swim up, although the yolk sac was not yet completely absorbed. On the 7-8th day the fry finally became free-swimming and began to feed. This proved to be the critical point, as they required immediate feeding but *Artemia* nauplii were too large, such that infusorians or other micro-organisms must be fed. If this hurdle can be overcome then further rearing should present no problems.

Remarks: Poor water quality, unsuitable water chemistry (too high a pH and hardness), and an inadequate diet will encourage the development of skin lesions on the head region, to which this species is very susceptible. For this reason optimal maintenance conditions should be provided, corresponding to the natural conditions, in order to keep these fishes healthy in the long term.

It should in addition be noted that *S. acuticeps* are periodically available in the trade that have a concavity on the head. No plausible explanation of this phenomenon has been offered to date, but it may be the result of the long period of hunger endured by the fishes between being caught and making their homes in our aquaria. This defect can, however be brought under control by a balanced diet and several feeds per day. In general *S. acuticeps* should be fed small amounts several times per day and the aquarist should make sure they actually get enough food, as they are slow and steady feeders and also inefficient food converters. These points all preclude accommodating this species with greedy feeders, as this will sooner or later lead to complications.

Further reading: Weidner (1995a: 141-142; 1997d: 152-157).

Satanoperca daemon
(Heckel, 1840)

Original description: Ann. Wien. Mus. 2 (1): 389-92.

Derivation of scientific name: daemon (Lat.) = spirit, ghost, and, by (ecclesiastical) extension, demon; translation of the Tupi name *jurupari* for this fish.

Distribution: The type locality of *S. daemon* is the Rio Negro in Brazil close to the border with Venezuela (Heckel, 1840). Further localities, in Colombia, are the Rio Inírida near the village of El Remanso (Stalsberg, 1991) and in the Lagune Cerro Mavecure (Hongslo, 1977), as well as in the in the Rio Guarrojo in the drainage of the Rio Viachada (Hongslo, 1972). *S. daemon* can also be found in the Orinoco region in Venezuela, for example in the Rio Guariquito drainage (Evers, 1992), in the state of Guarico, and in Caqo de Quiribana (Ternetz, 1925). Kullander & Ferreira (1988) found the species in the drainage of the Rio Casiquiare, the river that forms a connection between the Amazonas and Orinoco drainages, and in the vicinity of Solano. The species is also found in the Rio Negro (Haseman, 1914; Gosse & Léopold III, 1967; Thayer Expedition) and its tributaries, for example the Rio Uapés (Léopold III & Gosse, 1967); and in the Igarapé Mapiri on the Rio Trombetas (Marlier, 1963) and Lago Manacapuru (Léopold III & Gosse, 1962) in Brazil, although the last two localities must involve confusion with *S. lilith*.

Habitat: *S. daemon* is a blackwater species which prefers slow-flowing, tea-coloured, calm waters with sandy, muddy, or loamy bottoms. These fishes are usually found in shallow bank zones, but they may also frequent deeper areas. Extensive field observations are, however, lacking. The species may also frequent root tangles and stands of plants in order to find shelter from predators. However, Stalsberg found *S. daemon* in fast-flowing water near the township of El Remanso in the state of Guainía in Colombia. Whether this was a temporary exception, or whether *S. daemon* is actually more variable than supposed as regards the current in its habitat, cannot be stated with any certainty at the present time.

Size: In contrast to *S. acuticeps S. daemon* can grow very large in the aquarium, such that an eventual size of almost 30 cm is not unusual in males.

Characters of the species: The three lateral spots, which are present even in juveniles, are an unmistakeable character of this species. While two of these spots lie on the body, the third is on the upper edge of the caudal fin base and is bounded by a light ring. In aggressive specimens the lateral spots become very large, expanding above all in the vertical plane and then extending almost from the caudal base to the belly region. At the same time there may be up to seven additional spots on the back, extending down to the upper lateral line. Between the operculum and the first lateral spot, and at the height of the upper lateral line, there is a band which runs diagonally downwards in the direction of the head. The back and the ventral region appear rather darker than the rest of the body. Depending on mood a number of cross-bands may appear on the forehead, and there may

1. A semi-adult individual of *Satanoperca daemon*.
2. The Caño San Diego in Venezuela. A classic blackwater biotope.
3. *S. daemon* is characterised by three lateral spots.

be two parallel longitudinal lines running from the mouth in the direction of the eye.

The body base colour is green-olive. Some populations develop large reddish areas on the belly with age. The ventral and the anal, as well as the lower half of the caudal, are also red, or at least orange, in many populations. Juveniles are greenish and exhibit rows of iridescent bluish dots on the flanks. The dorsal is slightly bluish and there are numerous reflective reddish dots on the soft part of the fin. Adult males have prolonged anterior dorsal soft rays which are coloured bright red.

Sexual dimorphism: The sexes can be differentiated only on the basis of eventual size, as females remain a few centimetres smaller than males. The first soft dorsal rays may also be more prolonged in males, but this is not a reliable criterion.

Maintenance: *S. daemon* is very much a warmth-loving cichlid which should not be kept at temperatures of less than 26° C, and for which soft (<8° dGH) and acid (pH 4.5-6.5 max.) water is a mandatory requirement for good health. If these parameters are exceeded in the long term then these cichlids may lose their colours and skin lesions will be inevitable. In addition a balanced, very vitamin-rich, diet is essential. Almost any foods will be taken, but despite their size they prefer small foods such as *Mysis*, *Artemia*, and the various sorts of mosquito larvae, to fish and krill. Frozen crustaceans may often be lost via the gills (see also *S.*

Derivation of scientific name: The name is intended to denote the close relationship of this species with *S. daemon*, as Lilith was a nocturnal female demon in Babylonian folklore.

Distribution: *S. lilith* is often sympatric with *S. acuticeps*, and has thus been found near Manaus (Melin *et al.*, 1923) at the confluence of the Rio Negro and the Rio Solimões. Further localities are the Rio Tapajós drainage (Stawikowski *et al.*, 1992; Warzel *et al.*, 1992; own obs., 1996) and the Rio Arapiuns (Stawikowski *et al.*, 1992; own obs., 1996). It has also been reported from the Rio Branco, Rio Trombetas, Rio Uatuma, Rio Aripuana, and the Rio Canuma (by Mayland, 1995).

Habitat: Because *S. lilith* and *S. acuticeps* are often sympatric, *S. lilith* is also a clear- or blackwater fish, although it does not avoid white water either. Naturally the species prefers a fine-grained or muddy substrate, in which it can search for food. It often spends time in areas near submerse vegetation, into which it can retreat if danger threatens. By and large it is found in the immediate vicinity of the shore in places where there are accumulations of wood or leaf litter

1. *Satanoperca lilith* belongs to the most beautiful *Satanoperca* and an aquarium with a group of these fishes is a feast for your eyes.
2. *S. lilith* lacks any patterning on the head.
3. Although the mouth of *S. lilith* is rather large one should feed them fine food, given in small portions several times a day. *S. lilith* is a careful feeder and should not be accompanied with robust and eager species.
4. The characteristic lateral spot is visible in still young individuals of *S. lilith*.

close by. Now and then it is found in smaller streams, e.g. the small igarapés of the lower Tapajós.

The water is relatively acid (pH 5.5-6.5) and correspondingly soft. Only in exceptional circumstances does the conductivity measure more than 50 µS/cm in the natural habitat of *S. lilith*.

Size: *S. lilith* is another species that seems not to grow as large in the aquarium as in the wild, and hence 20-25 cm is a respectable size under aquarium conditions. In the natural habitat, however, these cichlids can attain a size as large as 35 cm. *S. lilith* is thus the largest known *Satanoperca* species.

Characters of the species: For a long time *S. lilith* was known to aquarists as the "one-spot daemon", and regarded as a population of *S. daemon*. And although common names often have no apparent relevance to the fish in question, in this case there was a clear reference to the chief characteristic feature of the species. In contrast to *S. daemon S. lilith* does indeed have just one lateral spot, which is situated on the central flank on or just above the upper lateral line. Like *S. daemon S. lilith* has a usually roundish caudal spot, surrounded by a light ring, on the upper edge of the caudal base. In some populations the caudal spot is more elongate and lies totally on the fin itself.

The base colour is yellow or olive-green with only a few light reflective spots. Individual in neutral coloration exhibit up to six faintly marked vertical bars on the flanks; the lateral spot is sited on the third of these bars. Two parallel light bands run from the lower edge of the eye to the corner of the mouth. A few individuals have very faintly marked traces of bluish spots on the opercula. The ventrals, anal, and the lower part of the caudal are red-orange. There are a number of spots and streaks in the dorsal, arranged in lines or randomly distributed depending on the population concerned. The first soft dorsal rays are somewhat prolonged and their tips are black. These extensions do not attain the dimensions usual in *S. daemon*.

Sexual dimorphism: The sexes can be differentiated only with great difficulty, and even in adults it is a matter more of luck than judgement. Males may have somewhat longer extensions to the first soft dorsal rays. Otherwise the best indication is the lower body profile, which is rather more rounded in females.

Maintenance: In view of the eventual size the aquarium should have a capacity of at least 500 litres. Because stomach contents analyses have almost invariably yielded sand (Goulding, Carvalho, & Ferreira, 1988), the substrate should be as soft as possible, with very fine, rounded, grains. A few hiding-places — bogwood or thick clumps of plants — should be provided as cover, so the fishes have somewhere to retreat to if necessary. The plants should, of course, be properly rooted as otherwise they will very easily be dug up by these cichlids. Plus, only tough plants should be introduced, as *Satanoperca* will invariably nibble at fine-leaved or feathery foliage. The water should be soft (<10° dGH) and at least slightly acid (pH less than 7.0).

Because this species is a typical omnivore, the menu should include vegetable as well as animal food; as dried foods are accepted these can be used to provide for the vegetable element. That apart, any type of frozen or, of course, live food can be offered to *S. lilith*, with small portions fed as often as possible each day, as enormous quantities of food are required for growth. Feeding needs to be spread out over the entire day as one or two feeds per day will not permit these fishes to take in sufficient quantities of food. If there are other fishes in the aquarium then maintenance becomes more difficult, as these tankmates will compete with *S. lilith* for the food. In addition, care is required when feeding frozen *Artemia*, because *S. lilith*, just like *S. acuticeps*, is inclined to take in *Artemia* but eat only some of it, the rest often being ejected uneaten via the gills. *Mysis* and fine krill may be wasted in the same way, such that if greedy tankmates are present it is easy for *S. lilith* to go hungry.

S. lilith appears to be not so susceptible to the skin lesions that regularly occur in the other "spotted" *Satanoperca* species, but nevertheless optimal conditions should always be provided. This species too enjoys the company of conspecifics and thus should be kept only in a group. Besides which, a group of these elegant and rather retiring fishes is far preferable to a hotchpotch of mixed species. If, however, tankmates are desired, then there is a large choice available, as they will not harass even small fishes (5 cm and up). Only rapid-swimming and otherwise unsettling species — plus, of course, aggressive types — should be excluded, as their presence can very quickly send *S. lilith* into an eventually terminal decline.

Breeding behaviour: At present nothing is known of the breeding behaviour of *S. lilith*. It can, however, be assumed that it will not differ markedly from that of *S. acuticeps* and *S. daemon*.

Remarks: *S. lilith* is the largest known member of its genus. Attempts to breed the species may require a degree of experimentation as it cannot be ruled out that they may actually have quite different breeding behaviour. For example, leaf litter could be introduced in case the fishes prefer a transportable substrate.

Further reading: Goulding, Carvalho, and Ferreira (1988); Kullander & Ferreira (1988: 343-355); Mayland (1995: 550); Stawikowski (1989d: 265-266).

Satanoperca jurupari (Heckel, 1840)

Original description: Ann. Wien. Mus. 2 (1): 392-3.

Derivation of scientific name: The name *jurupari* is taken directly from the language of the indigenous local people and means, roughly, "devil".

Distribution: *S. jurupari* is one of the most widespread cichlids in South America, although the taxon may conceal a number of as yet undescribed species. Its distribution encompasses the entire Amazon basin and its northern and southern affluents, including the Rio Negro, the Ucayali drainage in Peru, the upper Rio Paraguay drainage, the Rio Guaporé in Bolivia, and the Orinoco drainage in Venezuela. In addition it has been reported from the Guianas. The type locality is Barra do Rio Negro on the lower course of the Rio Negro. Subsequently a number of rivers have been named: Brazil: Rio Solimões near Tefé (Agassiz, 1865); Obidos (Thayer Expedition, 1865); Rio Guamá (Warzel & Kilian, 1990), Rio Xingú drainage (Stawikowski, 1988) in the Igarapé Nazaré (Bergleiter, 1990); Rio Autaz (Roman, 1914); Rio Tapajós drainage, not only near Santarém (Kilian & Seidel, 1914; Stawikowski *et al.*, 1992) but also upstream to São Luis do Tapajós (Stawikowski *et al.*, 1992); Rio Javarí (Kullander *et al.*, 1984); Rio

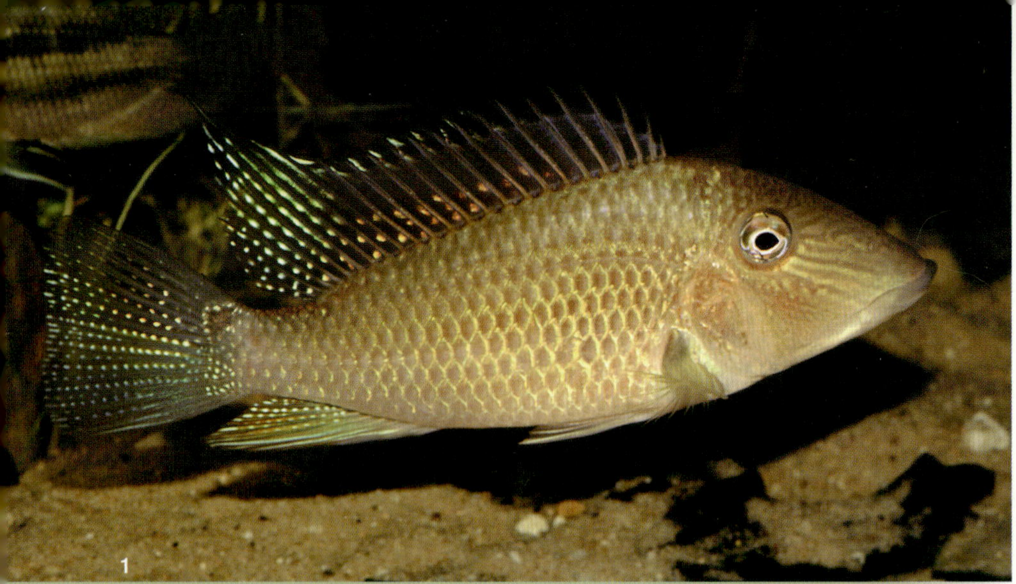
1

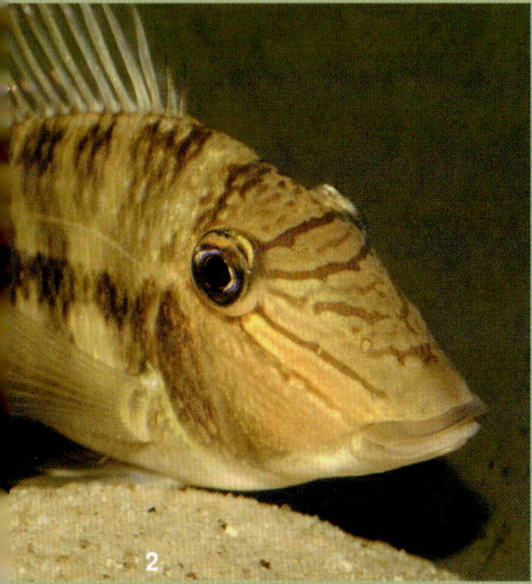
2

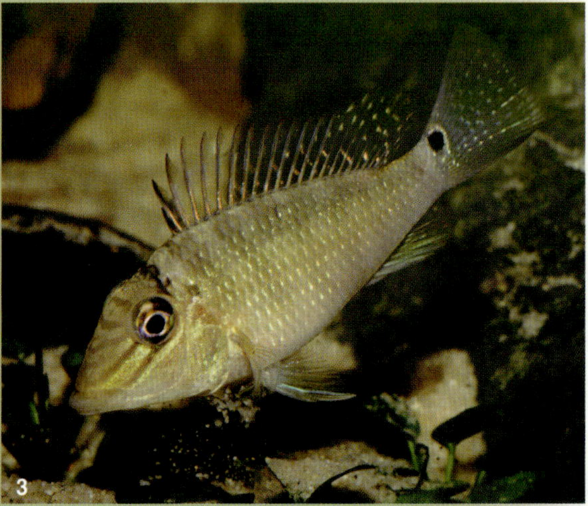
3

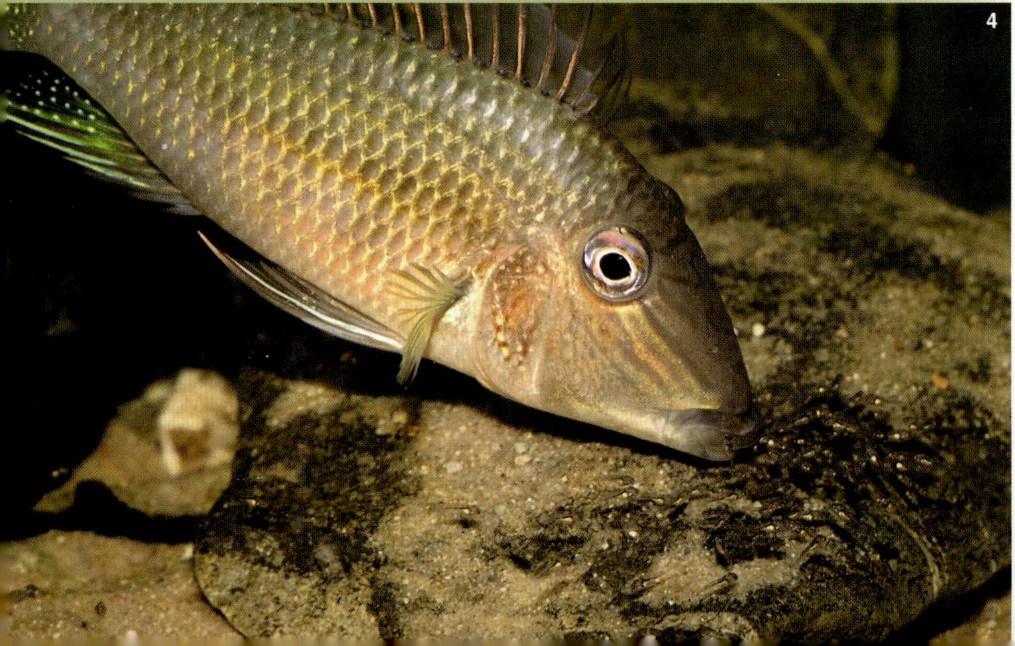
4

1. *Satanoperca jurupari* from the Rio Capim, a small tributary of the Rio Tocantins. These eartheaters can attain a total length of about 25 cm.
2. *S. jurupari* "Rio Capim" with stress pattern.
3. A juvenile *S. jurupari* "Rio Capim".
4. *S. jurupari* are ovophilous maternal mouthbrooders.
5. This *S. jurupari* was imported from Manaus.
6. These specimens from the Rio Xingú are also traded as *S. jurupari*.
7. According to body shape and colour pattern this juvenile eartheater from the Tocantins is a classic *S. jurupari*.
8. The same individual as in the previous photo but now as an adult.

Trombetas (Kilian & Seidel, 1914); Rio Negro drainage (Staeck, 1986); Lago Janaucá (Kullander *et al.*, 1980); Lago Utinga near Belém (A. Werner, 1987); Rio Moju (A. Werner, 1987); Rio Uatuma (Kullander *et al.*, 1987); Rio Tocantins (Goulding, 1983); Rio Itacaiznas; Rio Tefé (Stawikowski, 1993), Rio Curuá (U. Werner *et al.*, 1993); Rio Taciateha (U. Werner, 1994); Rio Gurupi (Andersen, 1994), as well as possibly also in the state of Amapá. Peru: Rio Ucayali (Kullander, 1981; Staeck, 1980); Rio Nanay drainage (Kullander *et al.*, 1981, 1983, and 1984; Urteaga, 1984); Rio Madre de Dios (Kullander *et al.*, 1983); Rio Napo (Kullander *et al.*,

1984); Rio Mazán (Kullander *et al.*, 1984); Rio Yavarí (Hongslo, 1976 and 1971; Kullander *et al.*, 1984); Rio Itaya (Staeck & Linke, 1985); Rio Tahuayo, Rio Putumayo, Rio Samiria, and Rio Corrientes (Kullander *et al.*, 1986); Rio Momon (Newman, 1993); Rio Yarapa (in Newman, 1995). Colombia: Amazon drainage (Hongslo *et al.*, 1971). Paraguay: Rio Paraná drainage (Kullander *et al.*, 1998). Bolivia: Rio Madre de Dios (Loubens & Lauzanne, 1982); Rio Mamoré (Loubens, 1984); Laguna Santa Rosa (Loubens, 1983). French Guiana: Comte River (Westin, 1992), as well as possibly in the Kourou River, the Sinnamary River, and the Approuague River. Venezuela: Rio Guarico drainage (own. obs., 1994) and possibly also the Rio Cuyuni drainage. In the event of a revision some of these populations will probably not be regarded as valid, but if only half of these localities are confirmed then the distribution of *S. jurupari* will still encompass almost the whole of northern South America.

Habitat: Given the enormous area across which *S. jurupari* is found, it is self-evident that a variety of habitats have been colonised by this species. Thus it is found in the immediate vicinity of fast-flowing water, although slow-flowing reaches are preferred, as in such areas the sandy bottom is in places densely vegetated and there are numerous accumulations of wood. *S. jurupari* is not restricted to a particular water type and is found in white-, black-, and clearwaters, with clearwater regions being preferred. The water parameters are equally variable. Conductivity may range from 10 µS/cm to 120 µS/cm, and these fishes are likewise apparently not fussy about the pH value, with values from 4.3 to 7.2 reported from the natural habitat, with hardness ranging from 0 to 8° dGH. Only as regards temperature is *S. jurupari* a little less adaptable, as only values between 25 and 30° C are tolerated in the long term.

Size: Because this species has an improbably large distribution and has thus formed separate populations, the eventual size varies with the population but has a range of 15-25 cm.

Characters of the species: *S. jurupari* has the plainest coloration of all the currently described *Satanoperca* species, although, depending on mood, every population may exhibit a more or less visible pattern of bars on the flanks. Thus, depending on mood, it may be possible to detect a horizontal lateral band that begins at the posterior operculum and ends on the caudal peduncle, as a number of vertical stripes on the flanks — viewed from above, these may be bilaterally offset. There is a more or less large ocellus on the caudal peduncle. Perhaps the most striking character is the head pattern. It is often possible to discern two dark brown or reddish parallel stripes running upwards from the corner of the mouth to the eye. In addition there may be two further parallel dark bars on the forehead, which appear to join the eyes together. Depending on the population the silvery base colour has a yellowish or bluish sheen.

Sexual dimorphism: As with all *Satanoperca* species, size in adults is the only clue.

Maintenance: *S. jurupari* is perhaps the hardiest member of its genus, as it can be kept in hard (20° dGH) and slightly alkaline water in the long term, though soft, slightly acid water is, of course, preferable. A temperature of about 28° C should be regarded as optimal.

S. jurupari should, like other *Satanoperca*, be kept in groups over a substrate of fine sand with bog-wood for cover and muted lighting. The aquarium should be at least 120 cm long. This species is rather more robust than other members of the genus as regards possible tankmates. Smaller species will not be harmed, yet *S. jurupari* are reasonably able to deal with somewhat more aggressive species. Even so, they will not thrive in the company of particularly aggressive species or powerful predators. Feeding presents no problems as this species is an omnivore.

Breeding behaviour: *S. jurupari* is a maternal ovophilous mouthbrooder which maintains a loose pair bond during brood care. Pair formation is extremely peaceful and in some cases barely noticeable. Instead you suddenly notice that the fishes are cleaning their chosen substrate, and spawning begins soon afterwards. The spawning substrate may be a stone or a piece of wood, provided it offers a horizontal surface. During the cleaning of the spawning site the partners circle each other a few times and during this phase synchronise their movements for the actual spawning. While the female busies herself very actively with the future spawning site, the male mainly guards the surrounding area and only sporadically helps with the cleaning of the substrate. Once the latter has been made ready by the female, then spawning follows immediately. Essentially, the eggs are laid in straight lines on the substrate, then fertilised by the male, again in a straight line, and then immediately taken into the mouth cavity of the female.

The actual brood care is exclusively the task of the female. In the aquarium the male always remains in the immediate vicinity, but he does not directly protect the female — this is not in fact necessary as the brooding female always seeks out the quietest part of the aquarium and stays out of the way of other fishes. I have never seen a male brood the eggs or larvae. At 28° C the larvae are released from their mother's mouth for the first time after about 10 days (the time depends on the temperature). At this stage the yolk sac is still clearly evident and the larvae do not take food. After another two days the er's mouth in the event of danger and at night, although by then there will no longer be room for all of them. Shortly afterwards the female ceases brood care and the fry are left to their own devices. They grow rather rapidly such that after a further 14 days they can be fed on lobster eggs and *Cyclops*.

Newman reports that his pair spawned rather high up on a horizontally-positioned root, previously thoroughly cleaned by the female. After a few "dummy runs" the female laid 4 to eight slightly brownish eggs on the root and then swam a little way away from the eggs so that the male could fertilise them. The eggs were somewhat larger and more numerous than those of *S. leucosticta*. After fertilisation the female returned and took the eggs into the protection of her mouth. The entire process was then repeated until after about 90 minutes the female's supply of eggs was exhausted. Thereafter the male showed no further interest in the female, who was left completely on her own. Because the male harassed the female very severely she ate the spawn. The male also behaved so oppressively after other spawnings with other females that successful breeding was never achieved. Newman describes his fishes as polygynous ovophilous mouthbrooders.

1. *Satanoperca pappaterra* with a bluish ground colour from an unknown locality. Photo: Uwe Werner.
2. *S. pappaterra* from Porto Velho.
3. Freshly caught *S. pappaterra* from the Pocóne, Mato Grosso, Brazil. Photo: Uwe Werner
4. *S. pappaterra* (from Porto Velho) spawn in a manner similar to that seen among many East African cichlids.

yolk has been absorbed to the point where feeding with *Artemia* nauplii can begin. For up to eight days thereafter the fry are taken into the moth-

Remarks: The photos illustrate a number of populations, perhaps even undescribed species, which vary slightly in their mode of brood care and in their markings.

Further reading: Kullander (1986: 147-154); Newman (1995: 6-11).

Satanoperca pappaterra (Heckel, 1840)

Original description: Ann. Wien. Mus. 2 (1): 396-399.

Derivation of scientific name: *pappaterra* is the name used by the people of the Mato Grosso for this fish, and translates as "eartheater".

Distribution: The type locality is the Rio Guaporé. The distribution of *S. pappaterra* lies in southern Brazil in Mato Grosso, specifically in the Pantanal at Poconé, in the Teles Pires, and in the Xingú drainage (Werner, pers. comm.), in the Rio Paraguay drainage (Staeck, 1986), and in the Rio Guaporé drainage (Heckel, 1840; Kullander *et al.*, 1989). Additional localities are the Rio typical of the species.

It cannot be ruled out that *S. pappaterra* has a wider distribution than hitherto assumed. Fishes which bear a close resemblance to this species are sometimes found in the main Amazon basin.

An extract from Kullander (1986), "The Cichlid Fishes of the Amazon River Drainage of Peru" nicely demonstrates the close relationship between *S. pappaterra* and *S. jurupari*, but also indicates the difficulty of determining the species within the *S. jurupari* complex:

"*Satanoperca* material from the Madre de Dios system cannot be distinguished specifically from *S. jurupari* in the Ucayali-Amazonas drainage. There are slight colour and shape differences, but not appreciably greater than amongst Ucayali-Amazonas *S. jurupari* from different localities. I have examined limited material of *S. pappaterra* from the Guaporé drainage, which differs from *S. jurupari* in having a contrasted colour pattern of black blotches along the side and back, the axial blotch series usually contained in a contrasted blackish band. Expect for coloration, I am unaware of any discrete distinguishing characters from *S. jurupari*. Haseman (1911) regarded colour differences in his *Satanoperca* material from the Paraguay, Mamoré, Guaporé, Manaus and Santarém as reflecting different water conditions and ontogenetic changes. Collections of *G. jurupari* from various biotopes in the Ucayali-Amazonas drainage would seem to support such a view, but the magnitude of variation referred to by Haseman is much greater than that amongst *S. jurupari s. s.*" KULLANDER

1. *Satanoperca leucosticta* from Guyana.
2. *S. leucosticta* spawning on a leaf.
3. After spawning *S. leucosticta* conceal their spawn with sand.

Satanoperca leucosticta
(Müller & Troschel, 1849)

Original description: in: Schomburgk, 1849, Reisen in British-Guiana in den Jahren 1840-1844. Part 3; Leipzig: 625.

Derivation of scientific name: *leucos* (Gr.) = white; *stiktos* (Gr.) = spotted, referring to the light reflective spots on the head, also on the dorsum in some populations.

Distribution: A widely distributed species in the Guianas. *S. leucosticta* is found both in Surinam (Nickerie

233

and Corantijn drainages) and Guyana (Demerara, Mahaica, and Mahaiconi, and Essequibo drainages). The type locality of the species is Lake Amucu in Guyana (Kullander & Nijssen, 1989). In redescribing the species Kullander & Nijssen (1989) used specimens from the Stondansi Val area in Surinam. It cannot be ruled out that the species occupies an appreciably wider distribution. Thus Kullander has also identified as *S. leucosticta* specimens in the Natural History Museum, Stockholm, from Colombia (Rio Orinoco drainage: Rio Inírida, Caño Conejo; Rio Metá drainage: Rio Yucao, Rio Manacacías; Rio Vichada drainage: Rio Guarroyo), Brazil (Rio Negro drainage: Puerto Samariapo). Because the Rio Branco in Brazil is connected with the Rio Essequibo system in Guyana, at least during the rainy season, it cannot be ruled out that *S. leucosticta* might also be found in this region (Chefalo, 1988) and in other Brazilian river systems. Whether these specimens will still be assigned to *S. leucosticta* after a further revision remains to be seen.

Habitat: The habitat of *S. leucosticta* is in the rivers of the coastal lowlands of Surinam and Guyana, where it inhabits woodland, savannah, and marshland streams. Despite the proximity of the coast the water is very soft.

Specimens caught in Colombia by Hongslo & Cruz (1972) were found in an inundated stream with clear, still, tea-coloured water. The bottom consisted of partially flooded grassland and scrub as well as the roots of large trees.

Size: Some populations can attain up to 25 cm.

Characters of the species: *S. leucosticta* can be distinguished from all other *Satanoperca* species by the absence of any dark elements on the body and head. There is only a small black caudal spot, occupying just a few scales, on the caudal peduncle, and, depending on mood, a faint lateral band may be seen on the flank. The cheeks, from the mouth to the posterior edge of the operculum, are covered in countless small whitish or iridescent bluish spots, often on a reddish background, and in some populations they may also extend onto the back. There are no white spots on the forehead, though there are often red-brown lines on a light background. The flanks are silvery blue-grey. The unpaired fins are patterned with whitish dots and streaks on a reddish or bluish background. The tips of the dorsal spines are black.

Sexual dimorphism: As in the case of many other eartheaters, the sexes in this species are very difficult to differentiate. In general males grow somewhat larger and have more prolonged fins. Females often exhibit a very short blunt genital papilla for long periods while in males the genital papilla is very pointed and relatively long, and appears only shortly before spawning.

Maintenance: Basically the same maintenance conditions apply to *S. leucosticta* as for other *Satanoperca*: a decor which includes plenty of wood, a few stones, and a fine sandy substrate, and maintenance in a small group, will be a good approximation of the natural environment. In addition leaf litter should also be included when keeping this species — this should be boiled beforehand. These fishes do not require leaves for their general well-being, but a transportable substrate is obligatory for breeding.

Because plants are not molested, a few well-rooted plants (choose species with a low light requirement as *S. leucosticta* does not particularly enjoy bright light) can be included. Although higher plants are not eaten, vegetable food in the form of scalded lettuce or boiled Brussels sprouts should be offered. Naturally the green food requirement can also be satisfied using a suitable dried food, and this will be eaten without demur. The species should be fed as varied a diet as possible, as in contrast to *S. jurupari*, *S. pappaterra*, and *S. mapiritensis*, *S. leucosticta* is rather prone to skin lesions; moreover for this reason excessively high pH (over 7.5) and hardness (more than 12° dGH) should be avoided. The aquarium itself should have a minimum length of 150 cm and a capacity of at least 350 litres.

Breeding behaviour: *S. leucosticta* is an ovophilous mouthbrooder which requires a movable substrate for breeding and takes its eggs into the mouth at a later stage. Small pieces of wood, leaves, or even cork insoles (as long as they sink!) will do. The important thing is that the intended substrate should not be too heavy and can be moved with the mouth. The best leaves are those which can be collected in autumn, and they should be boiled before they are introduced into the aquarium. The most suitable types are maple or beech leaves, which will slightly acidify the water and colour it brownish. The humic acid they contain will help prevent the eggs from

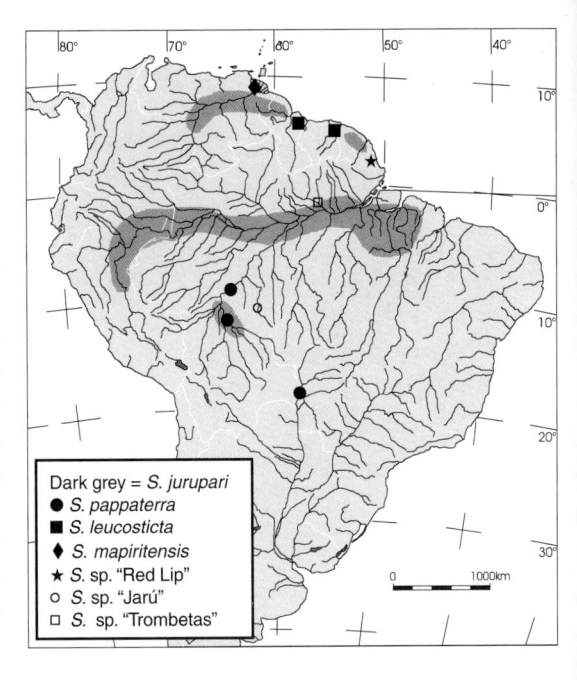

Dark grey = *S. jurupari*
● *S. pappaterra*
■ *S. leucosticta*
♦ *S. mapiritensis*
★ *S.* sp. "Red Lip"
○ *S.* sp. "Jarú"
□ *S.* sp. "Trombetas"

235

fungussing. Oak leaves are less suitable as they may acidify the water too much. The leaves should not be too small, bearing in mind that they may have to accommodate a clutch of up to 500 eggs.

If the leaves are introduced into the aquarium retrospectively, then immediately a sort of unrest can be observed among the ripe females. They threaten one another and there may sometimes be harmless quarrels. Once a female has laid claim to a leaf then she will court the male, who will previously have paid no attention to the future spawning site even if pairing has already taken place. From this point on the pair bond will, however, be obvious, as now both partners clean the spawning substrate almost immediately. Usually the substrate is transported to a quiet spot where the pair will be relatively undisturbed. The cleaning is interrupted by lateral threat and enemies are chased away by both parents. Once the substrate is prepared to the satisfaction of both future parents, then

1. *Satanoperca leucosticta* are best kept in large groups.
2. Gottwald, Seva and Zucker caught this *Satanoperca*, with a strong resemblance to *S. leucosticta*, near Rorainopolis, Roraima, Brazil (Rio Branco drainage). Photo: Antoine Seva

spawning takes place fairly soon after. The female deposits a batch of 4-8 eggs which in turn are fertilised by the male. If, however, there are enemies in the vicinity then the role of the male is to drive away these intruders. In this case the eggs are fertilised later.

The location of the leaf or other substrate plays a subordinate role. In essence a horizontal position is preferred, but spawning can take place at an angle of 45 or even 60 degrees. If the substrate drifts into a more vertical position then the parents tug it back to the horizontal. Once the spawning is finished then the substrate is covered in sand as camouflage. The parents now alternate in the tending of the spawn, hovering either over it or in the immediate vicinity and fanning fresh water over the eggs with the pectoral fins. After as little as about 24 hours the eggs are uncovered by both parents and taken into the protection of their mouths. Because no eggshells remain on the substrate the species is a (delayed) ovophilous mouthbrooder.

Over the next 2-3 days both parents spend most of their time in the shelter of a piece of wood. They

237

next take turns at the brood care, so that both of them can feed during the brooding period. The free-swimming fry are controlled and directed by jerking movements of the fins.

On the fifth day after first release the degree of brood care visibly diminishes. Initially the fry are left outside the mouth for increasingly longer periods, until eventually they are taken in only at times of extreme danger and at night. And because of their growth they soon no longer all fit into the parental mouths. After 14 days brood care is completely ended.

The young can take newly-hatched *Artemia* immediately, and after 14 days they can already manage lobster eggs and *Bosmina*. Given ample feeding the young can attain 2 cm in as little as a month, although the switch from live to "dead" (frozen and dried) food requires a degree of patience.

According to Rütz (1992) *S. leucosticta* has developed a special method of feeding its offspring. The parents dig little pits in exposed places where the water circulation will cause small particles (e.g. live *Artemia* nauplii) to accumulate. The young are then deliberately led to these "larders" where they find plenty of food.

Newman describes his fishes as ovophilous biparental mouthbrooders. At each session of egglaying the female laid 10-20 slightly brownish, rather elongated, eggs on a leaf, but the male fertilised these only after every second or third pass. The very close-packed spawn eventually numbered about 200 eggs. Newman too found that the spawn was concealed with a thin layer of sand and fanned by both parents, and his subsequent observations correspond with those recorded above.

Neumann (1999), however, describes his fishes as larvophilous biparental mouthbrooders. In addition he established that after the first spawning unpaired individuals stole some of the larvae, but the true parents kept stealing them back until eventually they brooded them alone.

In 1976 Cichocki was able to observe this species (which he calls *Geophagus jurupari*) brooding in the Rupununi and in the Essequibo drainage. He was able to follow the brood care of two pairs simultaneously in the bank region of Grani Pond. One pair had laid 1122 eggs on a shoe insole (!) while the other had attached 477 eggs to a small piece of wood. Both clutches were covered with a thin layer of sand. After spawning both pairs dragged their spawn into deeper water, covering a distance of several metres in the process and with the female always remaining close to the eggs during transportation and the male defending the territory. The next day both parents and substrates had vanished. Near Bartica, in a small tidal stream that emptied into the Essequibo, Cichocki was able to observe another pair who dragged their spawn, in this case deposited on a mangrove leaf, back into shallow water when the tide came in.

On the basis of these observations it can be assumed that the species has optimised its mode of brood care in order to be able to transport its eggs to safety in areas influenced by the tides or by general variations in water level. The mouthbrooding is undoubtedly a step towards compensating for variations in water level.

Remarks: It may be that the brood care behaviour described does not apply to all populations, as, on the basis of our current knowledge, the species' distribution extends over a wide area such that differences in breeding behaviour may have evolved.

Further reading: Cichocki (1976); Kullander & Nijssen (1989: 66-73); Mücke (1992: 232-235); Neumann (1999: 237); Newman (1998: 1-6); Rütz (229-231); Schaefer (1992: 237); Steinmann (1992: 236); Weidner (1995d: 134-140). The following references purport to refer to S. jurupari, but must, however, actually relate to S. leucosticta: Schumann (1975a: 39-43; 1975b: 86-88); Thomas (1973: 370-373).

Satanoperca mapiritensis (Fernandez-Yepez, 1950)

Original description: Mem. Soc. Cienc. Nat. La Salle, Caracas, 10 (26): 117-118.

Derivation of scientific name: This species was named after the type locality, the Rio Mapirito in Venezuela.

Distribution: To date the distribution of this species has not been clearly defined. It is true that the species is found in the Rio Mapirito in northeastern Venezuela, between the Paria peninsula and the Caño Manamo, the most northerly channel of the Orinoco delta (Mayland, 1995), but the limits of its range to the south and west are as yet unknown.

Habitat: Ploeger visited the area of the type locality in 1996 and describes the habitat thus (translated from the German original): "As I balanced on a fallen palm trunk which lay across the small, fast-flowing river, I discovered a group of adult devilfishes (*Satanoperca* sp.) in the deeper water. The clearance associated with the building of the bridge meant there was no shade from trees, hence water plants — *Heteranthera zosterifolia* and *Najas* sp. — as well as a group of submerse waterlilies (*Nymphaea* sp) were thriving on the sandy, in places muddy, river bottom." Unfortunately Ploeger (1997) does not mention water parameters, as these would doubtless have been extremely interesting as this was a tidal zone. But we can nevertheless assume that this species too is a typical softwater cichlid.

Size: Because to date no imports definitely from this region have reached Germany no definitive statement can be made as regards the eventual size of these fishes. However, this species probably grows to somewhere around the 20 cm mark.

Characters of the species: In contrast to *S. leucosticta*, which is the species most similar to this one, *S. mapiritensis* has a deeper body, fleshier lips, and an extremely fine and close-packed pattern of light, almost whitish, iridescent spots on the cheeks, extending from the lower jaw to the eye. The forehead is devoid of such markings. There is a small spot, occupying only a few scales, on the upper edge of the caudal base. The body base colour is a silvery beige, on which dots are arranged in longitudinal lines. Mayland (1995) has a photo of *S.* sp. cf. *mapiritensis*. If this fish should turn out actually to be *S. mapiritensis* then it will be easily recognisable by its twin-pointed caudal fin.

Sexual dimorphism: Males probably grow larger and have more prolonged unpaired fins and ventrals.

Maintenance: This species will not differ particularly from other members of the genus as regards its maintenance.

Breeding behaviour: Because there are no reliable records of this species being maintained in the aquarium, nothing is known of its breeding behaviour.

Further reading: Mayland (1995: 550); Ploeger (1997: 34-39); Schaefer (1992: 237).

Satanoperca sp. "Redlip"
or
Satanoperca sp. "French Guiana"
or
Satanoperca sp. "Amapá"

Distribution: To date this species has been found only in the state of Amapá, Brazil, as well as in French Guiana, which begs the question of how far its range extends to the west. Confirmed localities in Guiana are Kafisoca on the Oyapock, Crique Cacao (a tributary of the Comte), Crique Deflots, and the Approuague (von Drachenfels & Gottwald, pers. comm). Planquette (1982, 1986) and Le Bail (1984) also found this species in the Approuague drainage. Planquette (1984) also caught this species further west in the Maroni and Sinnamary drainages. I myself found the species in 1999 in Crique Boulanger near the township of Cacao in Guiana. We (Dotzer, Neumann, & Weidner) were also able to find this species in the Sinnamary reservoir, although those specimens appeared to differ somewhat from the Boulanger individuals and those from the Approuague-Oyapock drainage, in that the lips were not so intensely red and they also had somewhat different head markings.

In Brazil, Stawikowski *et al.* (pers. comm.) found this species in the state of Amapá in the Rio Amapá Grande drainage, in a *cachoeira*

1. *Satanoperca mapiritensis* from Venezuela. Noticeable are the fine, closely set spots on the cheeks and the high dorsal fin.
2. A freshly caught *Satanoperca* sp. "Red Lip" from the Rio Uaçá drainage. Note the red-coloured lips. Photo: Rainer Stawikowski.
3. *Satanoperca* sp. "Red Lip" from unknown locality. Photo: Hans-J. Mayland.

(rapids) about 3 km upstream of the bridge on the BR-156 road. They also caught the species in the Rio Macari and the Oyapock. Goulding (1984) found this species in the Rio Amapá, in inundated forest above the Cachoeira Grande.

Habitat: Stawikowski et al. describe the Rio Uaga, a tributary of the Rio Uruaca, as a shallow forest stream with fast-flowing clear water over a sandy substrate. In places the bottom was covered with mud and the biotope was affected by a few fallen tree-trunks. This species was found in the immediate vicinity of a *cachoeira* in the Rio Amapá Grande (Stawikowski et al., 1989, pers. comm) and the Rio Amapá (Goulding, 1984). Stawikowski et al., 1989, pers. comm.) also found this species in a right-bank tributary of the Oyapock, in shallow water over a sandy bottom. The bank zone of the section in question was vegetated with aquatic plants. From these observations one may conclude that the species has a general preference for moderately fast-flowing clear water.

Von Drachenfels (pers. comm.) found this species in the tidal zone of the Crique Deflots in water with a conductivity of 560 µS/cm, hence we may assume that it also thrives in hard and slightly alkaline water.

Crique Boulanger is a small stream with a moderate current and slightly brownish water flowing over a sandy or gravelly bottom. In 1999 a number of large stones formed little barriers over which the water ran somewhat more rapidly. At the end of the dry season the water temperature measured about 28° C. A number of roots and branches extended into the water and provided the fishes with cover. It was noticeable that adults of about 12 cm were seen only in pairs, moving over the sand and feeding, while younger individuals, while not actually shoaling, swam in small groups through the crystal-clear water. The population density was high. *S.* sp. "Redlip" shared this habitat with a quite unimaginable number of characins. The cichlids we found included *Crenicichla saxatilis*, *Krobia* sp. "Redeye", and a few small *Cleithracara maronii* (pers. obs., 1999).

The individuals that we caught in the Sinnamary reservoir were in a sorry state. The water temperature was at least 32° C and the severely emaciated fishes were found near the shore by a slipway used for oil changes and heavy work. Hence there was a thick film of oil all over the surface of the bay. The bottom consisted of a certain amount of sand but was mainly composed of such products of civilisation as cans, bits of glass, paper, plastic containers, and old tyres. In other parts of the reservoir the bottom was rather cleaner, but at every step the powdery red laterite created a cloud of particles which still hadn't settled after 30 minutes of waiting, as there was no water circulation. A biotope that is doomed thanks to Man.

Size: A length of 20 cm should be regarded as the minimum likely eventual size for this rather large species.

Characters of the species: Without doubt the most typical character of this species, and the one responsible for one of its names, is the orange to red colour of the lips and corners of the mouth. This can vary in intensity depending on the population concerned. In addition these eartheaters exhibit two to three rein-like stripes on the side of the head. In some individuals these stripes are interrupted, while in others there are traces of additional stripes on the head. There are two horizontal stripes on the head between the eyes. Depending on mood there may be seven vertical stripes on the flanks, sometimes interrupted approximately at the level of the upper lateral line. In addition these fishes may also exhibit a lateral band running from the operculum to the caudal peduncle. The peduncular spot is small but always clearly visible. There are a few indistinct reflective spots on the operculum. In the right light the ventral region is silvery, while the flanks from the lower lateral line to the back may have a beautiful metallic brass-coloured sheen. Otherwise the flanks appear slightly greenish.

The body is moderately elongate and the eyes are set relatively high on the very elongate-looking head. In general the body form resembles the norm for the genus. The fins are transparent and have no characteristic markings.

Sexual dimorphism: As in other *Satanoperca* species there are no secondary sexual characteristics.

Maintenance: Although von Drachenfels saw these fishes in a tidal region, they evidently prefer soft, slightly acid water, and the red lips are more prominent in such conditions. There are no special requirements as regards aquarium layout, nor are they particularly fussy as regards feeding. Plants are not eaten, but vegetable food should nevertheless be provided. This is best achieved using a dried food with a vegetable base. Like other *Satanoperca* they prefer rather fine foods, which should, however, be fed in large quantities.

Breeding behaviour: According to Gottwald (pers. comm.) this species is a biparental mouthbrooder. The eggs were picked up immediately by the female during the spawning and brooded by her alone for the next two days, but then the eggs/larvae (?) were transferred to the male. From then on the parents alternated in the brooding. The female was separated off five days after spawning so that no further observations of the role of the male could be made.

There are no problems as regards rearing, as he fry can take *Artemia* Nauplii on their first day of free-swimming.

Further reading: Goulding (1984).

Satanoperca sp. "Jarú"

Distribution: This species was found by Uwe Werner and his companions in the Rio Jarú. Further investigations are required to establish whether this species also occurs in the Rio Aripuana and the Rio Juma. In 1988 Minde (pers. comm.) caught this species about 50 km to the north of Porto Velho in a left-bank tributary of the Rio Madeira.

Habitat: Werner and his companions caught this species among stones and wood in slightly turbid water in a still side-arm and in the main channel of the Rio Jarú. The bottom was black sand. No data regarding the water parameters are available.

Unfortunately Minde (1988; pers. comm) was likewise unable to provide any water parameter data. The biotope, as reported by Minde, was a slow-flowing river with very murky water. The river broadened increasingly downstream of a bridge and then flowed through an area of low scrub before splitting into channels between reeds and islands of grass and finally emptying into the Rio Madeira. Minde described the area as being like moorland. The only syntopic ichthyofauna he was able to discover was a wimple piranha (*Catoprion mento*) and an *Aequidens* species.

Size: The specimens maintained in aquaria have to date attained a maximum of 22 cm.

1. *Satanoperca* sp. "Jarú".
2. *Satanoperca* sp. "Trombetas" possess a few but relatively large bluish spots on the cheek. Another character is found in the finely spotted caudal peduncle.
3. An irregular pattern of blotches and an incomplete midlateral stripe form the coloration of *S.* sp. "Trombetas" in an aggressive mood.

Characters of the species: *S.* sp. "Jarú" does not differ in form from *S. jurupari*, and there are only minimal differences as regards body pattern. Depending on mood there are up to seven narrow vertical bands on a silvery background; the beginnings of these are always visible above all on the back. In aggressive individuals there is a midlateral longitudinal band running from the posterior edge of the operculum to the start of the caudal peduncle. There is a rather small caudal spot, only partially surrounded by a lighter zone, on the upper part of the caudal peduncle. Depending on the angle of the light the flanks may have a silvery or blue-green sheen, and the dark centres of the scales give the impression of a reticulated pattern.

The most characteristic feature of this species is the head pattern. There is a pattern of lines on the forehead, which blend into an irregular vermiculate pattern. The background

245

Gymnogeophagus de Miranda-Ribeiro, 1918

Derivation of scientific name: *gymnos* (Gr.) = naked; *geos* (Gr.) = earth; *phagein* (Gr.) = eat; referring to the close relationship with the eartheaters of the Amazon region, from which they differ, however, in having an unscaled (= naked) anterior body. The genus, as originally defined, was thought to differ from the closely-related Amazonian *Geophagus* (at that time including *Satanoperca*) by having an unscaled head — it is now known that some Amazonian geophagines also exhibit this feature, and the genus has been redefined accordingly.

Distribution: The distribution of *Gymnogeophagus* starts in the southern part of the Amazonian region and includes southern Brazil, eastern Paraguay, plus Uruguay and northern Argentina, including the La Plata basin.

Ecology: *Gymnogeophagus* by preference inhabit calmer sections of rivers in which there are large areas of submerse vegetation. Large rivers are generally avoided, and if they are found in such waters then it is in the rather slower-flowing reaches. Instead the main habitats are flooded grasslands, lakes, lagoons, and also smaller streams. The bottom may be

1. This small brook — width about 80 cm — flows near Centurion, Uruguay. Its banks were partially rocky. Photo: Tonny Brandt Andersen.
2. These aquarium fishes are difficult to identify, either as *G. meridionalis* or as *G. rhabdotus*, because their collection locality is not known. Their caudal fin exhibits vertical as well as horizontal stripes. Photo: Uwe Werner

sandy or muddy and also include rocky areas. Accumulations of dead wood are also present and provide the fishes with cover.

Because of the southerly distribution climatic variations during the course of the year are noticeable. This fact should be borne in mind as regards the aquarium and the fishes should be kept for at least two months of the year in rather cool water (12-15° C). The fishes will then be livelier and more inclined to spawn. Temperatures above 25° C are to be strictly avoided. The water in these regions is not as soft and acid as is the case in some parts of the Amazon region, although pH values above 7.5 and hardness in excess of 10° dGH are rarely encountered.

Characters of the genus: Unfortunately the type species of the genus, *G. balzanii*, is somewhat atypical of the general pattern that characterises *Gymnogeophagus*. While all other members of the genus can be recognised by an only moderately ascending upper head profile and an elongate body, and show no pattern of vertical stripes in their normal coloration and are also relatively colourful, none of these points applies to

249

the type species. Dominant male *Gymnogeophagus* may exhibit a hint of a nuchal hump.

In contrast to members of the genus *Geophagus*, *Gymnogeophagus* exhibit marked sexual dimorphism which is already apparent in semi-adult individuals. Males are more colourful, while females exhibit only a more or less prominent black pattern on a grey to sand-coloured base. In addition *Gymnogeophagus* generally do not grow as large as *Geophagus*.

Ethology: Except during the spawning period *Gymnogeophagus* are extremely shy and retiring cichlids, which enjoy the company of their own kind in the aquarium and also form small groups in the natural habitat. It cannot be ruled out that some species form colonies and may incline towards harem-formation (Kirsten, 1991), although a certain distance is always maintained between individuals. During the breeding season females in particular can be very aggressive towards other occupants of the aquarium and also males who neglect to defend the territory may suffer at their partner's "hands". Injuries are, however, rare and almost never serious.

Within the genus there are only larvophilous mouthbrooders and open-brooders ("concealed-spawning open-brooders") that select a protected spot as their spawning site.

If these fishes are to be kept with other species, then it should be borne in mind when choosing tankmates that no bullies or boisterous species should be included. The best choice is other eartheaters, loricariid catfishes, and various characins, always bearing in mind the temperature requirements of the *Gymnogeophagus*.

All species can be regarded as omnivorous, which, even though they do not harm plants, should be provided with vegetable matter in the aquarium as otherwise they may suffer from deficiency diseases.

Remarks: All members of the genus should never be kept at constant temperatures, but maintained at temperatures of less than 20 °C for at least two months per year. The fishes will reward their owner for this with better colours, increased vitality and readiness to spawn. It is very easy to provide optimal conditions for *Gymnogeophagus* by keeping them in the summer months in a garden pond. During the winter months, however, they should be kept cool again, as otherwise with high room temperatures they will experience two "summers" per year, which would again be detrimental to their health.

G. cyanopterus was designated as the type species of this genus, but that species is now regarded as a synonym of *G. balzanii*.

Further reading: Darda (1995a: 4-7; 1995b: 17-18; 1997a: 22-26); Hensel (1870); Kirsten (1991: 168-171); Reis & Malabarba (1988).

Gymnogeophagus australis
(Eigenmann, 1907)

Original description: Proc. Wash. Acad. Sci. 8: 454.

Derivation of scientific name: *australis* (Lat.) = southern, referring to the distribution of the species.

Dark grey = *G. balzanii*
● *G. australis*
■ *G. gymnogenys*
○ *G. labiatus*
♦ *G. lacustris*
□ *G.* sp. "Rosario I + II"

Distribution: The distribution encompasses northern Argentina and Uruguay. According to Gosse (1975) the type specimens originated from Cerro Largo, Montevideo, Uruguay (Felippone, 1932) and from the Rio Santa Lucia, Dept. Canelones, Uruguay (Barattini, 1935), as well as Rosario Santa Fé, Paraná, Argentina (Arnold, 1937), from the Ludena Park, Rosario, Pcia. de Santa Fé (Ministry of Agriculture, 1946), and from the Rio Uruguay near Conception del Uruguay (Siccardi, 1947). Aschenbach found this species in the Largo del Parque Sud, Ciudad Santa Fé (1960) and in Arroyo Colorado, Dept. La Capital, Pcia. de Santa Fé (1958). In 1966 Foerster found *G. australis* in the Rio Soberbio, Missiones, Argentina. According to Eigenmann (1907) the type locality is Buenos Aires, which begs the question whether this means the city or the state.

Habitat: According to Schulz (1988) it would appear that a number of the known *G. australis* biotopes no longer exist (Cerro Largo, Montevideo, Uruguay) or are in a shocking ecological condition (Lago del Parque Sud, Santa Fé, Argentina. The Rio Santa Lucia at Montevideo contained murky, milky-coffee-coloured water, while further northwest in the direction of Rincon de Buschental it was very fast-flowing and hence he was able to fish only near the bank. He was unable to find *G. australis* in either place. Further attempts in the vicinity of Santa Fé, in both small streams and lagoons, were likewise unsuccessful (Stawikowski & Werner, 1988).

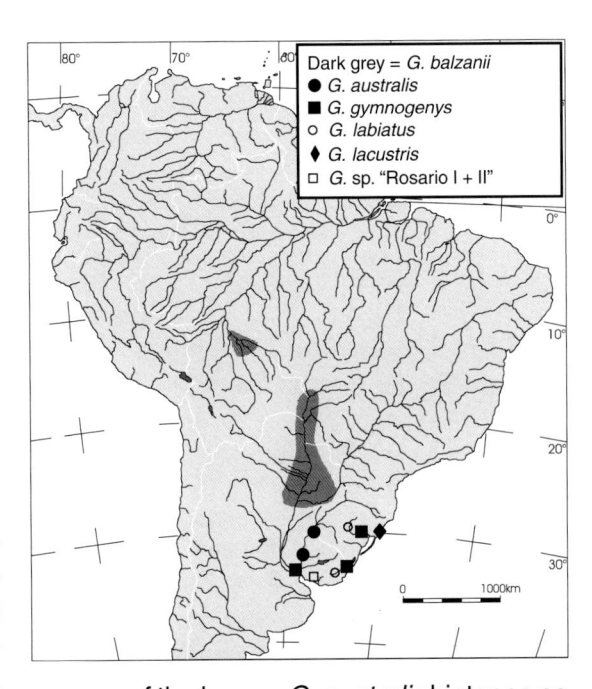

Size: The largest of Eigenmann's specimens measured 15.5 cm.

1. This *Gymnogeophagus* could be the elusive *G. australis*. The photo shows a female of *G.* cf. *australis*.
2. A male *Gymnogeophagus* cf. *australis*.
3. An adult male *Gymnogeophagus balzanii*. Photo: Rainer Stawikowski.

Characters of the species: No reliable data on live coloration are available at present. According to Reis & Malabarba (1988) preserved specimens have no lateral or caudal peduncle spot. There is a dark area on the back anterior to the dorsal fin. The bases of a few scales on the back are dark brown. Six vertical bars on the body, splitting into double bars with light intervals on the central flank. The pectorals are transparent, the ventrals blue-black; the dorsal is dusky with ascending light stripes which are replaced by light spots on the soft part of the fin. The caudal is likewise dark, with round glassy (transparent) dots on the soft rays, similar to those on the soft dorsal. The anal has comparable, but smaller and less numerous, little dots. Gosse regarded *G. australis* as being closely related to *G. balzanii*, but lacking the steep upper head profile; and distinguished from *G. gymnogenys* by its coloration.

Darda and U. Werner purchased fishes (via the trade) which share a series of characteristics with *G. australis* and which will here be designated as *G.* sp. cf. *australis*. A striking feature of these fishes is the double bands on the lower flanks, exhibited only by females and reminiscent of *G. balzanii*. Males, however, are more like *G. gymnogenys* in both markings and body form, except that *G.* sp. cf. *australis* are in general rather paler, the yellow forehead is completely absent, and the spotted pattern of the tail is not so prominent. In addition *G.* sp. cf. *australis* lack the interorbital bars, although the subocular stripe is clearly visible. The black markings are identical to those of *G. gymnogenys*.

Sexual dimorphism: Should Darda and Werner's fishes turn out actually to be *G. australis*, then males will have a clearly more steeply ascending upper head profile, sometimes even developing a nuchal hump, and are all in all more colourful, while females have the typical *G. australis* barring on a silvery-beige background. The sexual dimorphism and dichromatism are striking.

Maintenance: *G. australis* should be maintained in the same manner as other members of the genus. Darda (pers. comm.) reports that *G.* sp. cf. *australis* requires a regeneration period of a few weeks at a very low temperature (about 5° C).

Breeding behaviour: The fishes that Darda obtained via the trade spawn in the same manner as *G. rhabdotus* (see below). However, all the fry reared turned out to be females. Why this should have occurred has not been established. It may be that too high a temperature may have been responsible, as the proportions of the sexes in other geophagine cichlids, e.g. *Apistogramma nijsseni* (Römer, 1989), are dependent on temperature.

Remarks: It is at present unclear whether *G. australis* is a valid species, as the holotype is lost, the fishes can no longer be found at the type locality, and the redescription by Reis & Malabarba (1988) was on the basis of the paratypes, although these were totally faded.

Further reading: Darda (1977a: 22-26); Gosse (1975: 133-138); Reis & Malabarba (1988: 259-305); Römer (1989: 74-77); Stawikowski & Werner (1988: 177-180).

Gymnogeophagus balzanii (Perugia, 1891)

Original description: Ann. Mus. Civ. Stor. Nat. Genova, 2, 10: 623-624.

Derivation of scientific name: In honour of the collector, Professor Luigi Balzan, who provided Perugia with the type material.

Distribution: The type material originates from the Rio Paraguay at Villa Maria in the Brazilian state of Mato Grosso (Gosse, 1975). The species is otherwise rather widely distributed, and is found in the Rio Guaporé (Haseman, 1909) and in the Rio Paraguay drainage (Gosse, 1975; Haseman, 1909); Kullander *et al.*, 1992, 1993, 1995, 1996, 1998; Ahlander 1999). This species is also be found in the Rio Pilcomayo (Kullander *et al.*, 1994), as well as in the Rio Paraná drainage in the Rio Riachuelo (Körber, 1995) plus the Rio Uruguay system, Rio Grande do Sul (Gosse, 1975).

Habitat: *G. balzanii* inhabits almost exclusively slow-flowing or still waters such as ditches, ponds, swamps, or flooded grasslands. It can, however, also be found in the quieter parts of large rivers. In contrast to other eartheaters, *G. balzanii* is very common in areas with dense to rampant vegetation. Large expanses of sand are not the main habitat by any stretch of the imagination.

The water is very soft with a slightly acid to neutral pH. The adaptability of this species as regards optimum temperature is remarkable, as in the north of its range, in the Rio Guaporé region, average temperatures remain fairly constant throughout the year, while in the south considerable fluctuations are encountered during the course of the seasons. *G. balzanii* requires fairly warm conditions for a *Gymnogeophagus* and prefers temperatures between 20 and 28° C. For a few weeks of each year the temperature should be lowered to 15° C.

Size: Occasionally adult males attain 20 cm under aquarium conditions, but in normal circumstances they do not exceed the 16 cm mark. Females remain somewhat smaller.

Characters of the species: This species has a olive green to yellowish background with numerous vertical bars split into narrow double bands. The upper half of the body in males usually exhibits greenish to sometimes bluish shades, while the breast and throat region is vivid yellow. With the exception of the pectorals all the fins share the base colour. Adult dominant males exhibit numerous iridescent bluish-white dots on the fins, back, and head region.

A dark band runs from just in front of the dorsal origin to the posterior edge of the eye. The cheek is adorned with a dark vertical stripe connecting the eye with the lower part of the operculum. There is a dark, roundish, lateral spot between the upper and lower lateral lines.

The body is much compressed laterally and the very short body lends adult individuals an almost disc-shaped appearance. Adult males also have an almost vertical anterior upper head profile.

Sexual dimorphism: Females generally remain smaller, and are not as exquisitely coloured as males. The upper head profile is not as steep in females. Adult males have an almost vertical anterior upper head profile and may even develop a nuchal hump. In addition males exhibit more prolonged dorsal and anal fins. Males tend to lose the stripes when motivated; females lack spots in Fins and on the face, and the blue/green colour on the upper body.

Maintenance: If it is intended to keep a group of these fishes, then a 200 litre aquarium is suitable for 5-6 individuals. Because *G. balzanii* are very retiring cichlids any tankmates must be chosen with great care. Other eartheaters, various characins, catfishes, and the more robust labyrinth fishes can be kept with this species. A touch of greenery can be provided by a few tough plants, but fine-leaved types should be avoided as eventually they may succumb to the cichlids, although plants are not otherwise eaten. For this reason it is all the more important to provide a balanced diet. *G. balzanii* is one of the cichlid species that is susceptible to skin lesions (a sign of vitamin deficiency) and for this reason they should always be fed a good quality dried food with a vegetable content in order to regulate their vitamin uptake. Otherwise these fishes can be regarded as omnivores and fed any type of live or frozen foods. It is important to ensure they receive enough food in a community situation, as they are rather backward feeders.

No great effort is required as regards the aquarium decor, except for a fine substrate, luxuriant greenery around the edges, and hiding places made from wood and rocks. The lighting should be muted as these fishes do not enjoy too bright a light, and will not show their best colours. The filtration should be adequate but not too powerful, as *G. balzanii* prefers calm water.

It is possible to keep just a pair, but a small group of at least 6 is better, permitting study of their interesting social behaviour.

These fishes can be kept in practically any type of water, though extremes should, of course, be avoided. A pH around neutral and a hardness of less than 20° dGH may even be conducive to breeding.

Breeding behaviour: The choice of spawning substrate appears to be the prerogative of the male. Usually a flat stone, or one at a slight angle to the bottom, is chosen. The actual courtship is best described as restrained. The male merely performs a few brief quivering motions in front of the female, with a little tail-beating thrown in. The male leads the female

1. A young male *G. balzanii*. Although this individual has not reached full adulthood its extremely steep snout is obvious.
2. A young female *G. balzanii*. The lines on the ventral portion of her body are vaguely visible.
3. The Arroyo de las Averias near Treinta y Tres. Locality of *G. gymnogenys* and *G. labiatus*. Photo: Tonny Brandt Andersen.

to the spawning site by swimming to the substrate and mouthing it, as described earlier for *Geophagus steindachneri*. If the female accepts the choice of spawning substrate then both partners begin to clean it.

G. balzanii is a larvophilous mouthbrooder in which the care of eggs and fry is performed solely by the female. Thus it is the female who, after the spawn has been fertilised by the male, partially covers it with sand so that it is better protected from predators. Most of the time the female remains at a distance of about 20 cm from the spawn and visits it only briefly at intervals during the first 24 hours, after which she frees the larvae from their shells and takes them into the shelter of her mouth. After 8 days the fry are released from their mother's mouth for the first time and are ready to feed immediately. During the first days the female is nervous and straightaway picks up the brood in her mouth at the least disturbance. Depending on the circumstances brood care by the female can continue for quite a long time, with the fry being collected up as long as 20 days after first release.

The female can be described as exceptionally territorial throughout the entire brood care, as the shoal of fry is not led around the aquarium but released within a very limited area. The female merely positions herself over the brood; there is no leading behaviour.

Remarks: *G. balzanii* is the type species of the genus, although it is rather atypical of the members of the genus.

Further reading: Allgayer (1988: 18-22); Gosse (1975: 127-133); Schmelzer (1986: 58-60); Stawikowski (1981b: 174-175); Werner (1987a: 132-136).

Gymnogeophagus gymnogenys (Hensel, 1870)

Original description: Archiv für Naturgeschichte 36 (1): 61.

Derivation of scientific name: *gymnos* (Gr.) = naked; *genys* (Gr.) = cheek; referring to the unscaled cheeks of this species.

Distribution (unless otherwise stated, all from Reis & Malabarba, 1988): Brazil: Rio Cadea (Hensel, 1870); Rio Guiaba (Hensel, 1870); Rio Piratini (Malabarba & Stehmann, 1982); Dam on the Rio Jacui (Benvegnú, 1972); Rio Taquari; Rio Forqueta; Rio Cai (Buckup, Souto, Reis, & Malabarba, 1982); Rio Paranhama at its confluence with the Rio dos Sinos (Casada Neto, 1979); Rio da Ilha (Reis, 1982); Rio Saica (Lucena, Malabarba, & Reis, 1983; Lagoa de Cerquinha (Malabarba, 1981); Rio Santa Maria (Malabarba, 1982); Arroio do Ribeiro (Malabarba & Reis, 1982); Acude dos Garcia (Malabarba & Reis, 1982); Rio Ibuci da Cruz (Malabarba & Reis, 1982); Rio Negro (BR-153) (Malabarba & Lucena, 1982).

Brandt Andersen (1996) found *G. gymnogenys* in Uruguay, in the Arroyo de la India Muerta in the Rio Olimar Grande system near the town of Velasquez, and in the Arroyo de las Averias between Treinta y Tres and Valentines. Other sites in Uruguay are, according to Kullander (www. nrm. se) Arroyo Averias near Las Pavas (Canteras, 1996), the Rio Uruguay drainage (Canteras, 1997), and the Laguna Merin basin (Cantera, 1996, 1997).

The only recorded site in Argentina is the Rio Gualeguachu (Arnold, 1937), and in Uruguay the Cerro Largo (Felippone, 1932) as well as the Rio Santa Lucia at Canelones (Barattini, 1935).

Habitat: *G. gymnogenys* by and large inhabits slow-flowing to still waters. In general these fishes frequent the bank region among submerse- and emerse-growing vegetation. There may also be a covering of floating plants. The substrate is mainly muddy. The water is soft with a slightly acid pH.

In the state of Rio Grande do Súl the cycle of the seasons is clearly discernible, such that in winter (June/July) temperatures may be close to freezing, while in Summer water temperatures of 25° C are quite normal. This annual cycle should be taken into account during the aquarium maintenance of this species.

When Brandt Andersen caught *G. gymnogenys* in the Arroyo de la India Muerta he found the number of females was significantly larger than that of males. From this he hypothesised that males must hold large territories within which several females were tolerated.

Size: 15 cm can be taken as a realistic size datum for males of *G. gymnogenys*. It cannot, however, be ruled out that odd males may exceed the 20 cm mark. In general females remain 2-5 cm shorter than males.

Characters of the species: In both sexes the base colour is greenish beige to yellow. In the centre of the flank there is a dark, sometimes rectangular-looking lateral spot at the height of the body axis. In front of this, depending on mood, there may be an oval spot, often connected to the lateral spot itself. Traces of a mid-lateral band may be visible, again depending on mood. Males and dominant individuals have an interorbital bar and a saddle-stripe at the dorsal fin origin. The area between is coloured vivid yellow and may develop into a nuchal hump. In addition males exhibit iridescent bluish spots on the flanks. The unpaired fins as well as the ventrals are reddish with numerous iridescent bluish spots, unlike *G. rhabdotus*, whose fins exhibit a striped pattern of the same colour. The pectorals are colourless.

The upper head profile rises more steeply than in *G. rhabdotus* and *G. meridionalis*, both of which have a rather more pointed head.

Sexual dimorphism: The males are more colourful and may develop a nuchal hump.

Maintenance: Hardness and pH are of little importance as long as extremes are avoided. A neutral pH and a hardness of up to 10° dGH will be perfectly adequate.

Provided the aquarium capacity is no less than 200 litres and any tankmates are not too aggressive, then these are undemanding charges which should be kept in a group (Kirsten, 1991) and which require hiding places in the form of plants, wood, and rocks for their well-being.

G. gymnogenys should not be kept for long periods at temperatures in excess of 25° C. The annual cycle of seasons to which these fishes are exposed in the wild should be reproduced in the aquarium without fail. Thus during our winter they should be kept at temperatures not exceeding 15° C (for at least 2 months) and the temperature should be allowed to drop to 10° C for a few days. During the transitional periods the temperature should be lowered and raised, respectively, only slowly, to avoid temperature shock.

G. gymnogenys will eat almost anything as long as it is the right size. A good quality dried food and all sorts of frozen foods will just do the job. During the "winter phase" only a very little food will be taken, so only very small quantities should be offered and any uneaten food immediately removed before it pollutes the water unnecessarily.

Breeding behaviour: *G. gymnogenys* too is a larvophilous mouthbrooder. Because males need to court the favour of females by means of striking coloration, dominant males exhibit their finest colours almost all of the time in the aquarium. Courtship is, however, actually initiated by the female. She begins by cleaning the spawning substrate, and then butts the male in the side to draw his attention to her readiness to spawn. At this stage the male contents himself with the minimum of ritual, i.e. lateral threat and tail-beating. The most striking feature of courtship is the mouth snapping in front of the female, as described earlier for *Geophagus steindachneri*.

Egg deposition takes place in open-brooder fashion, with up to a hundred amber-coloured eggs, which adhere to the substrate on their long side and are then fertilised by the male. In general a slightly sloping or horizontal stone serves as substrate, and is often sited beneath overhead cover which provides additional protection. The eggs are not always arranged symmetrically so the clutch looks incomplete, with visible gaps. After spawning

1. A young male of *Gymnogeophagus gymnogenys* from an unknown locality.
2. *G. gymnogenys* from the Arroyo de las Averias between Treinta y Tres and Valentines, Uruguay. Photo: Tonny Brandt Andersen.
3. The Arroyo de la India Muerta near the city of Valezques. Photo: Tonny Brandt Andersen.
4. *G. gymnogenys* from the Arroyo de la India Muerta. Note the almost pure white ventral region and the large hump of this adult male. Photo: Tonny Brandt Andersen.

the female alone undertakes the care of eggs and fry. At the conclusion of spawning the eggs are sprinkled with sand to camouflage them. The female hovers above the eggs and fans fresh water over them with her pectoral fins. At a temperature of 22° C the female frees the larvae from their shells after 48 hours, and takes them into the shelter of her mouth. Once the female has picked up the larvae in her mouth she becomes extremely aggressive, and in a restricted space this can lead to the male being injured, as he is often the particular object of the female's attacks. However, heterospecific tankmates are attacked the most violently, such that it may be necessary to move the brooding female to another aquarium or use a divider.

After 12 days the free-swimming fry are released from the mouth and spat into a pit dug by beats of the mother's fins. The fry can immediately be fed with *Artemia* nauplii. Females are by and large conscientious in their brood care and guard their fry for a very long time. The fry grow very slowly but make few demands of the aquarist.

Further reading: Brandt Andersen (1999: 101-110); Darda (1994: 19-21); Gosse (1975: 117-126); Grad (1992: 43-44); Kirsten (1998: 168-171); Mayland (1987: 68-70); Reis & Malabarba (1988); Schulz (1986: 488-491; 1991: 771-774); Stieglitz (1987a: 15-17; 1987b: 238-243).

Gymnogeophagus labiatus (Hensel, 1870)

Original description: Archiv für Naturgeschichte 36 (1): 64-65.

Derivation of scientific name: labiatus (Lat.) = having (by implication, large) lips; referring to the greatly developed (thickened and swollen) upper and lower lips in this species.

Distribution: The type locality is the Rio Santa Maria in the Brazilian state of Rio Grande do Súl (Hensel, 1870). A further locality is the Rio Cadea in the same state (Hensel, 1870; according to Reis & Malabarba, 1988, Rio Cadeia). Specimens imported by Schulz originated from the Rio dos Sinos, some 10 km northwest of Santo Antonio da Patrulha (Stawikowski, 1989).

In 1996 Brandt Andersen caught a *Gymnogeophagus*, which he provisionally termed *G. labiatus* "Centurion", in a small river near the town of Centurion in Uruguay. And the presence of this species has been demonstrated in the Arroyo de las Averias, between Treinta y Tres and Valentines (Brandt Andersen, 1999; Cantera, 1997).

Habitat: *G. labiatus* inhabits fast-flowing water, whose bottom is covered with large rocks and coarse gravel. These fishes are very timid in both the wild and the aquarium and lead a relatively reclusive life close to the substrate.

Brandt Andersen (1999) describes the small nameless stream near the town of Centurion, Uruguay, as very narrow, with both the rocks and bottom composed of rock. The pH value in this biotope was 7.5 and the conductivity 60 µS/cm at 27° C.

Size: Males attain a total length of 18 cm, while females remain about 2-4 cm smaller.

Characters of the species: The most striking feature of this species in the wild state has to be the fleshy lips, which do not develop under aquarium conditions. Apparently the development of these lips is related to feeding, and because food does not have to be detected in the aquarium the lips do not develop fully. In contrast to *G. gymnogenys* the nuchal hump is rusty-red in colour and instead of spots in the unpaired fins this species has iridescent bluish streaks on a reddish background. The lateral spot lies on the centre of the flank below the upper lateral line. There is a dark band on the nape, ending at the posterior edge of the eye. A further dark band runs from the eye to the anterior operculum. Females are coloured an inconspicuous brown-beige and exhibit a pattern of 10 narrow vertical bars on the side. The bar on which the lateral spot lies takes the form of a double band.

Sexual dimorphism: Males grow significantly larger than females, are more vividly coloured, and develop an imposing nuchal hump.

Maintenance: Given the preference for fast-flowing waters, an adequate current should be provided in the aquarium. Because these fishes are rather timid then the decor — roots and stones — should offer as much privacy as possible in the way of cover and hiding-places. These potentially rather large cichlids also require large tanks at least 150 cm long. It is not necessary to provide very soft water, as even at 10-14° dGH they will remain healthy in the long term provided the pH does not drift too far into the acid or alkaline zones.

Feeding these cichlids is relatively easy, as they are omnivores. It is, however, particularly important to feed them adequate amounts of vegetable matter, as in the wild they browse cushions of algae and thus ingest plant material.

Stieglitz (1994) kept his fishes in a small group consisting of seven individuals, who seemed to do very well within the group and were exceptionally peaceful towards one another.

Of course *G. labiatus* should also have a rest phase of two to three months at cooler temperatures (8-12° C) before the temperature is again slowly raised to 25° C. The fishes will respond by increased readiness to spawn and brighter colours.

Breeding behaviour: According to Brandt Andersen (1999) the spawning behaviour resembles that of *G. gymnogenys*. According to Stieglitz *G. labiatus*, like *G. gymnogenys*, is a maternal larvophilous mouthbrooder. Further observations seem to indicate that even during brood care *G. labiatus* maintains close contact with conspecifics. Thus Stieglitz reports that (translated from the German): "further females, who had laid their eggs on a root, came to my attention only because they kept returning to this spot although they otherwise remained with the group." (Stieglitz, 1994).

After 48-72 hours the larvae free themselves from the egg shells and are picked up by the female. After seven days they are free-swimming and released from the mother's mouth and will immediately greedily feed on freshly-hatched *Artemia*.

According to Stieglitz (1994) *G. labiatus* females are not very good at brood care. Essentially, the female always remains a short distance from

1. A male *Gymnogeophagus labiatus* in the aquarium. Photo: Willem Heijns.
2. *G. labiatus* from the Arroyo de las Averias; male with an impressive hump. Photo: Tonny Brandt Andersen.
3. A freshly caught *G.* cf. *labiatus* from the Arroyo Catalancito in Uruguay. Note the thick lips. Photo: Wolfgang Staeck.
4. This *Gymnogeophagus* species was caught by Brandt Andersen near the city of Centurion in Uruguay and is named *G.* cf. *labiatus* "Centurion", because in many details it resembles *G. labiatus*. Photo: Tonny Brandt Andersen.
5. A spawning pair of *G.* cf. *labiatus* "Centurion". Their brooding behaviour resembles that of *G. gymnogenys*. Photo: Tonny Brandt Andersen.

her brood, in order to be on the spot immediately in the event of danger or disturbance. The fry are then taken into the protecting mouth with the speed of lightning. Often, however, she fails to react to disturbance so that fry-predators can easily help themselves.

Hensel (1870) appends extremely interesting observations in the natural habitat to his description of *G. scymnophilus*, today regarded as a synonym of *G. labiatus*. Although he did not observe the spawning itself and was not sure whether he was dealing with an open-brooder or a mouthbrooder, be assumed that the brood care was performed by the male. Thus the male (?) led his brood around in the shallow strip along the bank in areas where the current was significantly reduced by localised obstructions. When the observer approached the guarding fish, which kept watch a short distance from the brood, then it would immediately swim to the fry, who would gather lightning-fast around the parent's mouth and were then taken inside. The adult fish then fled and released the fry some distance away. Hensel managed to isolate the fry from their parent in the natural habitat by interposing a barrier between them. The parent waited a little way away until he spotted an opportunity to swim to them, whereupon he picked them up and fled once more. The only way Hensel could catch a mouthbrooding individual was stun or even kill the fish by firing a shot (!) into its immediate vicinity. He thus established that the fry were all brooded with their heads pointing in the direction of the parent's gills.

4

5

Remarks: *G. labiatus* is often regarded as a synonym of *G. gymnogenys*.

Further reading: Brandt Andersen (1999: 101-110, Darda (1995b: 17-18); Hensel (1870: 64-68); Kirsten (1993: 19-22); Mayland (1993: 46; 1995: 521); Reis & Malabarba (1988: 259-305); Stawikowski (1989b: 201); Stieglitz (1994: 9-12).

Gymnogeophagus lacustris Reis & Malabarba, 1988

Original description: Revista Brasil. Zool. 4 (4): 282-289.

Derivation of scientific name: lacustris (Lat.) = of/from lakes, referring to the fact that the type specimens, from which the species was described, all originated from lakes or the lake-like widenings at the mouths of rivers.

Distribution: The type locality is a canal between the Lagoa da Cerquinha and the Lagoa da Rondinha near the town of Pinhal, Tramandai, in the Brazilian state of Rio Grande do Súl (Reis & Malabarba, 1982). According to Reis & Malabarba (1988), additional localities are the Rio Maquini (Buckup, 1978; Reis, 1981), the mouth of the Rio Cornilios (Reiz & Penz, 1983), the Lagoa dos Quadros near Cornillios (Lucena, Tiago, & Morais, 1983), the Lagoa da Cerquinha (Malabarba, 1980; Buckup, Reis, & Malabarba, 1981), the Canal do Joco Pedro (Reis & Reis, 1981), and the Lagoa Itapeva. All these sites are in the state of Rio Grande do Súl, not far from the town of Pinhal.

Habitat: The specimens used by the describers came mainly from the Rio Grande do Súl and Santa Catarina regions. The lagoons had a sandy to muddy bottom with submerse vegetation. In the shore zones there were a number of emerse-growing plants (Graminacea and Cyperaceae).

Size: The standard length of Reis and Malabarba's largest specimen was 146 mm, so a maximum size of about 18-20 cm can be assumed.

Characters of the species: Preserved specimens are light olive green on the back and flanks, becoming somewhat lighter ventrally. There are usually nine double vertical dark bars, and a lateral spot on the third to fourth of these. A distinct dark band runs extends from the nape to the eye, and then usually ends on the inner corner of the preoperculum. Snout, cheeks, and operculum are darker than the body. There are nevertheless light blue spots, as well as a few scales, on the cheeks. The lips are fleshy and vivid orange in adults. The dorsal and anal are again olive green with a reddish tinge. There are also a few whitish to light blue stripes/oval spots, which may be rounder in shape on the anal.

The upper part of the caudal has a light reddish tinge on an olive green base.

Sexual dimorphism: Older adult males have a pronounced nuchal hump and also grow rather larger than females.

Maintenance: To date no aquarium details are available. It can be assumed that this species requires the winter rest recommended for its relatives.

Breeding behaviour: To date no observations on breeding behaviour are available. The describers mention that they netted an individual with larvae in February.

Remarks: According to Reis & Malabarba (1988) this species is very closely related to *G. labiatus*.

Further reading: Reis & Malabarba (1988: 259-305).

Gymnogeophagus meridionalis
Reis & Malabarba, 1988

Original description: Revista Bras. Zool. 4 (4): 259-305.

Derivation of scientific name: *meridionalis* (Lat.) = southern, referring to the southerly distribution of this species.

Distribution: The type locality lies in the Rio Negro on the road BR-153 in the Rio Uruguay drainage in the Brazilian state of Rio Grande do Súl (Reis, Malabarba, & Leyler, 1982). The paratypes originate from Argentina, specifically from the Laguna Camino Bella Vista and the Parque Ludena.

Further sites in Brazil are, according to Reis & Malabarna (1988), the Rio Uruguay near Itaqui (Garbe, 1914), Arroio Jaguari near São Francisco de Assis (Reis, Malabarba, & Lucena, 1983), the Rio Carai-Passo near São Francisco de Assis (Reis, Malabarba, & Lucena, 1983), Sanga do Rio Toropi (Reis, Malabarba, & Lucena, 983), the Rio Santa Maria (Malabarba & Lucena, 1982), and the Rio Negro in southern Brazil (Reis, Malabarba, and Lucena, 1982).

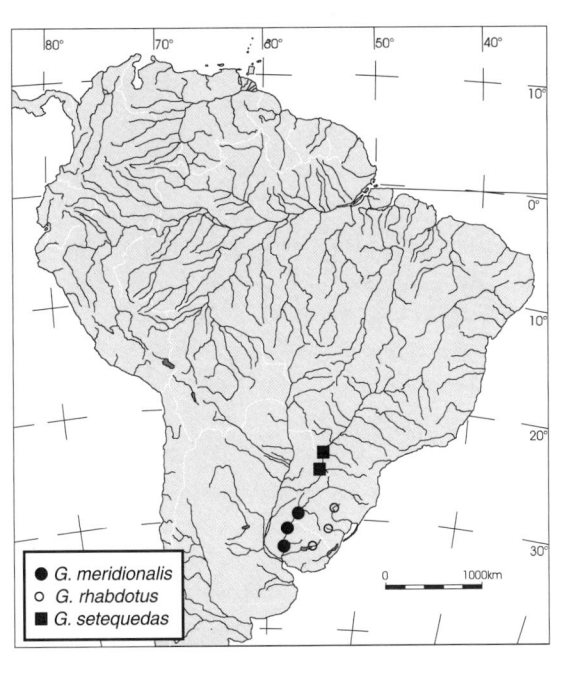

● G. meridionalis
○ G. rhabdotus
■ G. setequedas

1. A male *Gymnogeophagus* sp. "Yaguarón". This species resembles *G. meridionalis* in body shape and coloration. Photo: Tonny Brandt Andersen.
2. Also *G.* sp. "Rosario II" resembles *G. meridionalis* and Kullander has identified them as *G.* cf. *meridionalis*. Unfortunately they have not yet been bred in the aquarium. Photo: Tonny Brandt Andersen.
3. *G. meridionalis* in the aquarium. Photo: Tonny Brandt Andersen.
4. A small pool near Salinas, locality of *G. meridionalis*. Photo: Tonny Brandt Andersen.

In 1994 Körber found *G. meridionalis* in Buenos Aires in the Bosque de Palerma, and again, in 1995, in the Rio de la Reconquista, about 100 km upstream of the Represa La Reja (about 3 km south of the village La Resa).

In 1996 Brandt Andersen found this species in Uruguay in a small lake immediately outside of the town of Salinas, and a *G. meridionalis*-like species in the Rio Yaguarón, which he initially designated *G.* sp. "Yaguarón".

In 1996 Brandt Andersen caught a *Gymnogeophagus* very reminiscent of *G. meridionalis* in the Arroyo Colla (an affluent of the Rio Rosario) near the town of Rosario. Kullander designated these eartheaters *G.* sp. cf. *meridionalis* while Brandt Andersen (1999) provisionally called them *G.* sp. "Rosario II". In 1996 and 1997 Cantera caught specimens of the same species in the Arroyo Averías near Las Pavas, in Arroyo Valentín about 10-15 km west of the Ruta Nacional 7, in the Laguna Arenera de Carrasco near San José de Carrasco, and in a small pool in the basin of the Laguna Merín, 2 km from Centurión and 500 km from the Rio Yaguarón (in Kullander, www. nrm. se). Brandt Andersen (1999) called this species *G.* sp. Yaguarón".

Habitat: Reis & Malabarba (1988) characterised the sites for *G. meridionalis* as small pools, streams, and also large rivers with a sandy or muddy bottom. They inhabit clear as well as dark and murky water. The authors state nothing about the current. It can, however, be assumed that they prefer slow-flowing or still water.

According to Brandt Andersen, in December at 8 am the Rio Yaguarón had a water temperature of 20° C and a pH of 6.5. The following values were recorded in the Arroyo Colla: 26° C, pH 7.5, 365 µS/cm, and 8° dGH.

In the lake near Salinas *G. meridionalis* shares the biotope with '*Cichlasoma*' *facetum*, and the ichthyofauna also includes livebearing toothcarps such as *Jenynsia lineata* and *Cnesterodon decemmaculatus*.

Size: *G. meridionalis* appears to be the smallest member of the genus. The largest individual measured by Reis & Malabarba (1988) had a standard length of 88 mm, from which a maximum total length of 12 cm can be extrapolated. Females remain somewhat smaller.

Characters of the species: The base colour of these fishes is grey-brown with an olive tinge. The coloration becomes lighter ventrally, giving way to yellow. There are six vertical bars on the flanks, with the lateral spot on the third of these, between the two parts of the lateral line; this spot has a more roundish form. An eye-stripe runs from the nape to the eye and then vertically downwards to the front of the operculum. The pectorals are colourless. The ventrals exhibit bluish lines on an orange-yellow base. The unpaired fins, unlike in *G. rhabdotus*, exhibit iridescent bluish dots on an orange base. Males also exhibit reflective blue scales arranged in longitudinal lines on the flanks.

Sexual dimorphism: Males grow larger and are more colourful than females.

Maintenance: *G. meridionalis* is the most southerly representative of the genus, and unconditionally requires a rest period each year in which to regenerate. Individuals that are kept long-term at excessively high temperatures grow old very quickly and never achieve a good age. Moreover after just a year they lose their colour. Otherwise maintenance is by and large as for other members of the genus. Because the species remains rather small, tanks with a capacity of 160 litres are adequate for successful maintenance.

Breeding behaviour: Males occupy a territory and outside of the breeding season do not allow any conspecifics into this area. Females in the vicinity of the nest are courted by spreading the fins and opercula. If the female is ripe then she is allowed into the territory where she selects the future spawning site, which is almost always a vertical surface. This is cleaned chiefly by the female. In addition she digs a funnel-shaped pit in front of the stone, moving the sand in her mouth from the chosen area. This pit is usually very close to and almost immediately below the eggs, such that the hatching larvae automatically fall into it. The clutch can consist of up to 400 light brown to grey-brown eggs, which are guarded and tended by the female. The male guards the territory but is allowed in the vicinity of the eggs.

At a temperature of 20° C it takes about 120 hours for the larvae to hatch or be freed from the eggshells by the female. The larvae are then tended in the pit. Over the days that follow the female digs numerous further pits in order to move the larvae at least once per day. Körber (1998) has hypothesised that this is a survival strategy, as *G. meridionalis* is often found in still and even dirty water. The moving of the larvae is thus for reasons of hygiene, in order to avoid dirt accumulating in the pits.

At 20° C it takes 13 days from spawning for the fry to become free-swimming and to start searching for food. Freshly-hatched *Artemia* are too large at this stage, and thus an infusorian culture should be prepared in good time. Both parents lead the shoal of fry and play almost equal parts in the broodcare.

From these observations *G. meridionalis* is clearly an open-brooder, as moving the larvae around cannot be regarded as mouthbrooding.

On the other hand, Brandt Andersen watched the *G. meridionalis*-like species from the Rio Jaguarón in the natural habitat, and saw the female pick up her brood in her mouth when danger threatened. These fishes too always spawn on a vertical surface and both sexes take equal turns at looking after the brood (aquarium observation).

Remarks: *G. rhabdotus*, *G. setequedas*, and *G. meridionalis* form a special group which is distinguished from other members of the genus by the smaller number of scales in a longitudinal row (22-25 instead of 26-28).

Further reading: Brandt Andersen (1999: 101-110); Darda (1992: 13-14; 1995b: 17-18); Körber (1998: 156-158); Reis & Malabarba (1988: 259-305).

Gymnogeophagus rhabdotus (Hensel, 1970)

Original description: Archiv für Naturgeschichte 36 (1): 60-61.

Derivation of scientific name: *rhabdotos* (Gr.) = striped; referring to the horizontal banding.

Distribution: Reis & Malabarba (1988) list the following localities: Rio Cadea, Brazil, in the state of Rio Grande do Súl (Hensel, 1870; Rio Cadeia according to Reis & Malabarba, 1988); San José do Rio Negro and Chapada, Brazil, in Mato Grosso state. Further localities in Brazil include: Arroio Passo dos Buracos (Malabarba & Stehmann, 1982), Rio das Sinos near São Leopoldo (Leal, 1967); backwater of the Rio Jacui (Backup, 1976); Rio

Vacacai (Reis & Malabarba, 1982), Rio Pelotas (Leal, 1967); Rio Negro (Reis & Malabarba, 1982). In Paraguay this species is found in the Rio Acaray and Rio Carapi (Geneva Zoological Museum Expedition, 1979).

Brandt Andersen (1999) found this species in Uruguay by Route 7 near Valentines.

Cantera *et al.* caught *G. rhabdotus* in 1997 (Kullander, www. nrm. se) in Uruguay in the basin of the Laguna Merín, in the Arroyo Local near Valentines and at Paso El Santiago. In 1989 Kullander *et al.* caught this species in the Brazilian state of Rio Grande do Súl at Capoa da Canoa Lagoa dos Quadros near Praia do Barco.

Habitat: *G. rhabdotus* inhabits rather varied biotopes. It is found in lagoons, streams and small rivers with sandy, rarely muddy or stony, bottoms, with at most a moderate current. Waters with dense submerse vegetation are preferred.

However, in 1997 Kullander and Cantera caught this species in a fast-flowing stream in the Laguna Merín (Paso El Santiago). The water was 15 m wide and one deep, brownish, and unshaded. The banks were bordered by grass and low scrub.

Size: Even with optimal maintenance males attain barely 16 cm and females remain a few cm smaller.

Characters of the species: Because this species has a rather wide distribution, a number of different populations have evolved. The base colour of all populations is, however, olive-brown. On this scales with reflective dots are arranged in lines, giving the impression of longitudinal stripes. There is a lateral spot on the central flank; this can take the form of a transverse streak and is surrounded by a lighter zone. A dark band runs through the eye, extending from the nape to the anterior operculum. The pectorals are colourless. All the other fins have innumerable iridescent bluish spots and stripes on a flesh-coloured to orange base. The main distinguishing character from *G. meridionalis* is the presence of bluish stripes in the anal and dorsal fins.

The head of *G. rhabdotus* is distinctly more pointed than in other *Gymnogeophagus*.

Sexual dimorphism: Males grow larger and are significantly more colourful. In addition the dorsal and anal are more prolonged into points.

1. These fish come from an unknown location and are therefor difficult to identify. They could either be *G. meridionalis* or *G. rhabdotus*. Photo: Werner
2. *Gymnogeophagus rhabdotus* has fine blue lines in the tail which lack in *G. meridionalis*. Photo: Tonny Brandt Andersen.

Maintenance: If these fishes are kept constantly at temperatures of more than 24° C then they age rather rapidly and breeding is disturbed from its normal rhythm by the lack of a cool winter period. For this reason these fishes should be given a two months rest period at about 12° C. The fishes are then more likely to breed and livelier.

Other parameters are as for other members of the genus. The water does not necessarily need to be very soft and acid, as this species also thrives in hard alkaline water and will even breed. Hiding-places, muted lighting, and fine sand are all desirable. These fishes are omnivores, which do not, however, harm plants.

Breeding behaviour: *G. rhabdotus* is an open-brooder, which lays its eggs on horizontal surfaces of stones, roots, and even leaves. The clutch itself may number up to 500 eggs and a female of 5.7 cm SL has been recorded as producing more than 300 eggs (Loiselle, 1981). The female's role is the direct care of the spawn, while the male guards the territory. Should the male fail to do his job properly, then he is reminded of his duty by butts in the flank from the female. During brood care the colour of the male diminishes somewhat, while the female develops black markings.

The larvae hatch after 24-48 hours, after which they are moved around from pit to pit, as described earlier for *G. meridionalis*. At 23° C the yolk sacs of the larvae are used up after 6-7 days and the fry must then be fed with newly-hatched *Artemia*, or better, infusorians. Parent *G. rhabdotus* are exemplary in their brood care, and tend their fry devotedly for a long period. The fry seem to be less parent-oriented such that the parents are obliged to follow their offspring (Loiselle, 1981). During the entire brood care period (3 weeks) pits are dug repeatedly and the fry placed in them, particularly at night.

The further rearing of the fry may be difficult as this species should not be kept at the same high temperatures all the time. Thus dropping the temperature to 15° C stimulates the immune system in tank-breds as well, so that the young fishes remain distinctly more active and live longer.

Remarks: *G. rhabdotus*, *G. meridionalis*, and *G. setequedas*, form a distinct group within the genus.

Further reading: Brandt Andersen (1999: 101-110); Reis & Malabarba (1988: 259-305); Stieglitz (1986: 8-9). The following article must relate to *G. rhabdotus*: Loiselle (1981a: 31-35).

Gymnogeophagus setequedas
Reis, Malabarba & Pavanelli, 1992

Original description: Ichthyol. Explor. Freshwaters, 3, 3: 265-272.

Derivation of scientific name: Setequedas is derived from the proper name of the large waterfalls (Sete Quedas) which formerly lay in the type locality in the Rio Paraná, but which were swallowed up following by the construction of the Itaipú hydro-electric dam in 1983.

Distribution: As far as is known at present *G. setequedas* is widespread in the central drainage of the Rio Paraná in Brazil and Paraguay (Reis, Malabarba, and Pavanelli, 1992).

A number of affluents of the Rio Paraná in which this species is found, according to Reis, Malabarba, and Pavanelli, 1992, are the Rio Carapá, the Rio Pozuela, the Rio Acaray-Cué, the Rio Iguacú, the Rio Güyrauguá, and the Rio São Vicente.

In 1988 Ahlander (Kullander, www. nrm. se) visited Paraguay and collected *G. setequedas* at the following localities: Arroyo Zanja Pe; in a stream to the west of Lago Ypacarai, 1 km north of Iglesia Espiritu Santo Yukyry; Arroyo Yhú; in a number of residual pools by the Caaguazú-Yhú road; in the Iguacú reservoir in a bay near Juan E. O., Leary and Acara8 on Route 2; Arroyo Acapyta; Rio Güyrauguá between Caaguazú and J M Frutos.

In 1998 Kullander *et al.* found specimens of this species in the Arroyo Paso Há near the spa of the same name.

Habitat: According to Mayland (1995) this species is supposedly found in generally vegetated bank zones. Unfortunately no information is at present available on the water parameters of the natural biotope. It can, however, be assumed that low pH levels and very soft water are to be found in this region.

In 1998 Kullander found this species in the Arroyo Paso Há over a rocky substrate in brownish slow-flowing water with numerous eddies, and at the Embalse Acara8 dam in clear, still, water over a sandy, vegetation-free, bottom.

Ahlander (in Kullander, www. nrm. se) describes the Arroyo Zanja Pé in March as a stream with a slow to moderate current, 1-3 metres wide and 0.1-0.8 metres deep. The bottom was sandy and the water grey-brown. The surrounding area was farmed as pasture; plants (Poaceae and Cyperaceae) lined the banks.

Size: The standard length of the holotype (a female) is stated to be 81.3 mm, and the largest specimen in the type material 98.0 mm (SL), from which a total length of 12-14 cm can be assumed.

Characters of the species: *G. setequedas* is perhaps the least noteworthy *Gymnogeophagus* as far as coloration is concerned. Depending on the light, the base colour is a shade of blue-green, while a few rows of iridescent bluish spots on the flanks lend these fishes a rather attractive appearance. The ventral area is light yellow. All the fins are transparent and colourless, although the unpaired fins may be overlain with a reddish, sometimes yellowish, tinge, sometimes with a scattering of reflective bluish dots. This species has an elongate dark lateral spot on the central flank, below the upper lateral line and encompassing two rows of scales. In addition a broken lateral band runs from the posterior operculum to the caudal peduncle. Depending on mood there may be a small dark spot at the upper edge of the operculum. A dark suborbital streak runs from the eye to the edge of the gillcover, and there is another dark band on the forehead, ending at the posterior edge of the eye on either side of the head. Individuals in aggressive or breeding mood exhibit a pattern of usually five to six dark vertical bars on the flanks, with the third of these intersecting the lateral spot.

Sexual dimorphism: As in all other *Gymnogeophagus*, male *G. setequedas* are more colourful and are all-in-all rather larger. Darda (pers. comm.) indicates that the caudal spines in males are lines with red.

Maintenance: This species does not differ from other *Gymnogeophagus* as regards maintenance. Thus this species too should not

1. *Gymnogeophagus setequedas* is the least colourful species of the genus. Photo: Uwe Werner.
2. A brooding *G. setequedas*. Even the breeding coloration is rather plain. Photo: Werner Darda.
3. A male *G.* sp. "Rosario I" resembles *G. gymnogenys* in many aspects. Photo: Tonny Brandt Andersen.
4. Female *Gymnogeophagus* are noticeably less colourful than males. A female of *Gymnogeophagus* sp. "Rosario I". Photo: Tonny Brandt Andersen.

be kept at above 25° C in the long term. The longer the period at higher temperatures continues, the paler and more sluggish the fishes become. When this happens the temperature should be slowly lowered (down to 10° C) and only minimal food offered, to allow the fishes the possibility of regeneration. When the temperature is slowly raised again after two months then the fishes will respond with brighter colours and increased readiness to spawn.

Any aquarium that is to house *G. setequedas* should be provided with hiding-places in the form of wood, and a substrate of fine sand. A few flat stones lying horizontally on the surface of the sand will be readily accepted as spawning substrates. Plants will not be molested, so a little greenery can be introduced into the aquarium. There should be no problem in providing a varied diet, as these cichlids are omnivores that can be accustomed to any sort of food.

Breeding behaviour: In *G. setequedas* courtship is initiated by the male, who seeks to win the favour of the female with erect fins spread almost to tearing. During this lateral early stage by the development of the reflective spots on the unpaired fins, as juvenile and subordinate males appear as colourless as females.

Maintenance: *G.* sp. "Rosario I" does not differ from other *Gymnogeophagus* as regards maintenance. This species too requires a rest phase during which the temperature should not exceed 15° C, and the species should not be kept for long periods at above 26° C.

Breeding behaviour: According to Brandt Andersen *G.* sp. "Rosario I" is primarily a biparental mouthbrooder, with a strict division of labour between the two parents. Initially the female tended the spawn, which was at first concealed with sand. Depending on temperature the larvae were taken into the shelter of the mother's mouth after three to four days. Brandt Anderson speaks of the eggs disappearing, so it remains unclear whether this is an ovophilous or larvophilous species, although on the basis of the timing the latter seems more likely. Just a day later the male was leading the brood and taking them into his mouth when danger threatened, and thereafter the female no longer paid any attention to the offspring. After a week the fry were already so large that they could no longer all fit into their father's mouth. Even then the female played no part in the brood care.

In 1999 Brandt Andersen mentioned a friend whose female *G.* sp. "Rosario I" completed the brood care so the behaviour described above is not necessarily the norm for the species.

Further reading: Brandt Andersen (1997: 228-231; 1999: 101-110).

1. *Gymnogeophagus* sp. "Rosario I" is a biparental mouthbrooder. Photo: Tonny Brandt Andersen.
2. A male *Retroculus lapidifer*.

Retroculus Eigenmann & Bray, 1894

Derivation of scientific name: *retro* (Lat.) = backwards, towards the rear; *oculus* (Lat.) = eye; referring to the fact that the eyes are set relatively far back on the head compared with other cichlids.

Distribution: Species of the genus *Retroculus* have to date been found only in the Amazonian region, and it seems unlikely that they occur outside this area. So far *Retroculus* have been found only in the large southern affluents (Rio Xingú, Rio Tapajós, Rio Tocantins, and their drainages) of the Amazon as well as in the state of Amapá, Brazil, as far as the border region with French Guiana where they are found in the Rio Oyapock. To date there are no records for the northern affluents of the Amazon.

Ecology: These rheophilic cichlids are found mainly in fast-flowing reaches of the large clear- and blackwaters of Amazonia, although they also frequent areas of weaker current in the lee of large aggregations of rock or over sandy bottoms in shallow bank zones. And despite their rheophilic lifestyle they also frequent extensive sandbanks. It is often precisely these areas that are preferred for spawning and brood care, and thus many juveniles can be found in residual pools cut off from the main river, especially during the dry season. Because of their shallow depth and the bright sunshine these residual pools may have a water temperature of up to 35° C. The bottom consists of fine sand although larger river shingle may also form part of the substrate. Areas with large rocks complete the picture. Leaf litter is almost completely absent. Accumulations of wood are sometimes present, though *Retroculus* appear to prefer the open sand.

The water in the natural habitat is soft and has a slightly acid pH, although there are, of course, some areas where this generalisation does not apply. Thus *R. lapidifer* has also been found in decidedly acid water (pH 5.5) at a rather cool 22° C, in the Rio des Mortes, upper Araguia drainage, Brazil (Werner, 1990). The biological quality of the water seems to be more important, as *Retroculus* react very badly to any interruption in the nitrogen cycle (see Remarks, below).

Characters of the genus: In body form *Retroculus* are slightly reminiscent of members of the genus *Satanoperca*, only the head is even more pointed and almost forms an isosceles triangle. The mouth opening is horizontal and very large. The lips are fleshy and very well developed. Because *Retroculus* have a reduced swimbladder as an adaptation to fast-flowing regions in open water they appear rather clumsy and tend to swim in a rather jerky manner requiring a high energy expenditure. Usually they are seen "sitting" on the bottom, propped up on their strongly developed ventral fins. Because of the bottom-oriented lifestyle the eyes are high on the head. The body is moderately compressed laterally and the caudal peduncle noticeably powerful.

An additional character is the black spot in the soft part of the dorsal fin, rather reminiscent of a "tilapia spot".

The basal 60-75% of the caudal fin is scaled.

Ethology: *Retroculus* only very rarely seek out overhead cover. They have a very large flight distance, and if pursued then they take flight extremely rapidly despite the reduced swimbladder and the — to human eyes — clumsy mode of swimming, heading straight across the open sand towards a region of coarser river shingle in order to hide there. If they can see no other method of escape then they dig themselves lightning-fast into the soft sandy substrate. This happens so quickly that human eyesight is incapable of following their disappearance into the bottom in 100% detail. In addition, because these fishes are relatively flat and bury themselves with great rapidity, the place where they disappear is only in rare instances the "collecting site" where they can be dug out again.

The name of the type of the genus, *R. lapidifer* (Castelnau, 1855), translates as "stone-carrier" and relates to a peculiarity of the genus, all known members of which construct nests of coarse shingle for their brood care, and then spawn in them. Field studies indicate that these nests are constructed chiefly in the bank zones, which often lie above the water's surface during the low-water season, and it is thus often possible to find circular collections of pebbles, up to a metre in diameter, along the dried-up shoreline. This explains why so many juveniles are to be found in the residual pools mentioned earlier, which then heat up accordingly. What is also astonishing is the fact that these nests are often several metres distant from natural deposits of shingle, so that the fishes have to transport their little stones over long distances. *Retroculus* appear to form regular breeding colonies, as the individual nests are only a few metres apart. This may, of course, be a function of the limited amount of habitat available, and it may be that because of the nature of the terrain the rapids conceal a relatively high population density unknown to, or only suspected by, humans. Aquarium observations have shown that in *R. lapidifer* spawning over shingle is not obligatory (Kiefel, 1989) and that a pit dug in a fine substrate (Lucas, 1999; Kellner, pers. comm.) is also acceptable as a breeding site. My own observations indicate that *R. lapidifer* digs a pit in the substrate, exposing the bottom glass, and later spawns there. After 24 hours the pit is invariably still present, only the glass is now completely covered with coarser gravel, so "stone-carrier" is indeed an accurate description. The eggs are extremely adhesive such that small particles (e.g. sand) cling to them and the eggs themselves stick together. Unfortunately further broodcare has not yet been observed in the aquarium, so it is unclear whether the brood is taken into the mouth at a specific point in time, or whether after becoming free-swimming the brood is led simply in the open-brooder fashion.

Remarks: To date only a few imports of these fishes have proved successful, as they react very badly to any deterioration in water quality. In particular nitrite and ammonia appear to cause considerable harm, whereas nitrate plays a subordinate role. For this reason *Retroculus* should be treated with antibiotics only when absolutely necessary, as there is a strong possibility of antibiotics harming the bacterial fauna of the aquarium such that the nitrification process is interrupted. The result will be a rise in nitrite and ammonia levels and the fishes will be poisoned. For this reason these fishes should be treated with antibiotics only in the quarantine aquarium and then only with constant monitoring of the water parameters. Short term baths are preferable to long-term if the medicine allows. Treatment for *Ichthyophthirius* and other ectoparasites is readily tolerated. In order to avoid problems with internal nematodes and flagellates it is suggested that the fishes be treated prophylactically every three to four months as described earlier to prevent the proliferation of these pathogens.

Moreover it should be mentioned that young *Retroculus* (whether wild-caught or tank-bred) appear to go through a sort of adolescent stage which may result in repeated unexplained deaths in the aquarium. Usually the candidates for the hereafter can be recognised by small open lesions on their bodies and/or increased respiratory rate. In general the belly swells up a short time afterwards and death then follows rather rapidly. The

1. Courting *Retroculus lapidifer* — the male is in the foreground.
2. Shortly after deposition the eggs lie still scattered in the centre of the pit.
3. After spawning the eggs are collected.
4. Both parents actively collect the eggs.
5. Even after the eggs have been chewed clean by the parents sand still adheres.

usual medications against worms, bacteria, and parasites have no effect. So far the cause of these deaths has not been diagnosed. The reasons could be connected with the diet or perhaps attributable to stress, as this usually takes place in overpopulated rearing aquaria or during a phase where a lot of chasing is going on. It cannot be ruled out that a "peck order" may develop within a group, with the weakest individuals coming to grief, although these are basically very peaceful cichlids.

According to Kullander (1998) *Retroculus* should no longer be assigned to the subfamily Geophaginae, but instead to the extremely primitive subfamily Retroculinae.

Further reading: Gosse (1971: 7-11); Kullander (1998: 461-498); Lucas (1999: 8-14); Stawikowski (1989c:

347-352; 1991a: 149-154); Weidner (1999: 8-12); Werner (1990c: 129-140).

Retroculus lapidifer
(Castelnau, 1855)

Original description: Animaux nouveaux ou rares de l'Amerique du sud. Poissons; Paris: 16.

Derivation of scientific name: *lapis* (Lat.) = stone; *ferre* (Lat.) = to carry, referring to this species' habit, in the wild, of building a nest (in which to spawn) of pebbles which must first be brought to the site.

Distribution: So far the only confirmed localities for *R. lapidifer* are in the Rio Tocantins system, which includes the Rio Araguaia and its drainage. Additional localities are known from the Rio Capim (including the Rio Guamá), which empties into the Baía de Marajó at Belém. It cannot be ruled out that the species may be found in other tributaries of the

- R. lapidifer
- R. septentrionalis
- R. xinguensis

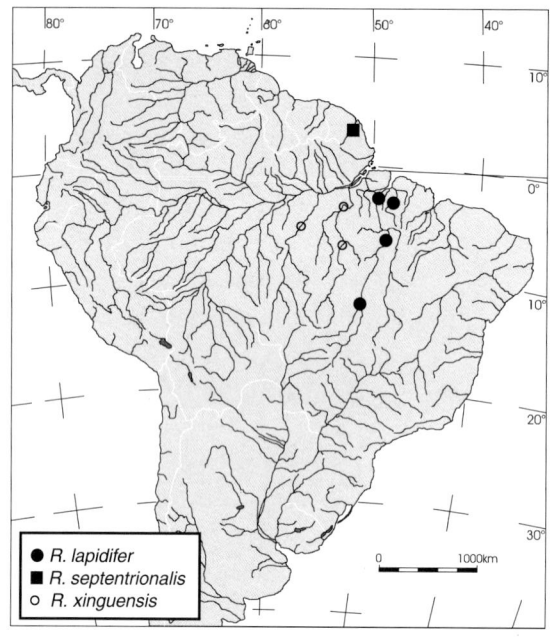

Rio Tocantins provided their topography includes fast-flowing reaches.

Habitat: Like all the species of the genus, *R. lapidifer* lives largely in fast-flowing rivers or reaches where the current increases appreciably on account of the topography, although during the dry season, when the water level falls to its minimum, these cichlids can also be found in residual pools. These pools are often only a few centimetres deep and can sometimes heat up to 35° C owing to their exposure to the sun. Normally, however, it is the permanent channels that are frequented, where temperatures over the course of the year average between 26 and 29° C. The water is soft and oxygen-rich. The pH lies between 6.0 and 6.8. However, Werner (1990) reports a water temperature of only 22° C and a pH sometimes as low as 5.5, from the Rio das Mortes in the Rio Araguaia system, Brazil.

R. lapidifer is a clearwater fish which requires water with minimal organic pollution. Sandy bottoms with areas of river shingle characterise the natural habitat. Leaf litter and wood are generally absent.

Size: A large species (up to 25 cm).

Characters of the species: *R. lapidifer* is relatively easy to distinguish from the other two described species, as it has no dark pattern in the caudal fin. Instead in adults the upper part of the caudal is yellow to orange, or even reddish. The dorsal spot is somewhat elongate in shape and lies at the lower edge of the dorsal fin and in direct contact with the ridge of the back, without there being any vestiges of its dark pigment on the back itself. The caudal, anal, and the hard rays of the ventrals often exhibit a dark edge. The caudal has as straight edge. These fishes exhibit an irregular, faded, pattern of dark markings on the body. A vertical bar begins on the back at the centre of the spinous dorsal base and runs downwards from the back downwards before kinking towards the head at the level of the upper lateral line. A further vertical bar at the end of the dorsal follows the same pattern. If the fish is happy and healthy then this irregular pattern changes to a normal stripe pattern with six bars visible, all extending down to the ventral region. The flanks of adults are covered in numerous iridescent bluish spots. Two stripes, again iridescent bluish, run below the eye and end about halfway to the upper lip. Depending on the population the lips may be yellow or bluish.

Sexual dimorphism: In general the females of *R. lapidifer* are not as large as males. The pectorals as well as the dorsal and anal are not prolonged anything like as greatly as in males. In dominant males the upper and lower edges of the caudal are also prolonged such that the tail looks slightly forked. Adult females may develop almost black upper and lower lips apparently signalling their readiness to spawn, but this statement must be considered in context, as it is based on observations of just one population and does not necessarily apply in every case. In this regard, however, it should be noted that males become noticeably more active when females exhibit this coloration.

Maintenance: A substrate of soft, fine sand is obligatory for this species, with a depth of at least 5 cm as these fishes often dive up to their eyes in the substrate while searching for food. The sand is picked up and masticated and then spat out in the same spot. The flight behaviour is another reason why the substrate should not be too coarse of sharp-edged, as in moments of panic these fishes will bury themselves in the bottom so that only their eyes remain visible. It is, however, advisable to include a number of pebbles as these will subsequently play an important role in the brood care. The rest of the decor can be minimal, as open sandy surfaces are the preferred habitat. Nevertheless a few hiding-places should be included to provide the *Retroculus* with a degree of cover. These fishes like a somewhat raised "perch", in the form of a rock or a horizontally-positioned flat stone, on which they can "sit" and inquisitively watch the world go by. Often several individuals will sit close-packed together on the same "plateau".

Plants can be included as long as they do not require much light, as *R. lapidifer* does not appreciate direct light. Given the eventual size of these fishes the aquarium must have a capacity of at least 600 litres with a bottom area of at least 150 x 60 cm. A minimum of four individuals should always be kept, as otherwise they may be very shy. Except at spawning time adults exhibit only minimal territorial behaviour and are thus easy to maintain in a group. However, when they are in breeding condition then their aggression increases and they are then capable of dominating too small an aquarium.

R. lapidifer will eat anything, but they prefer larger morsels such as pieces of fish, larger krill, mussel meat, and shrimp/prawn. Their appetites are unimaginable and they will feed practically all day long. A rounded belly is only rarely seen in adults. Even so it is important not to overfeed these fishes as they may easily become obese. Frequent feeds of small amounts of food throughout the day are more appropriate.

Oxygen-rich water is, of course, a prerequisite of the successful maintenance of these cichlids, but there is a tendency to attribute too much importance to oxygen content in relation to the "keepability" of these cichlids. Given that high temperatures (see Habitat, above) lead to a reduction in oxygen content, yet *R. lapidifer* nevertheless appears to thrive, without any increase in respiratory rate, under such conditions, the problems encountered with these cichlids in the aquarium must have another cause,

1. The eggs of *Retroculus lapidifer* are, after spawning is over, covered with pebbles.
2. Exposed nests (during the dry season) of *R. lapidifer* along the banks of the Rio Araguaia near São Bento. Photo: Frank Warzel.
3. Juvenile *R. lapidifer* prefer vantage points to rest.
4. Sometimes large numbers of juvenile *Retroculus* can be found in such pools (São Luis do Tapajós, Rio Tapajós, Brazil).

apparently deterioration in water quality (see Remarks, under the genus section, above).

Breeding behaviour: In 1989 Kiefel observed the first spawning known to have occurred in the aquarium. The aquarium in which these *Retroculus* spawned was decorated with fine sand plus pebbles and sparse rocks. Kiefel also constructed a few nests using a number of larger stones. In the course of time a pair eventually occupied one of these nests and began their courtship. They displayed to each other with their lower jaws fully lowered and all their fins spread. Now and then one of the pair would swim to the centre of the nest and pick up a mouthful of sand, which it then spat out again outside the nest. Eventually all that was left was the large pebbles, while a small rampart of sand now surrounded the outside of the nest. The other fish in the aquarium were chased only from the immediate vicinity of the nest and were not otherwise molested.

After a few days spawning was finally observed. First of all the female swam quivering over the nest and laid her eggs. Next the male followed and fertilised the spawn. The genital papilla of the male was small and pointed while that of the female appeared small and triangular. Kiefel surmised that the genital papilla of the female did not have any tactile function. The eggs were very light in colour, sank extremely rapidly, and were very adhesive, such that fine sand stuck all over the shell. Unfortunately Kiefel was unable to get any further with this breeding attempt, as by the next day the eggs which he had left with the parents had vanished, while those which he had removed fungussed within 40 hours despite strong aeration.

Three weeks later the same pair spawned again. This time Kiefel was able to follow the brood care behaviour for four days, but again the eggs fungussed. During this period a wall of sand was erected and then turned over and moved around, and Kiefel surmised it contained the eggs/larvae.

From my own observations *R. lapidifer* does not create a nest of large stones for spawning, but first of all prepares a large oval pit, at least 60 cm long and 40 cm wide. In the process the sand is removed down to the bottom glass (the bottom layer was 5 cm deep) and deposited in a sort of rampart around the nest. Once the bottom glass was exposed then spawning took place soon afterwards a short distance above this pit. Immediately after the spawning (7 pm) the following water parameters were recorded: Temperature 28.6° C, Nitrate < 5 mg/l, pH 5.2 (measured with Merck test strips), KH < 1° dKH, GH = 5° dGH, conductivity 240 µS/cm. Because spawning was completed within half an hour I saw only the behaviour immediately afterwards.

Immediately after spawning the approximately 200 eggs were collected together by both parents and carried to a spot measuring about 10 x 10 cm. A number of pebbles were individually carried and spat onto the heap of eggs. As noted by Kiefel, the eggs were yellowish to sand-coloured and very heavy, and sand stuck to them. It was noticeable that even when the eggs were taken into the mouth, chewed over, and spat out again, they were still covered in sand.

After the spawning both parents were very excited and drove potential predators away from the vicinity of the eggs with great gusto. At first they threatened the other fishes with fins spread almost to tearing and then attacked them by ramming them in the side, assuming they hadn't already made themselves scarce. If the front glass was touched with a finger then it too was threatened and eventually attacked. A pair of *Geophagus altifrons* in the same aquarium, who were already leading young, were very aggressively put in their place by the male. Both parents patrolled above their spawn, and each time a parent returned to the nest they greeted each other with lateral threat.

In general the female hovered directly over the spawn while the male guarded the territory. The eggs were repeatedly moved around by the parents and in addition the number of pebbles was continually increased, until by next morning the entire bottom of the pit was covered with them. The other 12 (!) occupants, all with a length of 15 cm, were confined to about 50 cm of the bottom area of the 160 cm aquarium. Only at feeding time did the other occupants venture out and even swim over the spawn. It was noticeable that the other fishes hardly ever went near the bottom so that it was easy for the parents to guard the eggs.

A "night-light" was provided at night so that the parents could guard the eggs, but despite this after 48 hours the eggs were no longer to be seen. I had, however, already siphoned off about 150 eggs and was endeavouring to hatch them artificially in a 12 litre aquarium with a small does of malachite green and gentle aeration. After 48 hours there was still no sign of pigmentation in the eggs although none of them had fungussed. The temperature in the hatchery was initially 25° C and was raised to 29° C after 48 hours. After a total of 96 hours the larvae began to hatch, and after 144 hours some were still in their eggshells. Apropos of which, it is worth noting that it is possible actively to assist in hatching by siphoning the eggs through a narrow tube. The brief change in pressure enables the larvae more easily to break through the shell. During the subsequent rearing I established that only the larvae that had hatched between the 96th and 120th hours were fully healthy. All the others exhibited deformities and were not viable. After 9 days the fry were already able to take food and could at this stage already manage newly-hatched *Artemia*.

Young *Retroculus* are extremely nervous and at the least hint of danger will flee in total panic. For this reason it is totally inadvisable to rear little *R. lapidifer* in aquaria with no substrate, as reflections from the bottom glass will stress them excessively. If, however, some substrate is introduced and the young are given somewhere to hide, then they will be calmer and losses smaller. The problems remains as to why individuals of 3-6 cm are so prone to illness that fails to respond to any medication (see Remarks, under the genus section, above). Unfortunately natural rearing under the protection of the parents has yet to be achieved.

Remarks: *R. lapidifer* is the type species of the genus and the species most often imported.

Further reading: Bernhard (1991); Kiefel (1989a: 393-395; 1989b: 455); Lucas (1999: 8-14); Stawikowski (1987: 573); Weidner (1999: 8-12); Werner (1990c: 129-140).

Retroculus septentrionalis
Gosse, 1971

Original description: Bull. Inst. Roy. Sci. Nat. Belg. 47 (43): 11-12.

Derivation of scientific name: *septentrionalis* (Lat.) = northern. The distribution of this species in northern Brazil to the border of French Guiana is more northerly than that of the other two described species.

Distribution: The type locality of *R. septentrionalis* is the Oyapock River (von Drachenfels & Bitter, 1987; Gosse, 1969: Planquette, 1986) and the Camopi River Gosse, 1969), in French Guiana, which form the boundary with Brazil. However, Werner (1988) and Stawikowski (1990) independently of one another found *R. septentrionalis* in the Rio Araguari in the state of Amapá, Brazil. At the present time it cannot be stated with certainty to what extent the distribution of this species extends to rivers emptying into the Atlantic.

Habitat: Von Drachenfels & Bitter (1988), who caught this species in the Oyapock at Saut Maripa, describe the habitat as fast-flowing water in which it was difficult to stand up in the current. The habitat of *R. septentrionalis* is, according to von Drachenfels (pers. comm.) full of rocks covered in dense growths of *Mourera fluviatilis*. But calmer areas in the lee of large rocks or root tangles are also preferred habitats of *R. septentrionalis*, as long as the bottom consists mainly of soft substrate material. Stawikowski (1991) caught this species in the Rio Araguari upstream of Porto Grande and describes the collecting locality as follows (translated from the German): "In general their [small islands in the river bed] edges are sand or gravel; only rarely did we find islands with muddy shores. In many cases the side of the island facing into the current had ac-

1. The Oyapock near Saut Maripa — locality of *Retroculus septentrionalis*. Photo: Ernst-Otto von Drachenfels.
2. Freshly caught *R. septentrionalis*. Photo: Rainer Stawikowski
3. *Retroculus xinguensis* may be the most attractive species of the genus *Retroculus*.

cumulated extensive piles of wood, including entire uprooted trees. Depending on the topography of the shoreline there were sections past which the water rushed very rapidly, but also places where the water was quite still."

Size: At present there are no confirmed data regarding the ultimate size of these cichlids. The specimen caught by Stawikowski had a total length of 25 cm.

Characters of the species: The body shape closely resembles that or *R. lapidifer*, i.e. again the upper head profile rises relatively gently and the outline of the head resembles an isosceles triangle. The body and fin coloration represents a link between the other two described species. Thus juvenile *R. septentrionalis* have a tail with vertical banding as in *R. xinguensis*, while the adult caught by

Stawikowski no longer exhibited any stripe pattern. Instead the upper edge of the tail has a reddish hue, as is seen in *R. lapidifer*. Then again, juveniles exhibit a body pattern reminiscent of *R. lapidifer*, while adults by contrast display only a pattern of vertical bars. The most significant distinguishing character from the other two described species is the form of the dorsal spot, which in *R. septentrionalis* is only faintly visible and appears to be broken up into individual stripes. In addition the dorsal spot is visibly offset from the ridge of the back, as is also the case in *R. xinguensis*.

Sexual dimorphism: At present unknown, as no reproductive activity has been observed and not enough specimens have been captured. However, it is extremely probable that in this species too the females remain smaller and are not as boldly coloured as are males.

Maintenance: At present insufficient aquarium observations are available, as the few individuals imported thus far have not been adequately studied. It can, however, be assumed that maintenance requirements will not differ appreciably from those of the other two described species.

Breeding behaviour: To date neither aquarium nor field observations have been made. The typical spawning nests found in the natural habitat lead to the supposition that this species spawns in a similar manner to *R. lapidifer*.

Further reading: von Drachenfels (1988: 16-21); Stawikowski (1991b: 56-59).

Retroculus xinguensis
Gosse, 1971

Original description: Bull. Inst. Roy. Sci. Nat. Belg. 47 (43): 7-11.

Derivation of scientific name: The name means of (or from) the Xingú, and refers to the provenance of the species.

Distribution: Until 1993 it was assumed that *R. xinguensis* was endemic to the Rio Xingú. But in 1992 Stawikowski, Müller, Kilian, Ludwig, and Schaefer found a *Retroculus* in the Rio Tapajós to the south of São Luis de Tapajós, and made specimens available to Kullander for investigation, and he identified them as *R. xinguensis*. The holotype was collected at Cachoeira de Martius in the Rio Xingú (Léopold III & Gosse, 1964) at the northern edge of the state of Mato Grosso in Brazil. But as *R. xinguensis* has also been found at Altamira which is much further downstream and relatively close to the confluence of the Xingú with the Amazon, the assumption is that this species is distributed throughout the Rio Xingú.

Habitat: The habitat of *R. xinguensis* does not differ significantly from that of *R. lapidifer*.

Size: This species too can attain a total length of up to 25 cm.

Characters of the species: *R. xinguensis* is probably the most attractive member of the genus. In particular, males have vivid red dorsal and ventrals. There is a pattern of vertical reddish lines on the caudal, and these are extraordinarily regular in their arrangement. The dorsal has a reddish edge and the genus-typical spot lies at the beginning of the soft part of the fin, about a scale's width from the ridge of the back. This spot appears somewhat rounder than in the other two species. The upper head profile of *R. xinguensis* rises rather more steeply than in the other species and the head thus appears somewhat more rounded.

Sexual dimorphism: In this species too the male has more prolonged ventrals, anal, and dorsal fin, which are also more vividly coloured. In addition females remain somewhat smaller and are in general more corpulent.

Maintenance: This species should be maintained in the same way as *R. lapidifer* and shares the susceptibility of that species to poor water quality.

Breeding behaviour: To date no detailed aquarium observations on the brood-care behaviour of this species are available. A pair have been observed during courtship and nest preparation, but they did not spawn. Their nest-digging behaviour corresponds to that of *R. lapidifer*. Field observations also suggest that this species breeds in the same manner as *R. lapidifer*. Here too nests up to a metre in diameter have been found in the natural habitat.

Further reading: Stawikowski (1993: 144-145); Weidner (1998b: 7-11).

1. *Retroculus xinguensis* is easily distinguished from the other members of the genus by the red anal fin.
2. Courting *Retroculus xinguensis*. This pair started to dig out a spawning pit.
3. *Acarichthys heckelii* of the round-headed form.

Acarichthys Eigenmann, 1912

The following section discusses genera and species which were for a long time numbered among the earth-eaters and the tribe Geophagini. The latest wisdom is, however, that they form a separate tribe, the Acarichthyini, within the subfamily Geophaginae (Kullander, 1998). The reasons for this include behavioural and morphological differences from the tribe Geophagini — for example, they have less pronouncedly developed epibranchial lobes.

Eigenmann (1912) regarded the genus *Acarichthys* as the "missing link" between *Aequidens* and *Geophagus* on account of the underdeveloped epibranchial lobe, and wrote: "This genus bridges the gap between *Aequidens* on the one side and *Geophagus* on the other." In the same work he regarded *Acarichthys heckelii* as closely related to *Retroculus* (Castelnau, 1855), as these cichlids likewise have a less pronounced epibranchial lobe, and also noted that the cichlid known at that time as *Acara geayi* (currently *Guianacara geayi*) possessed a similar body form. Regan (1905) formulated the close relationship between *Acarichthys heckelii* (at that time *Acara subocularis*) and *Acara geayi* rather more clearly, writing: "Consequently this species falls in the genus *Acara* and there can be no doubt that its position is next to *Acara Geayi*, Pellegr., which it resembles in many respects."

In spite of this, or precisely because of it, I propose to give full coverage to these cichlids here: firstly, because for many years they were numbered among the eartheaters, and secondly, because they have often been only inadequately dealt with elsewhere.

At present just two genera, the monotypic genus *Acarichthys* and the genus *Guianacara*, with two subgenera *Guianacara* and *Oelemaria* and a total of four species, are included in the tribe Acarichthyini. In this tribe we find the cave-brooding cichlids of the eartheater assemblage, although this designation must be used with great care. *Guianacara* are to some extent concealed substrate-spawners, as they produce eggs that are definitively I-type and never spawn on the ceiling of a cave, but always on vertical substrates; and are, moreover, easily satisfied with any spawning site that is fairly well concealed from view. *A. heckelii* must, however, be regarded as a cave-brooder, as its p-type eggs are attached to the ceiling of the cave.

Acarichthys heckelii
(Müller & Troschel, 1848)

Original description: in Schomburgk, 1849: 624.

Derivation of scientific name: Acara, a local name for cichlids, long used as a "catch-all" genus name and still valid in 1912 when Eigenmann erected *Acarichthys*; *ichthys* (Gr.) = fish. The specific name is in honour of the noted Austrian ichthyologist Jacob Heckel, who was also the author of the genus *Geophagus*.

Distribution: *A. heckelii* is a South American cichlid with a wide distribution. It is found along the Amazon in Peru near Quisto Cocha and in the northern and southern affluents of that river, as well as in the Rio Negro, the Rio Branco, and the Essequibo-Rupununi system in Guyana. This wide distribution has led to the evolution of different populations which may differ in their coloration as well as their body form. Thus forms with a distinctly pointed head were imported at the end of the 1980s, although today it is mostly a form with a rounder head that is imported, as the other type is resident in Guyana whence few importations are received.

Habitat: In 1971 and 1972 Cichocki studied *A. heckelii* in the natural habitat in the Rio Branco/Rupununi savannah, and established that *A. heckelii* is a monogamous cave-brooder. The caves, or rather tunnels, are dug by the fishes themselves and initially lead vertically down into the bottom, before usually ending in a horizontal tunnel 10-50 cm.

These nests are generally constructed in the vicinity of submerse vegetation which eventually provides shelter for the free-swimming young. The territory of *A. heckelii* has a diameter of about 2.5 metres. Astonishingly it is the females that occupy the breeding tunnels and court passing males. If a male is interested then he courts the female in turn; the pair bond is formed and the male is then allowed into the breeding tunnel. From then on the male takes over the territorial defence and is master of the territory.

The water in the natural habitat had a pH of about 6.0-6.75, though Cichocki (1976) also found these fishes in neutral and even alkaline waters (pH 7.0-8.0). During the rainy season (April to July) in 1971 the water temperature was around 28-30.5° C (Cichocki, 1976). The water is described by Cichocki as clear in all cases. The low hardness and slightly acid pH are evidence of the relatively low nutrient levels in the substrate.

Distribution of *Acarichthys heckelii*

Size: With good maintenance these fishes can attain a total length of 20-25 cm in the aquarium. Leibel (1984) cites a size of 150 mm SL and Cichocki (1976) 120 mm SL.

Characters of the species: Typical of *A. heckelii* are a very deep, laterally greatly compressed body and small terminal mouth, deep black anterior dorsal spines, greatly prolonged and red-coloured anterior dorsal soft rays, a black lateral spot, dark eye stripe, and thread-like extensions of the outer caudal rays. Even juveniles of only a few centimetres length can be differentiated from other geophagines (apart from *Guianacara*, to which *Acarichthys* is rather close) by the black anterior dorsal spines. There is a possibility of confusing juveniles with *Mikrogeophagus*, as these too have black anterior dorsal spines. There is a yellow to reddish (generally depending on the population) area behind the head. The pectorals are colourless. The ventrals may have threadlike extensions.

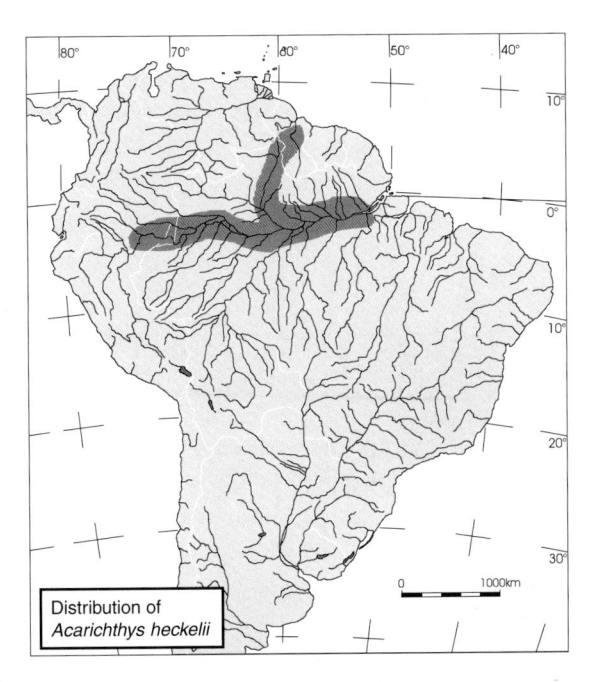

Sexual dimorphism: No secondary sexual characteristics can be discerned in juveniles. In adult, sexually mature, individuals the males may have more prolonged anterior dorsal soft rays.

During courtship the females exhibit a striking black pattern and at this stage the lateral spot has a light surround. In addition females are somewhat more rotund at this time.

Maintenance: *A. heckelii* is an omnivore which should be offered as varied a diet as possible. It will eat anything, and for this reason ample vegetable food should also be provided. Water parameters play only a subordinate role in maintenance. For breeding the pH should be slightly acid and the hardness less than 10° dGH, although Baran (1981) was able to breed his fishes in harder water. Because of the size of these cichlids the aquarium should have a capacity of at least 450 litres. The substrate should have a fine to medium grain size. Hiding-places and muted lighting will make an additional contribution to the fishes' wellbeing. Leibel describes his adults as unsociable and with a marked tendency to move the substrate around: "They are tremendous and incessant gravel movers, and the adults are unpredictably vicious towards conspecifics." Bader (1973), Baran (1981), Lucal (1996), Morche (1993), and Schneider (1987) all describe their *A. heckelii* as generally peaceful. It may be that the type of tankmates and/or the internal arrangement of the aquarium may have a significant effect on the behaviour of these cichlids.

Breeding behaviour: According to Cichocki (1976) sexual maturity is attained very late in this species. Thus females are ready to spawn only at two years old, while males need to be three years old before they are sexually active.

1. *Acarichthys heckelii*.
2. *A. heckelii* with a pointed snout — a form which was imported several decades ago. Photo: Peter Lucas.

If *A. heckelii* is to be stimulated to breed in the aquarium, then suitable caves must, of course, be provided. It is important that at least one of the fishes should be able to remain completely out of sight within the cave, and hence the entrance should be relatively restricted. Baran (1981) used a old sweet jar covered over and shaded with roots and rocks. Lucas (1996) positioned two flowerpots "mouth-to-mouth" and broke a piece out of the bottom of one of them. It is, however, also worth considering constructing a suitable tunnel from clay pipes of appropriate diameter. Leibel (1984) used an upturned flowerpot with a piece broken out of the side to serve as an entrance for the fishes.

According to Leibel, in order to bring these fishes into spawning condition large water changes are required each week. In addition Leibel raised the temperature to 35.5° C and kept it there for 3-4 days, after which he lowered it back to 25-26° C. He repeated this two weeks later, and during the interim fed the fishes mainly on live foods. Shortly afterwards they spawned.

During spawning the *A. heckelii* pair take turns to swim into the cave. The male usually fertilises the eggs directly inside the cave, or he may release his sperm outside the cave and it is then conveyed to the eggs by fanning movements on the part of the female. The female attaches the up to 2000 (Leibel, 1984; Cichocki, 1976) tiny whitish eggs to the ceiling and/or the walls. To date no more than a maximum of 250 fry have been achieved under aquarium conditions. It is not clear whether this is the result of a low fertilisation rate or an overestimate of egg numbers. Leibel noted that after a few hours (about 24) the eggs came away from the substrate and lay on the bottom, where they were further tended.

At 27° C the larvae hatch after about 60 hours. A further five days later the fry become free-swimming and must be fed immediately with the tiniest of foods (rotifers and other infusorians). Only three days later are they able to manage freshly-hatched *Artemia*. *A. heckelii* are not particularly good parents and brood care generally ends after 14 days at most.

Remarks: Older specimens of *A. heckelii* are prone to develop growths on the head and in the mouth region. To date it remains unclear what causes these growths or whether they can be treated.

Further reading: Bader (1973: 409-413); Baran (1981: 185-190); Cichocki (1976); Kullander (1986: 134-139); Leibel (1984: 15-19); Loiselle (1981b: 80-83); Lucas (1996: 28-32); Morche (1993: 76-79); Schneider (1987: 134-137).

Guianacara Kullander & Nijssen, 1989

Derivation of scientific name: Kullander & Nijssen's genus name refers to the basic distribution zone, the Guianas, with *acara*, the Tupi indian name for some cichlids, added as a suffix.

Distribution: The distribution of the genus is restricted to northeastern South America, and includes eastern Venezuela, Guyana, Surinam, French Guiana, as well as the Rio Branco, the Rio Trombetas drainage, and the state of Amapá in Brazil. The best-known species, albeit rather rare in captivity, *Guianacara geayi*, comes from the Camopi-Oyapock drainage in French Guiana.

Ecology: To date only a few observations have been made of *Guianacara* species in their natural habitat, by ichthyologists and itinerant aquarists. However, these limited observations indicate that *Guianacara* species seek out the company of their own kind and are inclined to form colonies. I myself have been able to observe and catch a *G. sphenozona*-like species "on the spot" at the Paso Caruachi, a former and now ruined causeway across the Rio Caroni in Venezuela. The fishes were swimming in the immediate vicinity of the stone causeway in water up to 1.5 metres deep. Over the course of time the causeway had become filled with numerous cracks and holes, in which the *Guianacara* sought refuge when danger threatened. It can be assumed that these holes also served as breeding caves, as this species, like all other known *Guianacara* species, has proved to be a cave brooder (or "concealed-spawning open-brooder") in the aquarium. The area around the causeway was dotted with numerous pits. I was never able to observe whether these were used for the guarding of free-swimming broods. In the lee of the causeway, over an extremely fine substrate, exclusively semi-adult individuals could be seen in extremely shallow (maximum 30 cm deep) water. The water was mineral-depleted (30 µS/cm), very acid, and very slow-flowing.

Characters of the genus: These cichlids can be recognised by their characteristic "saddle-spot", which varies in shape and size from species to species. *Guianacara* possess a more or less pronounced eye stripe on a silvery-beige background; this stripe begins on the nape and extends to the anterior edge of the operculum. The upper head profile rises steeply, but no nuchal hump is developed. The species can attain a length of up to 20 cm maximum, with females remaining slightly smaller. Apart from this size difference there are no secondary sexual characteristics.

In their description of the genus Kullander & Nijssen (1989) simultaneously erected two subgenera, *Guianacara* and *Oelemaria*. As far as aquarists are concerned the most important distinctions between them lie in the form of the "saddle" and the structure of the dorsal fin. While in *Guianacara* (the subgenus) the saddle takes the form of a vertical stripe, which may be reduced to a spot on the back region in adults, *Oelemaria* instead have a lateral spot on the centre of the side. Moreover *Guianacara* have produced anterior dorsal-fin lappets, while *Oelemaria* do not.

Unfortunately the description of these cichlids was (as usual) made on the basis of preserved material, and as a result identification of live specimens can be very difficult. The fact that the extent of the saddle can alter very rapidly with mood may overtax the aquarist. But, because coloration is very similar at times of high motivation (battle or brood care) or fear or stress, identification is best performed during threat display or spawning. The species descriptions include characters taken from the genus description. Thus the coloration of the anterior dorsal rays in adult *Guianacara* is mentioned, but this is definitely mood-dependent and not relevant in living individuals. Kullander & Nijssen, however, state that only adult *G. owroewefi* and *G. oelemariensis* possess black anterior dorsal rays, and that this characteristic is absent in other members of the genus.

Ethology: Field observations to date lead to the indubitable conclusion that *Guianacara* species are exclusively monogamous cichlids, which are inclined to form colonies. *Guianacara* can be found in areas with abundant rocks, as well as over sandy and muddy bottoms, provided a number of hiding-places are available in the form of roots and/or branches. They occupy not just stillwater zones but also areas with a rather faster current, and can even be found in rapids.

In the aquarium all the species imported thus far have proved to be exceptionally hardy cichlids that can be kept in hard (up to 20° dGH) and alkaline (up to pH 8.0) water even in the long term. In keeping with their natural habitat they prefer a fine substrate and hiding-places (plants, wood, and/or rocky structures) in the aquarium. As regards diet, they are omnivores with no special requirements. Although plants are not harmed, the food should nevertheless include vegetable matter in order to avoid deficiency symptoms. That apart, any type of flake, frozen, or — of course — live foods can be offered. The lighting should not be too strong and the temperature should not fall below 25° C in the long term. Various authors have stated that *Guianacara* have a rather high oxygen requirement, though I have never noticed any evidence of this myself.

1. Locality of *Guianacara geayi*, Saut Mapao, Approuague River, French Guiana.
2. A freshly caught *G. geayi* (Saut Mapao, Approuague river). The eye stripe is prominent while the saddle-spot is somewhat pale.
3. *G. geayi* several hours after collection. The eye stripe is now restricted to a spot on the gill cover; the saddle-spot is only vaguely visible.
4. The identification of *Guianacara* species is, without detailed collection data, very difficult. Here *G. geayi* (Saut Mapao).

In a restricted space battles may occur between males, and weaker individuals may come to grief. For this reason these fishes should be provided with ample space in the aquarium, particularly where a small group is to be kept, when a bottom area of 100 x 50 cm is the lower limit. Aquaria of 100 litres capacity are adequate for a pair.

Under these conditions there will not be long to wait before the fishes proceed to breed. Courtship is performed largely by the male, who courts any female who enters his territory. If the female is ready to spawn then she responds to his wooing. The two fishes position themselves side by side and head to tail and start tail-beating. Shortly thereafter there may be frontal threat with mouth-wrestling, though this is the exception rather than the rule. However, injuries almost never occur. Once pair formation has taken place then both sexes select the future spawning site and rearrange its immediate vicinity according to their particular preferences. In general the site is a hole which is protected from view on at least four sides. The eggs are always attached to vertical surfaces by their long sides. While the female assumes direct responsibility for care of the spawn, the male busies himself with defending the territory. When, after about 14 days (depending on water temperature), the larvae become free-swimming the male is tolerated in the immediate vicinity of the fry by the female and is allowed to participate in the leading of the young. Now and then small pits are constructed by the parents, and the young are then assembled in these for more effective supervision (see also Ecology, above). In particular just before "lights out" the larvae or fry are collected up by the parents and transported to such pits. On becoming free-swimming the fry can immediately be fed with *Artemia* nauplii. The subsequent rearing is not difficult as long as attention is paid to water quality. The growth of the fry is rather slow and it may be a year (maximum) before they are in turn sexually mature.

Further reading: Kullander & Nijssen (1989: 90-130); Schaefer (1994).

Guianacara geayi (Pellegrin, 1902)

Original description: Bull. Mus. Nat. Hist. Paris, VIII: 417-419.

Derivation of scientific name: The species was named in honour of the collector, F. Geay, who provided Pellegrin with the material used for the description in 1902.

Distribution: The localities from which this species was described lie in the Camopi and Oyapock drainages. But it is also found in the Approuague drainage in French Guiana (pers. obs., 1999) and in the Rio Caciporé drainage in Brazilian state of Amapá (Stawikowski *et al.*, 1991; pers. comm.).

Habitat: This species is usually found at the periphery of fast-flowing waters, but can also be found in rapids (Approuague, French Guiana, pers. obs., 1999). The sometimes muddy bottom at the Approuague site consisted largely of sand with large areas dotted with large rocks. For this reason progress through the waist-deep, murky, 32° C water was slow and difficult, and every step had to be taken with care in order to avoid losing one's footing. Only now and then did twigs and branches extend into the water, making it easy to fish with the cast net. Within an hour 18 fishes had been netted. As well as *G. geayi* we regularly captured *Cteniloricaria fowleri, Geophagus camopiensis*, and various *Leporinus*.

According to Mayland (1995) the sites for this species in the Oyapock and Approuague drainages are softwater rivers with a strong current, occasionally rapids and rocky terrain. Only where there are bays in the banks and the current is less strong are there deposits of sand and occasionally wood and leaf litter. The eroded cavities in the rock near the bank are much favoured by the cichlids as places to live and breed.

Von Drachenfels found *G. geayi* among stones in calmer parts of the Oyapock rapids, in slack water and back-eddies where the current was not so strong.

- *Guianacara geayi*
- *G. oelemariensis*
- *G. owroewefi*
- *G. sphenozona*
- *G.* sp. "Rio Caroni"
- *G.* sp. "Red Cheek"

Size: Adult males of *G. geayi* can attain a total length of 20 cm, while females remain 2-4 cm smaller.

Characters of the species: According to Kullander & Nijssen (1989) adult *G. geayi* do not have dark anterior dorsal rays, while juveniles do exhibit this character. The lateral spot is wedge-shaped as in *G. sphenozona* but in contrast to that species *G. geayi* has larger spots in the soft dorsal. A most important character is that the spots in the dorsal are not limited to the soft part, but are on the spinous part as well. *G. geayi* has a distinctive suborbital stripe which extends downwards in a straight line to the lower edge of the operculum and then turns slightly upwards again, creating a small black angle on the cheek. The body base colour is yellowish.

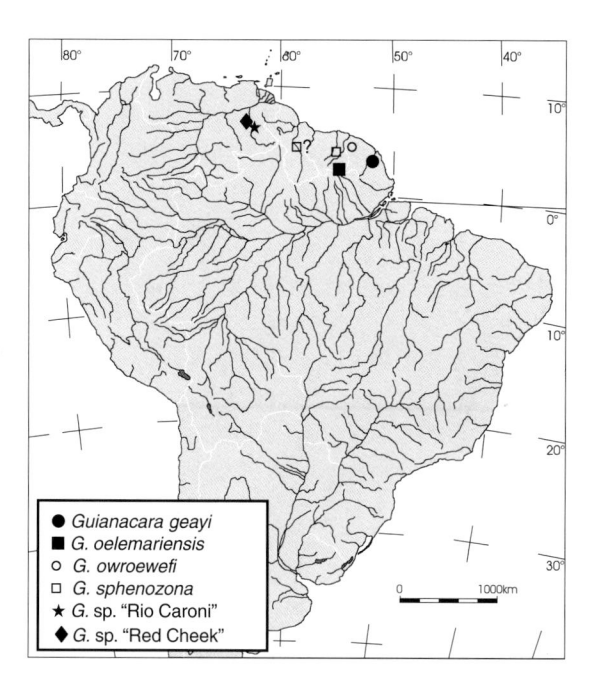

Sexual dimorphism: *G. geayi* does not exhibit any pronounced sexual dimorphism, apart from the fact that males grow large and may have more pointed and elongated tips to their fins. In addition males may have a larger number of light spots on the unpaired fins and the ventral profile does not appear as rounded.

Maintenance: An aquarium with a capacity of 100 litres is adequate for keeping a pair of these fishes. If, however, they are to be housed with other fishes, or perhaps even several pairs are to be kept together, then the bottom area of the aquarium should under no circumstances be less than 100 x 50 cm, as otherwise the pairs will squabble excessively. This may not necessarily lead to injuries, but the long-term stress will be too great. In addition the aquarium should be provided with as many hiding-places as possible; wood is particularly suitable, but stones will do as a substitute. When arranging the aquarium it is important to make sure that there are caves which the pair can excavate to suite their preferences. If suitable caves are not available then a lot of digging may take place, especially in the corners, with small ramparts of sand being erected and then vehemently defended.

The water parameters required for maintenance will be found above, under the description of the genus. *G. geayi* is an omnivore which has no specialised feeding requirements, except that it should be borne in mind that these fishes have a high metabolic rate, so the filtration should have a corresponding capacity and regular water changes should be carried out.

Breeding behaviour: If the aquarium has been set up in accordance with their requirements, then *G. geayi* will proceed to breed without problems. The pair formation is initiated by the male through lateral display, but it is the female who makes her choice of mate and is often dominant within the partnership. However, the male does not always take well to being "under her thumb", and this often results in small quarrels between the pair. The partners almost always indulge in lateral threat when they meet, and often the opercula are spread as well while the pair circle nose to tail. At the same time there is often a greeting ceremony with an exchange of small gestures by which the partners recognise each other. If two unpaired individuals meet then they very rapidly start delivering small bites to each other's flanks, and if the argument is not resolved in this fashion they face each other and threaten each other frontally with opercula outspread, and they may even resort to mouth-fighting.

Once a pair has formed then they very soon seek out a well-protected home in which to spawn after it has been excavated by both partners to their mutual liking.

After intensive courtship, during which the pair circle nose to tail with all fins spread, the spawning takes place in the cave (or sheltered spot), with the female attaching her eggs mainly to vertical surfaces and only extremely rarely to the overhanging "ceiling". The numerous (up to 400) green-grey eggs are very small (1-1.5 mm) and adhere by their long side. After four days the larvae are freed from their shells by the female and collected together on the floor (of the cave). During the next seven days the

1. The yellow colour of *Guianacara geayi* is even noticeable in juvenile individuals.
2. The eye stripe of *G. geayi* is often reduced to a spot on the gill cover.

wrigglers are tended almost entirely by the female, while the male guards the immediate vicinity of the breeding cave. If the male should stray too far from the cave, the female dashes out and reminds him of his paternal duties in no uncertain terms, by ramming him several times in the flanks.

The female is very fond of hiding the larvae in little nooks and crannies where they are better protected from attacks by predators. After a total of 11 days at 26° C the now free-swimming fry are led around by their mother in the immediate vicinity of the breeding cave. The male now also participates in the direct care of the brood, and alternates with the female in leading the young. The parents are extremely vigilant in their leading of the young, and both parents guide their offspring in the desired direction. The coloration of the opercula is undoubtedly very helpful in so doing, as the eye-stripe is now reduced to an opercular spot, very prominent during this phase, and which can be used by the fry for orientation as the parents invariably remain above them. Often the lips too are very dark, and this, together with the conspicuous black ventral spines, is an additional help in orientation. The fry are guided by means of jerking of the body, twitching of the fins, and leading; fin twitching clearly indicates danger, as on this signal the fry sink to the bottom and remain there motionless. When the parental fins are spread the fry rise up again. At nightfall the fry are collected together by the female and concealed in nooks and crannies in the floor of the cave. Although the male repeatedly tries to enter the breeding cave he is never allowed to do so.

The rearing of the fry is not particularly difficult, as once free-swimming they can manage *Artemia* nauplii immediately and do so extremely greedily. Unfortunately they grow only very slowly, so that a lot of time and effort must be invested before they are large enough to go to new homes. The good news is that they are themselves in turn sexually mature at a length of 8 cm, i.e. at 9-12 months old.

Remarks: Without exact details of the collecting locality it is very difficult to tell the species apart, as the characters differentiating the species are dependent on mood and may vary very rapidly.

Further reading: Mayland (1995: 517); Pellegrin (1902: 417-419); Schmettkamp (1979: 586-589); Werner (1980: 226-229). The following article may refer to *G. oelemariensis* (see articles appendix), although the photos show *G. geayi*, Rio Caciporé, Amapá, Brazil: Stalsberg (1991: 106-111).

Guiancara oelemariensis
Kullander & Nijssen, 1989

Original description: The Cichlids of Surinam. E. J. Brill, Leiden, Holland.: 126-130.

Derivation of scientific name: Named after the only river system in which the species is known to be found, the Oelemari river in Surinam.

Distribution: To date the only known locality is the eponymous Oelemari River and its tributaries, an affluent of the Marowijne (Maroni) in southeastern Surinam.

Habitat: Unfortunately no observations on the habitat of *G. oelemariensis* are available at present.

Size: The largest specimen documented by Kullander & Nijssen (1989) measured 81.0 mm Standard Length, which would signify a maximum total length of 11-12 cm. An aquarium strain of a species referred to *G. oelemariensis*, imported by Stalsberg (1991) but not positively identified as this species, is said not to exceed 15 cm.

Characters of the species: *G. oelemariensis* can very easily be differentiated from other members of the genus, as in contrast to the other species *G. oelemariensis* does not have a saddle-spot as such, but instead exhibits a black lateral spot, rectangular in appearance, that lies on the centre of the flank. In addition *G. oelemariensis* does not have produced anterior dorsal fin lappets.

An additional character, not very helpful to aquarists, is the possession of one rather than two supraneurals.

Sexual dimorphism: Females remain somewhat smaller and look rather more dainty. Males have rather more prolonged and pointed dorsal and anal fins and have a larger number of light spots on these fins and the caudal.

Maintenance: Although *G. oelemariensis* has yet to appear in the aquarium hobby, it can be assumed that it will not make any appreciably different demands on its owner than do the other species, and can be reckoned among the easy to keep species. Should the fishes kept by Stalsberg (1991) prove actually to be *G. oelemariensis*, then this species can be kept just as for other *Guianacara*.

Breeding behaviour: To date there are no confirmed observations regarding the breeding behaviour of *G. oelemariensis*. It can, however, be assumed that it is a concealed-spawning substrate-brooder. In the event that Stalsberg (1991) really kept and bred *G. oelemariensis* (see Further reading, below) then brood care does not differ particularly from that of other members of the genus. Stalsberg estimated clutch size at 200-300 light grey, opaque, eggs, which were laid at a total hardness of 2° dGH, a pH of 5.2, and a temperature of 26.3° C. The larvae hatched after 24 hours and were next transported to a pre-dug pit. After a further 6 days the fry became free-swimming and were immediately fed with *Bosmina* and *Cyclops* nauplii, which they were able to manage without difficulty. Stalsberg indicates that the species is not particularly fast-growing.

Further reading: Kullander & Nijssen (1989: 126-130). The following article may refer to *G. oelemariensis* (see articles appendix), although the photos show *G. geayi*, Rio Caciporé, Amapá, Brazil: Stalsberg (1991: 106-111).

Guianacara owroewefi
Kullander & Nijssen, 1989

Original description: The Cichlids of Surinam. E. J. Brill, Leiden, Holland: 97-118.

Derivation of scientific name: *owroewefi* is a Latinisation of a local name for this cichlid, *owroe wefi* (alternative spellings *ooroe wefi*, *owroe wiffi*) meaning "old wife". This name is supposedly given to this cichlid (and a whole series of others) because of the dedication with which they look after their offspring.

1. *Guianacara owroewefi* from Petit Laussat are characterised by the reddish colour in the cheek and the red-orange ground colour.
2. The Petit Laussat in French Guiana — locality of *G. owroewefi*.

Distribution: In their original description Kullander & Nijssen (1989) cite the Maroni River, as well as the upper Coppename drainage and the middle Saramacca, as localities for this species and also indicate that it is found in the River Oelemari sympatric with *G. oelemariensis*. Kullander & Nijssen indicate that *G. owroewefi* is, not surprisingly, also found in French Guiana as the Maroni River forms the border between that country and Surinam.

cies with a bright red head region which is often labelled *Guianacara* sp. "Petit Laussat" in the more recent aquarium literature. Gottwald (pers. comm.) found this species in the Crique Balante in the Maroni drainage as well. All these fishes are *G. owroewefi*, and these must be the most easterly localities for the species, as it is replaced by *G. geayi* in the Approuague.

In the Mana drainage, in the Crique Voltaire, in the Crique Petit Laussat and the Crique Grand Laussat Von Drachenfels found a *Guianacara* spe-

Habitat: Von Drachenfels (pers. comm.) found his red-headed *G. owroewefi* in the calmer reaches of fast-flowing rivers. In general the fishes frequented sandy bottoms covered with mud and mulm in the bank region. Mainly clearwaters, but during the rain season sediment was sometimes washed down such that the visibility was appreciably reduced. Driftwood, rocks covered in vegetation, and accumulations of boulders sheltered the shore zone such that the current there was not so violent, and in addition provided the fishes with shelter from predators and large numbers of caves, overhangs, crannies where parents could tend their young in relative safety. Von Drachenfels repeatedly saw pairs leading their broods among the piles of rocks. The distance between individual brooding pairs was very small. In the Crique Voltaire *G. owroewefi* was found in slow-flowing water above waterfalls. The bottom was sandy and dotted with aquatic plants. The water was slightly brownish in colour. No large stones could be seen in the area where the species was observed; such rocks were found only further downstream in the waterfall zone. The holotype was found below rapids but the species has also been found in the Brokopondo reservoir (Kullander & Nijssen, 1989).

In Petit Laussat *G. owroewefi* can be found in a comparable biotope to that described by von Drachenfels, except that the water temperature was, at about 25° C, remarkably low.

At the end of October 1999 we (Dotzer, Neumann, & Weidner) found *G. owroewefi* in the Maroni at 32° C. The water was extremely murky and the bottom was an absolute morass near the bank and in the still backwater where we netted *G. owroewefi* as well as numerous *Geophagus surinamensis*. Numerous twigs and branches extended from the bank into the water and made collecting hard, sweaty work. Further upstream we also found this species in the middle of the river among large stones, but here too the water was very murky such that more detailed observation was practically impossible. However, because the drag net generally yielded just two large specimens at a time, the assumption is that *G. owroewefi* is a monogamous cichlid.

Size: Like all other *Guianacara* species *G. owroewefi* attains a maximum size of 15 cm in males, while females remain about 2-3 cm smaller. The largest specimen recorded by Kullander & Nijssen (1989) measured 107.3 mm Standard Length, while the largest female was just 76.7 mm SL.

Characters of the species: *G. owroewefi* can be told from *G. geayi* by the smaller spots on the soft dorsal, and from *G. geayi* and *G. sphenozona* by the extent of the saddle spot. Thus *G. owroewefi* exhibits a vertical stripe on the centre of the body, most strongly marked on and just below the upper lateral line. If the typical saddle spot is exhibited then unlike in *G. geayi* and *G. sphenozona* it does not appear wedge-shaped, but rather like a narrow band. In addition some preserved material has silvery or pale centres to the scales, not seen in any other member of the genus.

Live specimens from Petit Laussat have a reddish body coloration, not seen in *G. owroewefi* from the Maroni (at Maripasoula).

In their original description, Kullander & Nijssen (1989) state that juvenile *Guianacara* exhibit black anterior dorsal spines, but that this character is retained only by adults of *G. owroewefi* and *G. oelemariensis*. However, this statement applies only to preserved material, as adult *G. geayi* and *G. sphenozona* also exhibit this character, depending on mood, so that the coloration of the dorsal rays does not represent a distinguishing character. A better character is the suborbital stripe, which in *G. owroewefi* is about as wide as the pupil and runs down vertically in a straight line across the cheek and the edge of the preoperculum and the lower, preopercular, part of the subopeculum.

Sexual dimorphism: The sexes can only with great difficulty be differentiated on the basis of coloration. During brood care females do in fact exhibit a more contrast-rich colour pattern, with the suborbital stripe, the throat, and the lips shiny black. The reddish coloration on the head diminishes in females but becomes brighter in males. Only when the fry are free-swimming does the male exhibit a more contrast-rich pattern on the head, which probably serves the young as an orientation aid.

In addition males grow somewhat larger and have longer and more pointed tips to the unpaired fins.

Maintenance: *G. owroewefi* does not differ from other members of the genus in its maintenance requirements.

Breeding behaviour: Once pairs have occupied their territories then every day there will be small confrontations at the territorial boundaries, but these run their course with no harm done and usually end at the frontal and lateral threat stage. More rarely there may be short bouts of mouth-fighting, but these, like the mutual threatening, are generally only between individuals of the same sex. Only very rarely is a male seen to fight with a neighbouring female for any length of time.

Once a pair has formed it is practically impossible to stop them from breeding. In general first of all the male occupies a territory and welcomes any female that approaches with tempestuous lateral display. The partners swim side by side and head to tail and fan water at each other with their tails while circling at great speed. Sometimes short bouts of mouth-fighting may be seen as the pair test out each other's fitness to breed. Ultimately the partner must be capable of defending the brood, so only appropriately strong individuals are accepted as partners. Once pairing is completed then the female busies herself enthusiastically with the breeding cave, which she enlarges to her liking. The substrate is removed and used to build a rampart close by. The actual spawning substrate is cleaned exclusively by the female, as the male is not allowed near the offspring until the time comes to guard the fry. Until that time his role is to defend the territory.

Once the female has completed her preparations then spawning follows fairly soon after. The female usually lays her dark green eggs on a vertical surface, only very rarely on an overhanging one, and they are immediately fertilised by the male. After 4 days the eggs are freed from their shells by the female, and first of all just deposited on the bottom, but later on the female collects them up and moves them around from one prepared niche to the next. The female moves them around in this way several times per day. After a further nine days at a temperature of 26° C the fry become free-swimming and can immediately manage *Artemia* nauplii. The offspring, which may number up

1. *Guianacara owroewefi* was found between the rocks near the bank. Maripasoula, French Guiana.
2. These young adult *G. owroewefi* have already formed pairs and defend territories. Territorial fights usually take place between individuals of the same sex (the males are in the foreground).
3. This, from Guyana imported, individual probably belongs to *Guianacara sphenozona*.
4. *G. sphenozona* from Guyana. Depending on mood the saddle spot can be reduced to a lateral spot. However, the light metallic blue sheen on body and fins seems to be typical for *G. sphenozona*.

to 250, are now led around the aquarium by both parents, and, as in *G. geayi*, the contrast-rich coloration of the parents plays an important role. From time to time the shoal of fry is collected together in a small pit where they can be better supervised. In such situations the female generally remains a short distance away in order to avoid drawing attention to the fry. If the parents twitch their fins this indicates danger to the fry, who immediately drop lightning-fast to the bottom. When the parents spread their fins the fry rise up again and begin to search for food.

G. owroewefi are very well able to look after themselves and can put even larger assailants to flight if the latter threaten their offspring, so a number of the fry will invariably survive without any great effort on the part of the aquarist.

Remarks: Study of specimens preserved in formalin indicate that the fishes imported from Petit Laussat must be *G. owroewefi*. Thus in formalin these cichlids lose the red colour on the head and breast. The dark markings mentioned by the describers agree with this species in all details. Bernhard (1992) likewise compares his fishes with *G. owroewefi*, but they are, however, probably a new, undescribed, species (see *G.* sp. "Red Cheek", below).

G. owroewefi is the type species of the genus *Guianacara*.

Further reading: Von Drachenfels (1988a: 236-239); Kullander & Nijssen (1989: 97-118); Schwer (1999: 41-45). It is unclear at present whether or not *G.* sp. "Red Cheek" is the same species as *G. owroewefi*, but nevertheless the reference will be mentioned here: Bernhard (1992).

Guianacara sphenozona
Kullander & Nijssen, 1989

Original description: The Cichlids of Surinam. E. J. Brill, Leiden, Holland: 120-125.

Derivation of scientific name: *sphen* (Gr.) = a wedge; *zone* (Gr.) = girdle; referring to the ventrally tapering, and hence wedge-shaped, midlateral vertical band.

Distribution: According to the describers this species is found in the River Sipaliwini and the middle Corantijn drainage, and probably occurs further west, in Guyana, as well.

Habitat: Unfortunately no concrete data are available on the localities where this species is found. Because Kullander & Nijssen do not rule out that *G. sphenozona* may also be found further west, i.e. in Guyana or even in Venezuela, it is possible that the *Guianacara* from the Rio Caroni in Venezuela must also be assigned to *G. sphenozona*. At any rate these fishes also have a wedge-shaped saddle-spot and fine spots on the soft dorsal (see characters of the species, below).

Size: The largest male examined by Kullander & Nijssen (1989) had a size of 84.8 mm Standard Length, while the largest female measured 81.1 mm. A total length of 12 cm can thus be regarded as a possible maximum.

Characters of the species: *G. sphenozona* exhibits a flank stripe which is most strongly marked on and above the upper lateral line and may extend some distance into the dorsal. The flank stripe may take the form of the tapering black wedge that gives the species its name, or be reduced to a spot on the lateral line. In contrast to *G. geayi*, *G. sphenozona* exhibits smaller spots on the dorsal fin, and these spots are restricted to the soft part of the fin. According to the original description adult *G. sphenozona* supposedly do not have black anterior dorsal rays, but because coloration is mood-related — all *Guianacara* imported to date have exhibited black anterior dorsal rays during brood care — this character is not reliable. *G. sphenozona* belongs to the subgenus *Guianacara* and hence has prolonged anterior dorsal lappets. A better method of identifying *G. sphenozona* is by the bluish base colour of the flanks. In addition the suborbital stripe can serve as an identification character: in *G. sphenozona* this stripe, which runs across the cheek to the preoperculum, is slightly curved and indistinct at its edges.

Sexual dimorphism: Males grow larger and appear significantly "beefier" than females. No other sexual differences can be discerned.

Maintenance: Like all other known *Guianacara* species, *G. sphenozona* is very easy to keep in the aquarium. This omnivore greedily accepts every kind of food; it also enjoys vegetable food although it does not molest higher plants.

Several pairs can be kept together in aquaria with a capacity of at least 300 litres and a length of no less than 120 cm. If the aquarium is smaller then the aquarist should limit himself to one pair. Intraspecific aggression is generally quite high, although battles do not lead to injury and the combatants usually limit themselves to threat. Only very rarely do they go as far as mouth-fighting, but without any harm coming to the loser.

If these fishes are to be kept with other species, then the tankmates should be very agile swimmers and have greedy appetites, as otherwise they will not be able to compete with *G. sphenozona*.

A wide range of water parameters will suit both maintenance and breeding — these cichlids do well in any water as long as the level of organic pollution is only slight. The temperature should relate to the natural habitat and not drop below 25° C.

Breeding behaviour: Like all other known *Guianacara*, *G. sphenozona* is a concealed-spawning substrate-brooder. After a short courtship and intensive cleaning of the substrate the eggs are attached to a vertical surface by their long side. While the female tends the eggs the male guards the territory. The larvae hatch after about 6 days and are moved around from pit to pit by the female for a further 5 days. The fry then become free-swimming and should now be fed with newly-hatched *Artemia*. During brood care the division of labour follows the pattern normal in other *Guianacara* species.

Further reading: Kullander & Nijssen (1989: 120-125). The following articles may refer to a form from the Rio Caroni, which may be an undescribed species although there is some evidence to suggest that it may be a local variant of *G. spheno-* *zona*. See also *G.* sp. "Rio Caroni" below.

Guianacara sp. "Rio Caroni"

Distribution: The Rio Caroni in eastern Venezuela is the home of this species, which has been found in the Caroni reservoir as well as at Paso Caruachi on the lower course of the river.

Habitat: In 1994 I found a colony of about 100 individuals of varying sizes close to a disused and eroded causeway at Paso Caruachi. While the larger individuals used holes in the former causeway as hiding-places,

1. *Guianacara* sp. "Rio Caroni" has, like *G. sphenozona*, a wedge-shaped saddle spot — the ground colour, however, is beige.
2. Like all other members of *Guianacara G.* sp. "Rio Caroni" are devoted to protect their offspring.
3. The Rio Caroni at Paso Caruachi — locality of *G.* sp. "Rio Caroni".

juveniles inhabited shallow zones with a depth of only a few centimetres. The bottom was sandy and dotted with numerous pits. I was unable to establish who was responsible for these excavations. Higher plants were completely absent, though along the bank numerous bushes, and roots extending into the water, provided a degree of cover. The water was slightly acid and had no measurable hardness. The conductivity at a temperature of 29° C measured 30µS/cm.

This species was also found in a nameless tributary of the Rio Caroni. This stream was about 6 metres wide and rather cooler (26° C) as it was shaded by dense forest. The conductivity here measured 300 µS/cm and we found practically every type of "civilised" rubbish on the stony bottom. The water itself had a musty smell, although no nitrite or nitrate could be detected. It would appear that waste water was discharged into the brook further upstream.

Size: The largest of the specimens I maintained attained a total length of 15 cm.

Characters of the species: In contrast to *G. sphenozona* G. sp. "Rio Caroni" has more of a beige-grey base colour. The saddle-spot and the coloration of the unpaired fins are similar to those of *G. sphenozona*. The first ventral spine is black. The suborbital stripe is only faintly marked and lies in the same position as in *G. sphenozona*.

Sexual dimorphism: Males grow larger and exhibit a weakly-developed nuchal hump.
Maintenance/Breeding: As for *G. sphenozona*, above.

Remarks: It remains to be clarified whether this is a new species or a local variant of *G. sphenozona*. Many features of the colour pattern suggest that it is *G. sphenozona*.

Further reading: Weidner (1995b: 7-14); 1996: 14-17).

Guianacara sp. "Red Cheek"

Distribution: In 1986 Köpke discovered these cichlids near Ciudad Piar on the road to Ciudad Bolivar in Venezuela. He also named the Rio Caroni drainage as a locality for this species. These fishes were not discovered again until 1998, when A. Werner (pers. comm.) found them in a pool to the west of the Rio Caroni. This pool lay about as far downstream of the Caroni reservoir as Mount Bolivar, which could be seen on the opposite shore of the Caroni.

Habitat: In spite of its depth of 160 cm, the biotope discovered by A. Werner was extremely warm. It was fed by a small stream, which had, however, already dried up by the time of the visit. The bottom of the pool was described as "muddy". As well as *G.* sp. "Red Cheek", *Hoplias* spp, *Cochlioden* spp, and several turtles were found in the pond.

Size: This species too grows no larger than 15 cm.

Characters of the species: Bernhard (1992) compared the individuals he was maintaining to *G. owroewefi*, and the accompanying pictorial material was generally reminiscent of that species, as Bernhard's fishes too exhibited a black vertical saddle-spot which was most boldly coloured on or below the lateral line. The red opercular spot was likewise reminiscent of a poorly-coloured *G. owroewefi* from French Guiana.

However, the specimens depicted in an article by Dick (1989) and in Schaefer (1994) are more reminiscent of *G. sphenozona*, which would be more reasonable in terms of geography.

Sexual dimorphism: Dick indicates that females are smaller and generally darker in colour. In addition they have a darker saddle (?).

Maintenance: Dick maintained his fishes at a pH of 6.7, a hardness of 8° dGH, and a temperature of 28° C. The aquarium was decorated with a few pieces of slate and a ceramic cave. Plants were not harmed, although the species liked to dig a lot. Unfortunately no further observations were recorded.

Breeding behaviour: As was only to be expected, both Dick's and Bernhard's fishes turned out to be cave brooders. The fry were free-swimming after 14 days, measuring some 5 mm and able to manage *Artemia* nauplii immediately. In this species too the fry were shepherded by spreading and twitching of the fins.

Bernhard also indicates that the female did not leave the breeding cave between spawning and the fry becoming free-swimming. In addition a territory was defended even when no fry were present. The pair bond is relatively strong and continues after brood care is ended.

Remarks: So far it has not been possible to clarify whether this is a new, undescribed, species or a population of an already described species.

Further reading: Bernhard (1992: 84); Dick (1989: 32-33); Schaefer (1994).

1. A breeding pair *Guianacara* sp. "Rio Caroni".
2. *Guianacara* sp. „Red Cheek" is restricted to a relatively small area in the Rio Caroni drainage and has a more conspicuous colour pattern than *Guianacara* sp. „Rio Caroni". Photo: Ad Konings.

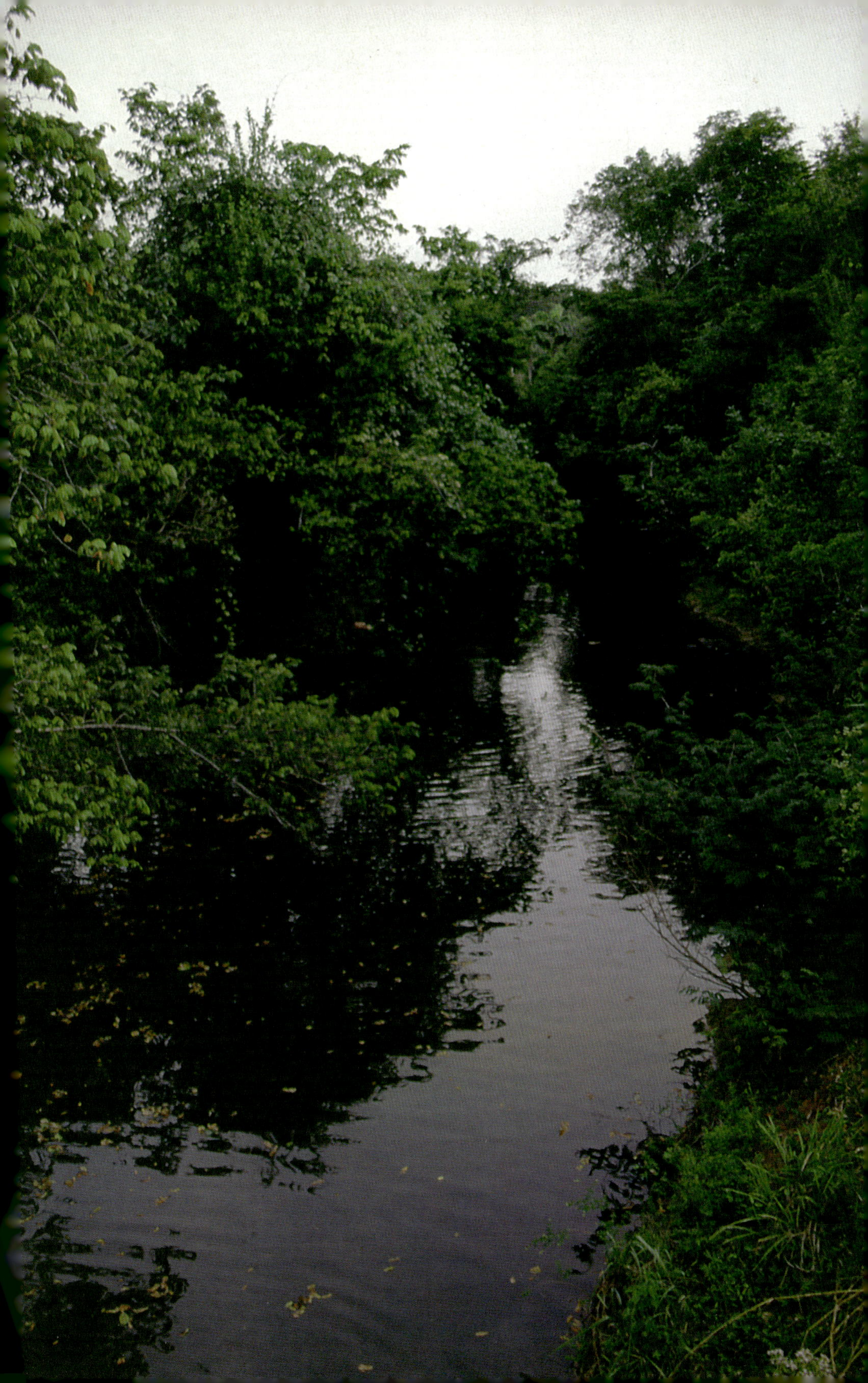

Glossary

anal fin: the unpaired fin on the underside of a fish immediately behind the anus.

anatomy: the study of the structure of organisms. This involves the dissection of plants, animals, and even humans, in order to gain insights into the form, position, structure, and function of the different parts, organs and organ systems, tissues, and cells. Anatomy is generally regarded as a sub-section of morphology*, although the distinction is fluid and differs between botany and zoology.

antero-: front; in front of.

branchial arch: a component of the branchial skeleton*.

branchial skeleton: in vertebrates with gills, the skeletal elements of the series of branchial arches that enclose the branchial cavity, supporting and protecting the soft gill tissue. Each arch is composed of a set of 4 individual elements: dorsally a small bone termed the pharyngobranchial, below which lie the two main elements, the epibranchial and then the ceratobranchial, and finally the small hypobranchial at the bottom. Each pair of gill arches (i.e. corresponding arches on either side of the body) is joined together ventrally by an unpaired basibranchial or copula (plural copulae).

caudal: of or relating to the tail; towards the tail (relative to some other point); the tail.

caudal fin: the tail fin.

ceratobranchial: an element in the branchial skeleton*.

cleithrum: flat, triangular bone in the shoulder girdle.

cranial floor: the cranial floor is the lower part of the skull (not including the lower jaw) and forms the supporting surface for the brain in the form of the anterior, central, and posterior cranial depression. All the bones of the skull, including those of the palate, unite to form the cranial floor.

distal: of fins: away from the point of attachment to the body; of the body: away from the median point or axis of the body

dorsal fin: an unpaired fin on the back of a fish.

detritus: waste material; fragments of dead animal and/or plant material, often mixed with inorganic sediment.

epibranchial: a component of the branchial skeleton*.

infraorbital: a small bone beneath the orbit (= eye socket).

lateral: of or relating to the side

littoral: the (shore) zone in a body of water where light is able to penetrate to the bottom

monophyletic: adjective used of a group of species whose members are all descended from a single ancestral species, and thus have a shared ancestry. The members of a monophyletic group can be recognised by synapomorphies*.

morphology: the branch of biology that deals with the form of the body and the structure and relative positions of its parts.

neural: of the nerves or nervous system

neural arch: in vertebrates, a pair of cartilaginous or bony elements extending dorsally from the main part of each vertebra and fused to form an arch enclosing the neural canal, through which runs the spinal cord. In fishes the neural canal disappears in the caudal part of the spinal column. On both outer sides of each neural arch there is a transverse process (projection), to which the ribs are attached. The fused apex of each arch is extended into a single, unpaired, spinal process

operculum: gill cover.

orbit: eye socket.

parapatric: term describing species which are geographically isolated but whose distributions are directly adjacent.

pectoral: of or on the breast, in the breast region.

pectoral fin: a paired fin, normally located on the side behind the gills.

pelagic: found in open water.

pelvic fin: see ventral fin.

pharyngeal: of the pharynx.

phylogeny: the evolutionary history of a taxon.

polygamous: having multiple sexual partners.

polygynous: having multiple female sexual partners.

premaxillary: the anterior bone in the upper jaw.

preoperculum: the anterior bone of the operculum*.

profundal: in freshwater, the region of the bottom where rooted plants cannot grow through lack of light, deeper than the littoral*.

subspecies: a taxonomic subdivision of a species, differing in minor details from the typical form and often having a different geographical range.

supracranial: above or on the top of the cranium.

supraneural: small bone(s) at the front of the dorsal fin.

supraorbital: above the orbit (eye socket).

sympatric: of species or populations: living in the same geographical region.

synapomorphy: the expression of a shared, unique, heritable character.

syntopic: living in the same biotope.

systematics: the branch of biology which deals with the classification and nomenclature of living (or formerly living) things.

taxon (plural *taxa*): a biological category (e.g. genus, species) and/or its scientific name.

tribe: a group of closely-related genera within a taxonomic family.

ventral: of the belly or underside; towards the belly (relative to another point).

ventral fin: a paired fin located on the ventral surface between the gills and the anus.

ventrally: towards the underside.

References

References of localities which are not listed here were taken from Dr. Sven Kullander's website (www.nrm.se) or from the original descriptions and revisions.

Allgayer, R. (1988): Les Mangeurs de Terre ou *Geophagus*. AQUARAMA 104. 18-22.

Anderson, K. (1993): Kolumbien, ein Paradies für Cichlidenliebhaber. Teil 2: Die Provinz Chocó. The Cichlids Yearbook, Vol. 3: 88-90.

Andersen, K. (1994): Kolumbien: Zurück im Paradies. The Cichlids Yearbook, Vol. 4: 78-83.

Andrews, C., A. Exell & N. Carrington (1990): Gesunde Zierfische. TETRA-Verlag, Melle.

Arendt, K. (1995): Schillernde Juwelen — *Biotodoma cupido* "Santarém". D. Aqua. Terr. Zeit. (DATZ) 48 (2): 85-88.

Bader, H. (1973): Aus Heimat und Leben des Buntbarsches *Acarichthys heckelii*. D. Aqua. Terr. Zeit. (DATZ) 26 (12): 409-413.

Bailey, M. (1993): Südamerikanische Cichliden. Enjoying Cichlids. Cichlid Press.

Baran, G. (1981): Erstmals gelungen: Die Zucht von *Acarichthys heckeli*. DCG-Info 12 (10): 185-190.

Barel, C.D.N., M.J.P. van Oijen, F. Witte & E.L.M. Witte-Maas (1977): An introduction to the taxonomy and morphology of the Haplochromine Cichlidae from Lake Viktoria. Neth. J. Zool. 27 (4): 333-389.

Bassleer, G. (1983): Bildatlas der Fischkrankheiten. Neumann-Neudamm, Melsungen.

Bernhard, R. (1991): *Biotodoma* sp. "Santarém". The Cichlids Yearbook, Vol. 1. Cichlid-Press, St. Leon-Rot.

Bernhard, R. (1991): *Retroculus lapidifer* (de Castelnau, 1855). The Cichlids Yearbook, Vol. 1. Cichlid-Press, St. Leon-Rot.

Bitter, F. (1998): Neuheiten und Raritäten — *Geophagus camopiensis*. Aquaristik aktuell 6 (11-12): 39.

Boguth, R. (1975): *Geophagus brasiliensis*. DCG-Info 6 (13): A - Z.

Brandt Andersen, T. (1997): *Gymnogeophagus* sp. "Rosario I" - Haltung und Zucht eines aquaristisch neuen Erdfressers aus Uruguay. DCG 28 (12): 228-231.

Brandt Andersen, T. (1999): *Gymnogeophagus* aus dem südlichen und östlichen Regionen Uruguays. DCG-Info 30 (6): 101-110.

Casciotta, J. R., & Arratia, G. (1993): Jaws and Teeth of American Cichlids (Pisces: Labroidei). J. Morp. 217: 1-36.

Castelnau, F. de (1855): Animaux nouveaux ou rares receullis pendant l,expédition dans les parties centrales de l,Amérique du sud, de Rio de Janeiro à Lima, et de Lima au Para, exécutée par odre du gouvernement français pendant les années 1843 à 1847, sous la direction du Comte Francis de Castelnau. Poissons. Paris, XII 13-19.

Cichocki, F.P. (1976): Cladistic History of cichlid fishes and reproductive strategies of the american genera *Acarichthys*, *Biotodoma* and *Geophagus*. U.M.I. Disseration, Michigan.

Cope, E. D. (1870): Contribution to the ichthyology of the Marañon. Proc. Am philos. Soc. , Vol. XI: 559-570.

Cope, E. D. (1872): On the Fishes of the Ambyiacu River. Proc. Acad. nat. Sci. Phil., Vol. 23: 250-294.

Cope, E. D. (1894): On the Fishes Obtained by the Naturalist Expedition in the Rio Grande do Sul. Amer. philos. Soc. Philad. 33: 84-108.

Cuvier, G. & Valenciennes, A. (1831): Histoire naturelle des poissons. Tome septième. Paris XXIX + 531 pp.

Darda, W. (1992): Gesucht: *Gymnogeophagus gymnogenys* — Gefunden: *Gymnogeophagus meridionalis*. Das Aquarium 278: 13-14.

Darda, W. (1994): Der dunkle Erdfresser: Erlebnisse rund um *Gymnogeophagus gymnogenys*. Das Aquarium 302: 19-21.

Darda, W. (1995a): Ein Gartenteich für *Gymnogeophagus*-Arten — Teil 1: Entstehungsgeschichte. Das Aquarium 311: 4-7.

Darda, W. (1995b): Ein Gartenteich für *Gymnogeophagus*-Arten — Teil 2: Fische. Das Aquarium 313: 17-18.

Darda, W. (1995c): *Geophagus argyrostictus* — Ein Offenbrüter aus dem Rio Xingu, Brasilien. Aquaristik aktuell 4: 42-44.

Darda, W. (1997a): Ein Gartenteich für *Gymnogeophagus*-Arten — Teil 3: Umbau, Vergrößerung und Bau eines Sumpffilters. Das Aquarium 338 (8): 22-26.

Darda, W. (1997b): Der gelbe Wangenstrich-Erdfresser — *Geophagus taeniopareius*. Aquaristik aktuell 4: 52-54.

Dick, A. (1989): Ein neuer "*Acarichthys*"? Pflege und Zucht von "*Acarichthys*" spec. Wangenfleck. DCG 20 (2): 32-33.

Drachenfels, E. O. von (1988a): *Acarichthys geayi*. DCG-Info 19 (12): 236-239.

Drachenfels, E. O. von (1988b): Abenteuer Oyapock. Aqua. Mag. 1988 (3): 16-21.

Eckinger, D. (1987): Nachzucht von "*Geophagus*" daemon. DCG-Info 18 (7): 132-134.

Eigenmann, C.H. (1910a): Catalogue of the fresh-water fishes of tropical and south temperate America. Repts. Princeton Univ. Exped. Patagonia 1896-1899. Zool. 3 : 375-512.

Eigenmann, C.H. (1910b): The localities at which Mr. John Haseman made Collections. Ann. Carnegie Mus. Vol. VII 1: 299-314.

Eigenmann, C.H. (1912): The freshwater fishes of British

Guiana, including a study of the ecological grouping of species and the relation of the fauna of the plateau to that of the lowlands. Mem. Carneg. Mus. 5: XXII + 578 p.

Eigenmann, C.H. & W.L. Bray (1894): A Revision of the American Cichlidae. Annals N. Y. Acad. Sci., VII: 607-624.

Eigenmann, C.H. & R.S. Eigenmann (1891): A Catalogue of the Fresh-Water Fishes of South America. Proc. U. S. Nat. Mus. 15 (842): 1-81.

Elias, J. (1982): *Geophagus surinamensis* (Bloch, 1791), der Surinam-Perlfisch. D. Aqua. Terr. Zeit. (DATZ) 35 (4): 139-142.

Fink, W. L. & S.V. Fink (1979): Central Amazonia and its Fishes. Comp. Biochem. Physiol. 62 A: 13-29.

George, M.R. (1995): Intraovarielle Aspekte und Laichstrategien von Knochenfischen. In Fortpflanzungsbiologie der Aquarienfische. Bornheim: Birgit-Schmettkamp-Verlag: 27-32.

Glaser, U. & W. Glaser (1996): Aqualog — Southamerican Cichlids I. Mörfelden-Walldorf.

Gosse, J.P. (1963): Description de deux ciclides nouveaux de la region amazonienne. Bull. Inst. r. Sci. nat. Belg. 39 (35): 1-7.

Gosse, J.P. (1971): Revision du genre *Retroculus* (Castelnau, 1855) (Pisces, Cichlidae) designation d'un neotype de *Retroculus lapidifer* (Castelnau, 1855) et description de deux especes nouvelles. Bull. Inst. Royal Sci. Nat. Belgique 47 (43): 1-11.

Gosse, J.P. (1975): Révision du genre *Geophagus* (Pisces Cichlidae). Acad. Roy. Sci. d'Outre-Mer, Brüssel. 71-76.

Goulding, M., M.L. Carvalho & E.G. Ferreira (1988): Rio Negro — Rich life in poor water. SPB Academic Publishing, The Hague, Nederlands.

Grad, J. (1987): *Geophagus brasiliensis*, ein Schmuckstück im Aquarium. DCG-Info 18 (1): 12-15.

Grad, J. (1992): Anmerkungen zu *Gymnogeophagus gymnogenys*. DCG-Info 23 (2): 43-44.

Günther, A. (1862): Catalogue of the Fishes in the British Museum, Volume IV. London, 278-315.

Hagenmeier, H. E. (1995): Das enzymatische Schlüpfen von Fischen. In Fortpflanzungsbiologie der Aquarienfische. Bornheim: Birgit-Schmettkamp-Verlag: 101-113.

Haseman, J. D. (1911): An Annotated Catalogue of the Cichlid Fishes Collected by the Expedition of the Carnegie Museum to Central South America, 1907-1910. Annals Carneg. Mus. Vol. 7: 329-373.

Heckel, J. (1840): Neue Flussfische Brasilien's nach den Beobachtungen und Mittheilungen des Entdeckers beschrieben. Erste Abteilung, die Labroiden. Ann. Wien. Mus. Naturges. 2: 327-470.

Hensel, R. (1870): Beiträge zur Kenntnis der Wirbelthiere Südbrasiliens. Archiv für Naturgeschichte 36 (1), S. 64-68.

Hoffmann, W. (1996): *"Geophagus" brasiliensis*. DCG-Info 27 (4): 78-80.

Jacobi, B. (1981): Untersuchungen zur Ethologie von *Geophagus hondae* Regan, 1912 (Teleostei, Cichlidae). Darmstadt: pp. 105.

Jacobi, B. (1985a): Zur Biologie des Rothaubenerdfressers *Geophagus steindachneri* Eigenmann & Hildebrandt, 1910 (Pisces, Cichlidae): 2. Kieferapparat und Ernährungsweise; Evolution der Maulbrutpflege. DCG-Info 16 (4): 73 80.

Jacobi, B. (1985b): Zur Biologie des Rothaubenerdfressers *Geophagus steindachneri* Eigenmann & Hildebrandt, 1910 (Pisces, Cichlidae) — Schluß. DCG-Info 16 (5): 95-98.

Jorgensen, J. & A. Stalsberg (1988a): *Satanoperca daemon* (Heckel, 1840). DCG-Info 19 (3): 51-55.

Jorgensen, J. & A. Stalsberg (1988b): *Satanoperca daemon* (Heckel, 1840). DCG-Info 19 (4): 75-78.

Kiefel, H. (1989a): Teilerfolge bei der *Retroculus*-Zucht. D. Aqua. Terr. Zeit. (DATZ) 42 (7): 393-395.

Kiefel, H. (1989b): Nochmals: *Retroculus lapidifer*. D. Aqua. Terr. Zeit. (DATZ) 42 (8): 455.

Kiefel, H. (1992): Der "Tränenstricherdfresser" aus dem Rio Xingu. D. Aqua. Terr. Zeit. 45 (3): S.152-154.

Kirsten, G. (1991): Die *Gymnogenys*-Story. DCG-Info 22 (8): 168-171.

Kirsten, G. (1993): Ein neuer *Gymnogeophagus*. DCG-Info 24 (1): 19-22.

Klinkhardt, M. B. (1998): Fische aus ethologischer Sicht. In Verhalten der Aquarienfische. Bornheim: Birgit-Schmettkamp-Verlag: 27-58.

Knopf, M (1996): "Rotmaul-Erdfresser": *"Geophagus"* cf. *brasiliensis*. DCG-Info 27 (4): 73-78.

Körber, S. (1998): Pflege und Zucht von *Gymnogeophagus meridionalis*. D. Aqua. Terr. Zeit. (DATZ) 51 (3): 156-158.

Koslowski, I. (1984): Anmerkungen zum *Biotodoma*-Aufsatz von Friedrich Kuhlmann. D. Aqua. u. Terr. Z. (DATZ) 37 (1): 17

Kuhlmann, F. (1984): *Biotodoma* erfolgreich im Aquarium nachgezogen. D. Aqua. u. Terr. Z. (DATZ) 37 (1): 14-17

Kullander, S.O. (1980): A taxonomical study of the genus *Apistogramma* Regan, with a revision of brazilian and peruvian species (Teleostei: Percoidei: Cichlidae). Bonn. Zool. Monogr., 14: 1-152.

Kullander, S.O. (1986): Cichlid fishes of the Amazon River drainage of Peru. Swed. Mus. Nat. Hist.: pp 147-154.

Kullander, S.O. (1991): *Geophagus argyrostictus*, a new species of cichlid fish from the Rio Xingu, Brazil.

Cybium 15 (2): 129-138.

Kullander, S.O. (1994): Amazonische Cichliden — Jenseits der Flußbiegung. DATZ-Sonderheft — Amazonas: 53-59.

Kullander, S.O. (1998): A Phylogeny and Classification of the South American Cichlidae (Teleostei: Perciformes). Pp. 461-498 in Malabarba, L. R., R. E. Reis, R. P. Vari, Z.M.S. Lucena, & C. A. S. Lucena (eds), Phylogeny and Classification of Neotropical Fishes. Edipucrs, Porto Alegre.

Kullander, S.O. & E.J.G. Ferreira (1988): A new *Satanoperca* species (Teleostei, Cichlidae) from the Amazon River Basin in Brazil. Cybium 12 (4): 343-355.

Kullander, S.O. & H. Nijssen (1989): The Cichlids of Surinam. Brill — Leiden: 48-56.

Kullander, S.O., R. Royero & D.C. Taphorn (1992): Two new species of *Geophagus* (Teleostei: Cichlidae) from the Rio Orinoco drainage in Venezuela. Ichthyol. Explor. Freshwaters 3 (4): 359-375.

Leibel, W. S. (1984): Heckel's Thread-Finned Acara *Acarichthys heckelii* (MUELLER AND TROSCHEL, 1848). Fresh. Mar. Aqua. Mag. (1). 15-19.

Linke, H. & W. Staeck (1997): Amerikanische Cichliden I — Kleine Buntbarsche. Tetra-Verlag. Melle.

Loiselle, P.V. (1981a): A Jewel Of Unexpected Provenance *Gymnogeophagus australis*. Fresh. and Mar. Aqua. Mag. May 1991: 31-35.

Loiselle, P.V. (1981b): Südamerikanische Erdfresser: Die Gattung *Geophagus* und ihre Verwandtschaft. D. Aqua. Terr. Zeit. (DATZ) 34 (3): 80-83.

Lowe-McConnell, R. H. (1969): The cichlid fishes of Guyana, South America, with notes on their ecology and breeding behaviour. Zool. J. Limn. Soc., 48, pp. 255-302.

Lowe-McConnell, R. H. (1991): Natural history of fishes in Araguaia and Xingu Amazonian tributaries, Serra do Roncador, Mato Grosso, Brazil. Ichthyol. Explor. Freshwaters 2 (1): 63-82.

Lucas, P. (1996): Die Geschichte vom hässlichen Entlein. TI-Magazin 131:28-32.

Lucas, P. (1999): *Retroculus* sp. — Eine kleine Buntbarsch-Sensation aus Südamerika. Das Aquarium 363: 8-14.

Lüling, K. H.: Südamerikanische Fische und ihr Lebensraum. Engelbert Pfriem, Wuppertal-Elberfeld.

Mayland, H.J. (1987): Neu: Der Rotflossen-Perlmutterbuntbarsch. Aquarien Magazin 21(2): 68-70.

Mayland, H.J. (1993): Kurz vorgestellt: *Gymnogeophagus labiatus*. Das Aquarium 285: 46

Mayland, H.J. (1995): Cichliden. Landbuch-Verlag GmbH, Hannover: 550 pp.

Mayland, H.J. & D. Bork (1997): Zwergbuntbarsche. Landbuch-Verlag. Hannover. 189 pp.

Morche, H. (1993): *Acarichthys heckelii* Müller & Troschel, 1848.DCG-Info 24 (4): 76-79.

Mücke, J. (1992): *Satanoperca* cf. *leucosticta* — ovophiler oder larvophiler Maulbrüter? D. Aqua. Terr. Zeit. (DATZ) 45 (4): 232-235.

Müller, J. (1997): *Geophagus* sp. "Orange Head". Das Aquarium 340 (10): 9-10.

Neumann, D. (1999): *Satanoperca leucosticta*. DCG-Info 30 (11): 201-208.

Newman, L. (1993): Maintenance and breeding of the Red Hump Eartheater, *Geophagus steindachneri* Eigenmann & Hildebrand 1910. Cichlid News Magazine 2 (4): 14-16.

Newman, L. (1995): Spawning the Peruvian *Satanoperca jurupari* — A case of immediate mouthbrooding. Cichlid News Magazine 4 (2): 6-11.

Newman, L. (1996): The spotted Demonfish, *Satanoperca daemon* Heckel 1840. Cichlid news magazine 5 (3): 19-23.

Newman, L. (1998): *Satanoperca* cf. *leucosticta* (Müller and Troschel) — A Colombian Speckled-Faced Demonfish. Buntbarsche Bulletin 183: 1-6.

Nieuwenhuizen, A. van den (1977): Spaß an *Geophagus brasiliensis*, dem Brasilperlmutterfisch. D. Aqua. Terr. Zeit. (DATZ) 30 (6): 194-199.

Ortega, H. & R.P. Vari (1986): Annotated Checklist of the Freshwater Fishes of Peru. Smiths. Contr. Zool. 437: 1- 25.

Patzner, R. A. & F. Lahnsteiner (1995): Männliche Keimzellen von Knochenfischen. In Fortpflanzungsbiologie der Aquarienfische. Bornheim: Birgit-Schmettkamp-Verlag: 59-68.

Pellegrin, J. (1902): Cichlidé nouveau de la Guyane Française. Bull. Mus. Nat. Hist. Paris, Vol. VIII: 417-419.

Pellegrin, J. (1903): Description de Cichlidés nouveaux de la collection du Muséum de Paris. Bull. Mus. nat. Hist. nat. Paris, IX: 120-125.

Peters, H. M. & S. Berns (1978a): Über die Vorgeschichte der maulbrütenden Cichliden. I. Was uns die Haftorgane der Larven lehren. Aqua. Mag. 12 (5): 211-217.

Peters, H. M. & S. Berns (1978b): Über die Vorgeschichte der maulbrütenden Cichliden. II. Zwei Typen von Maulbrütern. Aqua. Mag. 12 (7): 324-331.

Ploeger S. (1997): Unterwegs im Orinoco- Delta: Estado Bolivar, Estado Monagas, Territorio Federal Delta Amacuro. DCG-Info 28 (2): 34-39.

Ploeger, S. (1999): Blaupunktbuntbarsche aus dem Maracaibobecken. D. Aqua. Terr. Zeit. (DATZ) 52 (2): 24-27.

Plösch, T. (1988): Juwel Kolumbiens — der Rothaubenerdfresser, *"Geophagus" steindachneri*. DCG-Info 19

(6): 115-118.
Plösch, T. (1991): Eine wichtige Präparationstechnik: Die Alizarin-/Alcianblau-Färbung nach Dingerkus & Uhler. D. Aqua. Terr. Zeit. (DATZ) 44 (4): 252-254.
Quoy, J.R.C. & P. Gaimard (1824): Voyage autour de monde. Zoologie, capitre IX. Poissons. Paris: 286-287.
Regan, C. T. (1905): Description of *Acara subocularis*, Cope. Ann. Mag. nat. Hist. (7) 15: 557-558.
Regan, C. T. (1906): Revision of the South-American Cichlid Genera *Retroculus, Geophagus, Heterogramma* and *Biotoecus*. Ann. Mag. Nat. Hist., Ser. 7, Vol. 17: 49-66.
Reis, R.E. & L.R. Malabarba (1988): Revision of the neotropical cichlid genus *Gymnogeophagus* RIBEIRO, 1918, with description of two new species (Pisces, Perciformes). Revta bras. Zool., S. Paulo 4 (4): 259-305.
Reis, R.E., L.R. Malabarba & C.S. Pavanelli (1992): *Gymnogeophagus setequedas*, a new cichlid species (Teleostei: Labroidei) from middle rio Paraná system, Brazil and Paraguay. Ichthyol. Explor. Freshwaters, Vol. 3, No. 3.: 265-272.
Richter, H.J. (1979): Cichlide mit "Kardinalshut": Pflege und Zucht des Rothauben-*Geophagus*. Aqua. Mag. 13 (3): 128-134.
Riehl, R. (1991): Die Struktur der Oocyten und Eihüllen oviparer Knochenfische — eine Übersicht. Acta Biol. Benrodis 3: 27-65.
Riehl. R. (1995): Die Eier und Eihüllen von Knochenfischen. In Fortpflanzungsbiologie der Aquarienfische. Bornheim: Birgit-Schmettkamp-Verlag: 11-27.
Römer, U. (1989): Zur Problematik der Geschlechterverteilung von Nachzuchttieren bei *Apistogramma nijsseni* KULLANDER, 1979. DCG-Info 20 (4): 74-77.
Römer, U. (1998): Cichliden-Atlas. Band 1. Melle.
Rütz, N. (1992): Mobile Kinderstube — Die Zucht von *Satanoperca* cf. *leucosticta*. D. Aqua. Terr. Zeit. (DATZ) 45 (4): 229-231.
Schaefer, C. (1992): Anmerkungen zu einer unbeschriebenen *Satanoperca*-Art. D. Aqua. Terr. Zeit. (DATZ) 45 (4): 237.
Schaefer, C. (1994): Erfolg mit Zwergcichliden. Bede-Verlag, Rühmannsfelden.
Schindler, I. (1995): Die Vertreter der Gattung *Cichlasoma* aus Nordost-Brasilien. DCG-Info 26 (4): 80-95.
Schmelzer, G. (1986): Erfahrungen mit *Gymnogeophagus balzanii* (Perugia, 1891): D. Aqua. Terr. Zeit. (DATZ) 39 (2): 58-60.
Schmettkamp, W. (1979): Gesattelt und gezäumt*: "Aequidens" geayi*. Aquarien - Magazin 13 (12): 586-589.
Schmettkamp, W. (1981): Notizen über ein Verhaltensexperiment mit Jungen von *Geophagus hondae*. DCG-Info 12 (6): 108-110.
Schmettkamp, W. (1986): *Acarichthys geayi*. DCG-Info 17 (8): A - Z.
Schmettkamp, W. (1998): Zur Bedeutung der orangefarbenen Knötchen in den Mundwinkeln der Männchen des Rothauben-Erdfressers, *Geophagus steindachneri*, und über ein Verhaltensexperiment mit seinen Jungfischen. In Verhalten der Aquarienfische. Bornheim: Birgit-Schmettkamp-Verlag: 199-204.
Schneider, R. (1987): Der "Paradiesfisch" unter den Buntbarschen: *Acarichthys heckeli*. DCG-Info 18 (7): 134-137.
Schoenen, P. (1981): Beobachtungen bei der Maulbrutpflege von *Geophagus hondae* REGAN, 1912. DCG-Info 12 (6): 101-108.
Schraml, E. (1975a): *Geophagus steindachneri*. DCG-Info 6 (13): A - Z.
Schraml, E. (1975b): *Geophagus steindachneri* EIGENMANN & HILDEBRANDT, 1910. DCG-Info 6 (13): 230-232.
Schumann, W. (1975a): *Geophagus jurupari* — die Teufelsangel. D. Aqua. Terr. Zeit. (DATZ) 28 (2): 39-43.
Schumann, W. (1975b): *Geophagus jurupari* — die Teufelsangel II. D. Aqua. Terr. Zeit. (DATZ) 28 (3): 86-88.
Schulz, T. (1986): Neu: Ein alter Hut — *Gymnogeophagus gymnogenys*. D. Aqua. Terr. Zeit. (DATZ) 39 (11): 488-491.
Schulz, T. (1991): *Gymnogeopohagus gymnogenys* — ein Zuchtbericht. D. Aqua. Terr. Zeit. (DATZ) 44 (12): 771-774.
Schwer, P. (1999): "Alte Weiber",... gesattelt und gezäumt. DCG-Info 30 (3): 41-55.
Staeck, W. (1990): Der Wangenstrich-Erdfresser: Natürliche Lebensräume und Pflege. Aqua. Heute 8 (1): S. 8-10.
Staeck, W. (1992): Zwerg-Erdfresser. Die Gattung *Biotodoma* im Biotop und im Aquarium beobachtet. Buntbarsch Jahrbuch 1993: 72-78.
Staeck, W. (1999): Betrifft: *"Geophagus" brasiliensis* (DCG-Info 8/1999). DCG-Info 30 (9): 180.
Stallknecht H. & H.-J. Herrmann (1998): Verhaltensbeobachtungen an Aquarienfischen und Ethotaxonomie. In Verhalten der Aquarienfische. Bornheim: Birgit-Schmettkamp-Verlag: 59-62.
Stalsberg, A. (1991a): Neu importiert: *"Geophagus" pellegrini*. D. Aqua. Terr. Zeit. (DATZ) 44 (11): 687.
Stalsberg, A. (1991b): *Acarichthys* cf. *geayi*. DCG-Info 22 (5): 106-111.
Stalsberg, A. (1993): *"Geophagus" pellegrini*. D. Aqua. Terr. Zeit. (DATZ) 46 (9): 556-558.
Stawikowski, R. (1979): Beobachtungen zum Ablaich-

verhalten von *Geophagus hondae*. Das Aquarium 118 (4): 159-162.
Stawikowski, R. (1981a): Aquaristisch neu: Der Wangenstrich-Erdfresser. Aqua. Mag. 15 (3): S.184-189.
Stawikowski, R. (1981b): Fischportrait: Der Paraguay-Erdfresser. Aquarien-Magazin 15 (3): 174-175.
Stawikowski, R. (1981c): *Geophagus brasiliensis* paßt nicht so ganz in das Erdfresser-Schema. DCG-Info 12 (10): 190-199.
Stawikowski, R. (1983): Offen- oder Höhlenbrüter? Beobachtungen über das Laichverhalten des Perlmutterfisches. Aquarien Magazin 17 (9): 454-461.
Stawikowski, R. (1986): *Acarichtyhs geayi* (Pellegrin, 1902). DCG-Info 17 (8): A - Z.
Stawikowski, R. (1987): Erstmals lebend eingeführt: *Retroculus*! D. Aqua. Terr. Zeit. (DATZ) 40 (12): 573.
Stawikowski, R. (1989a): Ein Erdfresser mit verschiedenen Gesichtern — *Geophagus altifrons*. D. Aqua. u. Terr. Zeit. (DATZ) 42 (8): 476-480.
Stawikowski, R. (1989b): Neu importiert: *Gymnogeophagus labiatus*. D. Aqua. Terr. Zeit. (DATZ) 42 (4): 201.
Stawikowski, R. (1989c): Steinträger — Beobachtungen an *Retroculus*-Arten. D. Aqua. Terr. Zeit. (DATZ) 42 (6): 347-352.
Stawikowski, R. (1989d): *Satanoperca lilith* Kullander & Ferreira, 1988. D. Aqua. Terr. Zeit. (DATZ) 42 (5): 265-266.
Stawikowski, R. (1990a): Fische im Biotopaquarium. Franckh-Kosmos, Stuttgart.
Stawikowski, R. (1990b): Neu importiert: Wieder Fische vom Xingú. D. Aqua. Terra. Zeit. 43 (1): 7 -8.
Stawikowski, R. (1990c): *Geophagus* spec., ein ovophiler Maulbrüter aus dem Rio Tocantins. DCG-Info 21 (4): 73 - 80.
Stawikowski, R. (1990d): Offenbrütende *Geophagus*. D. Aqua. Terra. Zeit 43 (9): 519.
Stawikowski, R. (1991a): "Steinträger": Neue Beobachtungen an *Retroculus*-Arten. DCG-Info 22 (7): 149-154.
Stawikowski, R. (1991b): Araguarí — ein Fluß und seine Cichliden. DCG-Info 22 (3): 56-69.
Stawikowski, R. (1993*): Retroculus* im Tapajós. D. Aqua. Terr. Zeit. 46 (3): 144-145.
Stawikowski, R. (1994a): *Geophagus proximus*. D. Aqua. Terr. Zeit. (DATZ) 47 (4): 222-228.
Stawikowski, R. (1994b): Amazonas: Der Regenwald und seine Fische. DATZ-Sonderheft — Amazonas: 5-9.
Stawikowski, R. (1995a): Die Gattung *Biotodoma*. D. Aqua. u. Terr. Z. (DATZ) 48 (2): 82-85.
Stawikowski, R. (1995b): Fortpflanzung südamerikanischer Erdfresser (Gattung *Geophagus*). Fortpflanzungsbiologie der Aquarienfische. Birgit Schmettkamp-Verlag, Bornheim.
Stawikowski, R. (1996): Rio Arapiuns — Ein Fluß und seine Cichliden (Teil 1). DCG-Info 27 (12): 269-277.
Stawikowski, R. (1997a): Rio Arapiuns — Ein Fluß und seine Cichliden (Teil 2). DCG-Info 28 (3): 53-58.
Stawikowski, R. (1997b): Rio Arapiuns — Ein Fluß und seine Cichliden (Schluß). DCG-Info 28 (4): 61-66.
Stawikowski, R, (1998a): *Geophagus proximus* (Castelnau, 1855). DCG-Info 29 (6): A - Z.
Stawikowski, R. (1998b): *Geophagus* sp. "Tapajós". DCG-Info 29 (3): 41-48.
Stawikowski, R. (1999): Erdfresser aus dem Rio Tocantins und dem Rio Araguaia. DCG-INfo 30 (3): 56-59.
Stawikowski, R. & U. Werner (1988): Die Buntbarsche der neuen Welt — Südamerika. Edition Kernen. Essen.
Steindachner, F. (1875): Beiträge zur Kenntnis der Chromiden des Amazonasstromes. Sitz. Ber. Akad. Wiss. Wien, Bd. 71, I. Abt.: 61-137.
Steindachner, F. (1880): Zur Fischfauna des Cauca und der Flüsse bei Guayaquil. Denkschr. Akad. Wiss. Wien, XLII: 55-104.
Steinmann, R. (1992): Das Fortpflanzungsverhalten einer *Satanoperca*-Art. D. Aqua. Terr. Zeit. (DATZ) 45 (4): 236.
Sterling, T. (1973): Der Amazonas. Time Life Books B.V. 183pp.
Stiassny, M.L.J. (1991): Phylogentic intrarelationships of the family Cichlidae: an overview. In: M. H. A. Keenleyside (Hg.) (1991): Cichlid fishes Behaviour, ecology and evolution: London, New York; Tokyo, Melbourne, Madras.
Stieglitz, K. (1986): Liebt es etwas kühler: *Gymnogeophagus rhabdotus*; der gestreifte Erdfresser. TI 78: 8-9.
Stieglitz, K. (1987a): *Gymnogeophagus gymnogenys*: Der dunkle Erdfresser ist ein Maulbrüter. TI-Magazin 82: 15-17.
Stieglitz, K. (1987b): *Gymnogeophagus gymnogenys* ist Maulbrüter. DCG-Info 18 (12): 238-243.
Stieglitz, K. (1994): Neu bei uns: Der Lippen-Erdfresser. TI-Magazin 118: 9-12.
Thomas, M. (1973): Erfahrungen mit *Satanoperca jurupari*. D. Aqua. Terr. Zeit. (DATZ) 26 (11): 370-373.
Torbecke, T. (1996): Beobachtungen an *Satanoperca daemon*. DCG-Info 27 (6): 129-133.
Tresnak, I. (1979): *Geophagus hondae* Regan 1912. D. Aqua. Terr. Zeit. (DATZ) 32 (3): 88-91.
Warzel, F. (1998): Ein neuer *Geophagus* aus dem Rio Tocantins. TI-Magazin 143: 20.
Warzel, F. (1999): Aquaristisch neue Erdfresser aus Ostbrasilien. D. Aqua. Terr. Zeit. (DATZ) 52 (6): 18-19.

Weidner, T. (1993): Neu beschrieben: Zwei *Geophagus* aus Venezuela. D. Aqua. Terr. Zeit. (DATZ) 46 (11): S.687-688.

Weidner, T. (1994a): Wir können auch anders — Beobachtungen zum Brutpflegeverhalten einiger *Geophagus*-Arten. DCG-Info 25 (2): 39-42.

Weidner, T. (1994b): *Geophagus taeniopareius*. DCG-Info 25 (6): S.136-142.

Weidner, T. (1994c): Pflege und Zucht von *Geophagus proximus*. D. Aqua. Terr. Zeit. (DATZ) 47 (4): 228-229.

Weidner, T. (1994d): Zur Diskussion: "Löcher" — Einige Anmerkungen zur Entstehung von Hautläsionen bei Großcichliden. DCG-Info 25 (11): 256-264.

Weidner, T. (1995a): *Satanoperca acuticeps* ist kein Maulbrüter. D. Aqua. Terr. Zeit. (DATZ) 48 (3): 141-142.

Weidner, T. (1995b): Venezuela 1994 - Andere Gegenden, andere Fische. DCG-Info 26 (1): 7 - 14.

Weidner, T. (1995c): *"Geophagus" pellegrini*. DCG-Info 26 (3): 54-57.

Weidner, T. (1995d): *Satanoperca* cf. *leucosticta* — Funkelnde Juwelen im Aquarium. DCG-Info 26 (6): 134-140.

Weidner, T. (1996): Ein Sattelfleckbuntbarsch aus Venezuela. TI-Magazin 132: 14-17.

Weidner, T. (1997a): *Geophagus argyrostictus*, KULLANDER, 1991. DCG-Info 28 (4). A - Z.

Weidner, T. (1997b): *Geophagus taeniopareius* KULLANDER, ROYERO & TAPHORN, 1992. DCG-Info 28 (5). A - Z.

Weidner, T. (1997c): Hautläsionen bei Großcichliden — Ergänzungen zu meinem Bericht in DCG-Info 11/1994. DCG-Info 28 (1): 9-11.

Weidner, T. (1997d): Kweken met *Satanoperca acuticeps* (Heckel, 1840). NVC-Cichlidae 23 (6): 152-157.

Weidner, T. (1998a): Kweken met *Satanoperca acuticeps* (Heckel, 1840), deel 2. NVC-Cichlidae 24 (1): 20-24.

Weidner, T. (1998b): Seltene und wenig bekannte Grosscichliden aus Südamerika — II. Teil. TI 30 (4), Nr. 142: 7-11.

Weidner, T. (1998c): *Geophagus* cf. *brachybranchus* "Rio Caroni". D. Aqua. Terr. Zeit. (DATZ) 51 (8): 502-505.

Weidner, T. (1998d): Klein - bunt - schön: *Geophagus* sp. "Pindare". DCG-Info 29 (8): 150-155.

Weidner, T. (1999): *Retroculus lapidifer* — Steinträger und Grubenlaicher. D. Aqua. Terr. Zeit. (DATZ) 52 (9): 8-12.

Werner, U. (1980): Ein Cichlide mit zwei Gesichtern — Sattelfleckbuntbarsch, *Aequidens geayi*. Das Aquarium 133: 352 -353.

Werner, U. (1981): *Geophagus surinamensis*. DCG-Info 12 (10). A - Z.

Werner, U. (1983a): Verkannt und verleumdet: *Geophagus surinamensis* (I). Das Aquarium 17 (1): 14 -18.

Werner, U. (1983b): Nervenkitzel und Geduldsprobe: Zucht von *Geophagus surinamensis* (II). Das Aquarium 17 (2). 74-80.

Werner, U. (1983c): Die "anderen" Surinam-Perlfische (III). Das Aquarium 17 (3): 118-123.

Werner, U. (1985): Sattelfleckbuntbarsches — *"Aequidens" geayi*, gepflegt und gezüchtet. Das Aquarium 191: 226-229.

Werner, U. (1987a): "Erdfressender" Ballonkopferdfresser — *Gymnogeophagus balzanii* (Perugia, 1891): Das Aquarium 213. 132-136.

Werner, U. (1987b): *Geophagus brasiliensis* sind Fische auf lange Sicht. Das Aquarium 216: 298-304.

Werner, U. (1988a): *"Geophagus" crassilabris* Steindachner, 1877 — Dicklippiger Rothaubenerdfresser. DCG-Info 19 (8): A - Z.

Werner, U. (1988b): Riskiert eine dicke Lippe: *"Geophagus" crassilabris* Steindachner, 1876. D. Aqua. Terr. Zeit (DATZ) 41 (7): 212-214.

Werner, U. (1990a): Wangenstrich-Erdfresser: Es gibt zwei Arten! D. Aqua. Terr. Zeit. (DATZ) 43 (8): 453-454.

Werner, U. (1990b): Zum Fischfang im Mato Grosso — Teil 7: Im oberen Araguaia: DCG-Info 21 (5): 100-111.

Werner, U. (1990c): Zum Fischfang im Mato Grosso — Teil 8: Im "Fluß der Toten": DCG-Info 21 (5): 129-140.

Werner, U. (1992a): Fischfangabenteuer Südamerika. Landbuch-Verlag, Hannover.

Werner, U. (1992b): Der "Gelbe Wangenstricherdfresser" ist kein Maulbrüter! D. Aqua.Terr. Zeit. 45 (1): 7-8.

Werner:, U. (1994): *Geophagus* spec. "Rio Areões" — Ein neuer ovophiler Maulbrüter aus Südamerika. Cichliden-Jahrbuch 1994. Ruhmannsfelden: 62-67.

Werner, U. (1996): Der Gelbe Wangenstrich-Erdfresser. *Geophagus taeniopareius* gehört zu den Offenbrütern. TI-Magazin 129: S.19-23.

Werner, U. (1997): Erdfresser — Zwei neue *Geophagus*-Arten aus Brasilien. Das Aquarium 340: 4-8.

Werner, U. & R. Stawikowski (1988): Die Buntbarsche der neuen Welt — Südamerika. Edition Kernen. Essen.

Wickler, W. (1956): Der Haftapparat einiger Cichliden-Eier. Z. Zellforsch. 45: 304-327.

Winkelmann, H. (1975): Pflege und Zucht *Geophagus brasiliensis*. DCG-Info 6 (8): 99-100.

Winkler, W. (1956): Der Haftapparat einiger Cichliden Eier. Z. Zellforsch. mikr. Anat. 45: 304-327.

Wolf, G. B. (1988): Die Geschichte vom "Rotkäppchen" — *"Geophagus" steindachneri*. DCG-Info 19 (7): 126-130.

Wollenweber, G. (1971): *Geophagus surinamensis*. D. Aqua. Terr. Zeit. (DATZ) 24 (5): 152-155.

Index

Acara 9
Acarichthys 9, 15, 62
Acarichthys heckelii 9, 12, 15, 62, 70, 297, *297*, **298**, *300, 301*
agassizii 12
amoenus 11
Biotodoma 14, 46, 48, 62, 67, 69, **73**, 299
Biotodoma cupido 9, 12, 13, *13*, 15, *37*, *56*, 61, 69, 73, *73*, **75**, *76*, *77*, 82, 83
Biotodoma sp. „Aripuana" **81**, *81*, *84*
Biotodoma sp. "Guyana" **82**, *85*
Biotodoma wavrini 17, *17*, 73, **78**, *80*
boulengeri 13
brachyurus 14, 15
bucephalus 10
camurus 14, 15
Chromis 8
Chromys 9
Chromys lapidifera 10
cyanopterus 16, 250
duodecimspinosus 14
Geophagus 8, 11, 21, 67, 72, **86**, 171, 249
Geophagus altifrons cover, endpaper, *1*, 9, 10, 30, 43, 57, *65*, 67, 87, *88*, **89**, *89*, *92*, *93*, 95, 96, 110, 145, 150, 168
Geophagus cf. *altifrons* "Aripuana I" *8, 93, 153*
Geophagus cf. *altifrons* "Aripuana II" *153*
Geophagus argyrostictus 19, *33*, 87, 94, **99**, *100*, *101*,105, 110, 111, 118, 130, 142, 145
Geophagus cf. *argyrostictus* "Arapiuns" *104*, **106**, 109
Geophagus cf. *argyrostictus* "Aripuana" *104*, *105*, 107, **108**, *109*, 152, *153*
Geophagus cf. *argyrostictus* "Cumina" **112**
Geophagus cf. *argyrostictus* "Curuá" *108*, **110**
Geophagus cf. *argyrostictus* "Tapajós" *101*, **103**
Geophagus cf. *argyrostictus* "Trombetas" 111, **112**, *112*
Geophagus brachybranchus 19, *60*, *61*, 87, *117*, **118**, 121, 145
'*Geophagus*' *brasiliensis* 8, 12, 15, 18, 24, 57, 67, 86, 121, *192*, *193*, *196*, *197*, **198**, 200, *200*, 202, 203
'*Geophagus*' *brasiliensis* complex **191**
Geophagus brokopondo 19, 87, 145, **147**

Geophagus camopiensis 14, **128**, *128*, *129*, 145, 307
'*Geophagus*' *crassilabris* 12, 86, 171, **174**, *176*, *177*, 180,187
Geophagus grammepareius 19, 87, *133*, **134**, 145
Geophagus harreri 18, 88, **139**, *140*, 145
'*Geophagus*' *iporangensis* 15, 199, **200**, *201*
'*Geophagus*' *itapicuruensis* 15, **201**, *201*
Geophagus megasema 9, 10, 67, 122, 145, **150**, 151
'*Geophagus*' *obscurus* 9, 15, **202**, 203, *204*
'*Geophagus*' *pellegrini* 15, 22, 171, 175, **179**, *180*, *181*, 188
Geophagus proximus 9, 10, 11, 18, *64*, 67, 120, *120*, **121**, *121*, *125*, 126, 128, 145, 150
Geophagus sp. "Altamira" **94**, *96*
Geophagus sp. "Amapá Grande" **156**, *157*
Geophagus sp. "Araguaia-Orange Head" *72*, **168**, *169*
Geophagus sp. "Araguari" **158**, *160*
'*Geophagus*' sp. "Bahia Red" 199, **203**, *205*
Geophagus sp. "Columbia" *12*, *124*
Geophagus sp. "Madeira" **151**, *152*
Geophagus sp. "Maicuru" 116, **154**, *156*
Geophagus sp. "Parnaíba" **158**
Geophagus sp. "Pindaré" **158**, *160*, *161*
Geophagus sp. "Porto Franco" *113*, **115**, *116*
Geophagus sp. "Rio Areões" *13*, *40*, **95**, *97*
Geophagus sp. "Rio Negro I" 122, **125**, *125*
Geophagus sp. "Rio Negro II" **131**, *132*
Geophagus sp. "Stripetail" 122, **125**
Geophagus sp. "Tapajós" *165*
Geophagus sp. "Tapajós - Orange Head" *16*, 87, 118, **164**, *164*
Geophagus sp. "Tapajós-Red Cheek" **164**
'*Geophagus*' *steindachneri* 12, 15, 16, 22, 171, *172*, 175, 183, **184**, *184*, *185*, 256, 260
Geophagus surinamensis 8, 11, 15, 87, 140, **143**, *144*, 148, 150, 151, 155, 314
Geophagus taeniopareius 19, 36, 43, 87, **135**, *136*, *137*, 145
Guianacara 19, 21, 62, 70, 88, 140, **303**
Guianacara geayi 14, 19, 130, 297, *304*, 305, **306**, *308*, *309*, 314, 319
Guianacara oelemariensis 19, 304, **311**

Guianacara owroewefi 19, 70, 142, 144, 304, *312*, **313**, *316*
Guianacara sp. "Rio Caroni" *320*, **321**, *321*, *324*
Guianacara sp. "Red Cheek" 318, **322**, *324*
Guianacara sphenozona 19, 303, 314, *317*, **318**
Gymnogeophagus 10, 16, 18, 22, 50, 67, 69, 198, **248**
Gymnogeophagus australis 15, **250**, *252*
Gymnogeophagus balzanii 13, 15, 16, *17*, 22, 65, *68*, 69, 249, *253*, **254**, *256*
Gymnogeophagus gymnogenys 10, 14, 15, 252, **257**, *260*, *261*, 279
Gymnogeophagus labiatus 10, **262**, *264*, *265*
Gymnogeophagus lacustris 18, **266**
Gymnogeophagus meridionalis 18, *249*, 259, **267**, *268*, *272*, 273
Gymnogeophagus rhabdotus 10, 14, *249*, 253, 259, **271**, *272*, *273*
Gymnogeophagus setequedas 19, 271, **274**, *276*
Gymnogeophagus sp. "Rosario I" 269, *277*, **278**, *280*
Gymnogeophagus sp. "Rosario II" *268*
Gymnogeophagus sp. "Yaguarón" *268*, 269
gymnopoma 10
hondae 15
macrolepis 10
madgalenae 16
minuta 11, 198
Oelemaria 19
olfersi 18
pygmaeus 10
Retroculus 13, 18, 19, 30, 141, **281**
Retroculus lapidifer *5*, 9, 13, 18, *33*, *49*, 69, *281*, 282, *284*, *285*, **285**, *288*, *289*
Retroculus septentrionalis 18, **292**, *293*
Retroculus xinguensis 18, *293*, **294**, *296*
Satanoperca 10, 11, 21, 46, 48, 67, 68, 141, 171, 193, **206**, 282
Satanoperca acuticeps *8*, 9, 15, 18, *37*, 206, 207, **209**, *209*, *212*, *213*, 218, 220
Satanoperca daemon 9, 15, 18, 26, *28*, 30, *52*, *53*, 68, 207, 211, **215**, *216*, *217*, 221
Satanoperca jurupari 9, *9*, 15, 63, 94, 206, **223**, *224*, *225*, 232, 244
Satanoperca leucosticta endpaper, 9, 19, 206, 208, *224*, *225*, 228, **232**, 239
Satanoperca lilith 18, 107, 206, 207, 211, 215, **219**, *220*, *221*
Satanoperca mapiritensis 16, 208, **239**, *240*
Satanoperca pappaterra 9, 15, 18, 206, 228, *229*, **229**
Satanoperca sp. "Amapá" **240**
Satanoperca sp. "Französisch-Guyana" **240**
Satanoperca sp. "Jarú" *48*, **243**, *244*
Satanoperca sp. "Redlip" **240**, *241*
Satanoperca sp. "Tocantins" *68*
Satanoperca sp. "Trombetas" *245*, **246**
scymnophilus 10, 265
Sparus 8
subocularis 12, 15
thayeri 12, 15
tuberosus 18
ucayalensis 9
unimaculata 9, 198
unipunctata 9